PATENT IT YOURSELF!

PATENT IT YOURSELF!

How to Protect, Patent, and Market Your Inventions

DAVID PRESSMAN

McGRAW-HILL BOOK COMPANY

New York St. Louis San Francisco Auckland Bogofa Düsseldorf Johannesburg London
Madrid Mexico Montreal New Delhi Panama Paris São Paulo Singapore Sydney
Tokyo Toronto

Library of Congress Cataloging in Publication Data

Pressman, David, 1937–
  Patent it yourself.

  Bibliography: p.
  Includes index.
  1. Patents—Handbooks, manuals, etc.
2. Inventions—Handbooks, manuals, etc. I. Title.
T339.P73   608'.7   78-10232
ISBN 0-07-050780-5

234567890 HDHD 7865432109

The editors for this book were Robert A. Rosenbaum and Carolyn
Nagy, and the production supervisor was Thomas G. Kowalczyk. It was
set in Trump Mediaeval by Bi-Comp, Incorporated.

Printed and bound by Halliday Lithograph.

Contents

Preface

I f you're inventive or creative, or if you've made a one-shot invention, this book is for you! It's a complete do-it-yourself guide that will show you exactly how to take all of the necessary legal and commercial steps to safeguard and market your invention or practical idea, including protecting, evaluating, patenting, selling, and licensing.

However, even if you're not a do-it-yourselfer (many inventors, surprisingly, aren't handy), this book should save you much money and prove invaluable to you in working with and using professional help (patent attorneys, invention marketers, etc.) efficiently and intelligently, and should give you the requisite knowledge to forego many of the professional's services, as well as to keep you from being victimized by unscrupulous professionals, of which, unfortunately, there are many in practice.

There is a strong trend today to do it yourself, rather than to call on professional help, in such different areas as automobile repair, electrical work, plumbing, painting, carpentry, divorce, real estate sales, etc. This trend is probably due to many factors: The soaring costs of parts and skilled labor; the increase in the general level of knowledge and the desire for knowledge in our society; the publication of do-it-yourself guides; and the encouragement to do it yourself by publishers and replacement-parts manufacturers.

With regard to the cost of skilled labor, a look at the hourly rates charged in my city (San Francisco) will provide ample reason for doing it yourself. Automobile mechanics, electricians, and plumbing firms now charge about $35 per hour for the services of a journeyman. The rates of patent attorneys, however, make this figure seem small: Their hourly charges now run from about $60 to $150 per hour, depending upon the attorney's experience and prestige.

Although do-it-yourself guides abound in most fields where amateurs wish to avoid a professional's fee, I have not seen any complete and accurate guide available for the inventor wishing to bypass the patent attorney. Given the charges noted above, and the fact that inventors are inherently do-it-yourselfers, it is high time for this book.

A word of advice before you start. The preparation and prosecution of a patent application demands the ability to write detailed and extended explanations. If you haven't done much writing before, or if you feel that you lack the ability to explain in detail how things work, it would be wiser to use this book to aid you in working with a patent professional. Other requisites for the do-it-yourself invention exploiter are diligence and motivation. To patent and market an invention successfully requires what at first may seem to be a large amount of work and effort, but as with most new tasks you attack, "the first time is the hardest," and once you get well into it, the learning curve is downhill, and the satisfactions are immense. The important thing is to get into it, do it, and keep at it, and the rewards will follow. Ask any inventor who has received or is receiving royalty checks whether it was worth it!

David Pressman

PATENT IT YOURSELF!

CHAPTER ONE

Everyone Can Invent

WHAT IS AN INVENTION?

Traditional definitions of "invention" as "something originated by experiment" or "a new device or contrivance" are vague. Such an invention won't necessarily make you a millionaire or even bring you royalty checks. Also, as you'll see, even patentable inventions aren't limited to "things," products of experimentation, devices, or contrivances.

Obviously a more useful definition is needed. For our purposes, then, we'll call an invention any thing, process, or idea which is not generally and currently known; which, without too much skill or ingenuity, can exist in or be reduced to tangible form or used in a tangible thing; which has some use or value to society; and which you or someone else has thought up or discovered.

Note that an invention can be a process, or even an idea, so long as it can be made tangible in some way, "without too much skill or ingenuity." It can be as impalpable as a new wrinkle (or whatever else it is that stores information) in your brain, provided that it is practical or real enough for some artisan to make. On the other hand, the definition eliminates fantasies and wishes, such as time-travel or perpetual motion machines. An invention must have some use or value to society; otherwise what good is it, and how will you sell it? It must be generally unknown, and it must have been thought up or discovered by you or someone—otherwise it doesn't really have inventive value. Even if it is known in some remote corner, it can still be your "invention" if you invent it independently or discover it, and offer it in an area where it can be considered new. But, as you'll see later, to obtain a truly valid patent, your invention shouldn't have been known anywhere before you conceive it.

Why bother to define "invention" in such detail? So you'll begin to understand the term and have a better grasp and feel for it, and to define the limits of its usage in this book. As you'll see, we'll mostly be concerned with *patentable* inventions, but with what you'll learn, you should be able to market nonpatentable ones, so long as they're at least somewhat special and useful to society.

MAKING AN INVENTION

Now that we know what an invention is, how do we make one? The answer generally lies in a two-step procedure: (1) Recognize a problem, and (2) come up with a solution.

Although it may seem like duck soup, recognizing a problem is often 90 percent of an invention. In these cases, once the problem is recognized, creating the solution is the duck-soup part. Consider some of the Salton products—the home peanut-butter maker, for instance, or the warming tray, or the plug-in ice-cream maker for use in the freezer. Given the problem in each case, implementing the solution in an appliance merely involves electrification and/or size reduction, which any appliance designer can accomplish. True, during the implementation, ingenious and patentable inventions are often made, but in each case the basic idea was still at least 90 percent the recognition of a problem.

Of course in many other cases the recognition of a problem plays no part in the invention. Most improvement inventions fall into this category, for example, the improvement of the mechanism of a ball-point pen to make it cheaper, more reliable, stronger, etc. But in general you should go about inventing via the two-step process of finding a problem and solving it.

To exemplify, let's look at some very simple inventions made in recent years which have been commercially implemented, and note the problem (P) and solution (S) in each case.

1. *"Grasscrete."* P: Wide expanses of concrete or asphalt in a parking lot or driveway are ugly. S: Make many cross-shaped holes in the paving and plant grass in the earth below so that the grass grows up to the surface and makes the lot or driveway appear mostly green; grass is protected from the car's tires because of its subsurface position.

2. *Stick-On Transparent Watch Calendar.* P: Calendar watches don't display a full month's calendar. S: Print a set of transparent overlay stickers with the calendar for one month of the year on each; a new sticker can be placed on the watch crystal each month, yet the watch hands can still be seen.

3. *Car Lift Bag.* P: It is difficult to jack up a car to fix a flat. S: Provide a large, airtight cloth bag with a tube that can be fitted over the exhaust pipe; when the bag is positioned under the side or front of the car, the

exhaust gas will expand it enough to lift one side of the car without expenditure of physical labor.

4. *Buried Plastic Cable-Locator Strip. P:* Construction excavators often damage buried cables (or pipes) because surface warning signs often are removed or can't be placed over the entire buried cable. *S:* Bury a brightly colored plastic strip parallel to and above the cable; it serves as a warning to excavators that cable is buried below the spot at which they're digging.

5. *Magnetic Safety Lock for Police Pistols. P:* Police pistols are often fired by unauthorized persons. *S:* A special safety lock inside the pistol releases only when the pistol is held by someone wearing a finger ring containing a high-coercive-force samarium cobalt magnet.

The inventors of these inventions necessarily went through the problem-solution process (though not necessarily in that order) to make their invention. Even if an invention is thought to be spontaneous, it can usually be shown that problem-solution steps were somehow involved, even if they seem to coalesce.

So if you don't already have an invention, the first place to begin is to seek out problem areas. As you go through the day and perform or observe the performance of tasks, or solve or encounter problems, even if they're as simple as not having a full month's calendar on your calendar watch, learn to recognize and define them. Ask yourself if it can't be done more easily, cheaply, simply, or reliably, if it can't be made lighter, quicker, stronger, etc. Write the problems down and keep a list in your pocketbook, wallet, or notebook.

Then take time to cogitate on the problems you've discovered. Often the solution will be a simple expedient, such as electrification or reduction in size. Generally it will be more involved, as in the five examples listed above. But you don't have to be a genius to come up with a solution: Draw on solutions from analogous or even nonanalogous fields, experiment, meditate, look around. When one hits you, write it down, especially if it's in the middle of the night, since we tend to forget our nocturnal thoughts.

Also remember that sometimes the "problem" may be the ordinary way something has been done for years. Consider shower heads, devices which operated satisfactorily for about 50 years. But this didn't deter the inventor of water-massaging shower heads from recognizing the problem of an ordinary constant spray that didn't create any massage effect. He thus developed the water-massaging head that causes the water to come out in spurts from various head orifices, thereby creating the massaging effect. Similarly the invention of slow food cookers involved recognition of the problem that slow cooking could not easily be accomplished with ordinary pots and appliances, which most people believed operated satisfactorily. Is there a similar problem in your life or home which you can solve?

When you believe you've recognized a problem and figured out what you believe to be a unique solution, congratulations! You're an inventor!

RAMIFICATIONS

Once you've made an invention, write down the problem and the solution. This is not only so you won't forget it, but so it will be somewhere to remind you to do something about it. (As you'll see in Chapter 2, it's best to write it down in a special notebook.)

Then try to ramify it, that is, to do it or make it in other ways so it will be cheaper, faster, better, bigger (or smaller), stronger, lighter (or heavier), longer- (or shorter-) lasting, or even just different.

Why? First, our initial solution usually isn't our best, and sometimes isn't even workable, so you'll want to improve on your first effort. Second, even at this early stage you'll want to foreclose your future competitors from coming up with what you've omitted or with an alternative solution that avoids your patent. The best way to beat them is to think of it first. Third, even if you believe your first solution is the best and most workable, your potential producers or manufacturers may not see it that way, so it's best to have as many alternatives handy as possible, just in case. Fourth, when you apply for a patent, the more ramifications you have, the more psychological support you'll have for broader patent claims, and, as you'll see, the broader your claims, the better your patent will be. Fifth, and conversely, the broad claims of your patent application or the claims to your first embodiment may be anticipated by the prior art; but if you have narrower claims, or claims to other embodiments to fall back on, you'll still get a patent. This is sometimes of great value for psychological reasons, even if it doesn't cover a commercialized embodiment. Sixth, ramifications often illuminate your basic or first embodiment so you'll understand it better, see it in a new light, see new uses or new ways to do it, etc.

Some inventions, you'll find, can't be ramified: Your first embodiment will be your only one. But give it a try anyway for the reasons enumerated above.

And again, don't forget to record all of your ramifications in writing, as soon as possible.

WHAT LIES AHEAD

After you've thought up an invention and written it down, you've only started on the road to profitability. Lying ahead of you are patenting and marketing, which I'll describe in as much detail as possible so that your road to success will be smooth.

Patenting an invention is a time-consuming task, especially for a beginner. It involves a search and evaluation; the preparation of a patent application consisting of very formal drawings, description, claims, and declaration; and a filing fee. All these are followed by application prosecution, which involves studying letters from the U.S. Patent and Trademark Office and concomitant references, and drafting new claims and legal arguments.

However arduous patenting may seem, experience has taught me that this chore usually pales in significance when compared with the second chore of marketing an invention, whether you wish to manufacture and sell it yourself or sell your rights to an established manufacturer. An illustration of one especially difficult marketing story, which turned out successfully, can be found in *One Day at Kitty Hawk*, by J. E. Walsh (New York: Crowell Collier and Macmillan 1975), which shows how the Wright Brothers tried for years and years to sell rights to their "flying machine" to the government, finally achieving success, fame, and wealth after an almost unbelievable chain of disappointments. The herculean efforts and years they expended to market their invention and to convince a skeptical, incompetent military bureaucracy of its worth almost match the herculean efforts and years they spent developing and perfecting the machine. (The actual patenting, having been handled by a patent attorney, is not detailed in Walsh's book.)

The following chapters will provide a detailed, step-by-step guide to patenting and marketing, but you now know that very diligent efforts must be made and pursued if success is to be achieved.

DON'T BURY IT!

If you have a worthwhile invention, and you scrupulously follow all the advice and instructions given in this and the succeeding chapters, I believe you'll have a good chance of success. But following these instructions is not nearly as important as inventing something in the first place.

I believe that almost everyone, at some time in life, has a worthwhile invention, which if developed, can bring profit and be a benefit to society. And I believe that creative individuals, or even ordinary individuals who try to be creative by following the procedures outlined above, can come up with dozens of worthwhile inventions each year. But alas, most of these will not get so much as a second thought and will never be recorded, much less developed, and society will be deprived of the benefit and their inventors of the profit.

Don't bury yours or let it expire as an unused wrinkle on your brain: Give society the benefit of your creativity and you'll stand a very good chance of reaping the commensurate rewards due you.

CHAPTER TWO

Records Are Important

WHY SHOULD YOU MAKE A RECORD OF YOUR INVENTIONS?

There are at least four reasons for recording your inventions, and it's hard to determine which is the most important.

1. *In Case of Interference.*

   If your application becomes involved in an *interference* in the Patent and Trademark Office (PTO), you'll need to prove the dates you conceived the invention and built and tested if (if you did). As you'll find out later, an interference is a Patent Office proceeding between two or more patent applications (or a patent and one or more patent applications) which claim the same invention. Its purpose is to determine which application (or patent) was first.

   A detailed discussion of interferences is beyond the scope of this book. Suffice it to say here that the winner of an interference will be the applicant (or patentee) who first built and tested the invention in question, or filed a patent application on it, unless the other party conceived of the invention first and was diligent in building and testing it or in getting it on file. In the United States and Canada, unlike most countries, your Patent Office filing date is only one factor considered in an interference. Therefore it will be obvious that if your application becomes involved in an interference, the dates on which you conceived of the invention, built and tested it, and filed a patent application on it are crucial. To prove these crucial dates, it is essential to keep accurate, complete, dated, signed, and witnessed records of the milestones along your road of patenting.

2. *In Case of Theft.*

Records should be kept to prove ownership in case your invention is "stolen" by another. While thefts of inventions are rare, they do occur; some are intentional, some unintentional. In the lawsuits or other proceedings that follow cases of discovered theft or "derivation" (unintentional "theft"), the side with the best, most convincing, records and evidence will prevail.

3. *To "Swear Behind" a Cited Reference.*

Detailed invention records are needed in case you have to "swear behind" a cited reference during prosecution. As we'll discuss later, if the PTO examiner cites a reference against your application, you can eliminate the reference from consideration if (1) it was published or patented in the year preceding your filing date, and (2) you can show, by documentary evidence, that you built and tested, or conceived and were diligent in building and testing, your invention before the date of the reference. Similarly, if a U.S. patent is cited against your application, and it was pending when your application was filed, you can swear behind its filing date no matter how old the cited patent is. Naturally, to be effective and acceptable when swearing behind a reference, your records should be detailed, clear, and witnessed.

4. *For Good Engineering Practice.*

Patent and legal considerations aside, it is good engineering practice to keep accurate, detailed records. Good engineers and technicians record their developments in chronological order so that they can refer back to their engineering diary days, weeks, months, or even years later to shed light on subsequent developments, find needed data and details of past developments, and discover a base for new paths of exploration and ramifications, especially if failures have occurred.

HOW TO RECORD THE INVENTION—THE LAB NOTEBOOK

Now that you've been sold on the need to record your inventions, it's time to explain how to do it. As you've already guessed, the best, cheapest, most reliable, and most useful way to record your inventions is by the use of a standard laboratory notebook. If the term "laboratory notebook" seems redoubtable to you (it probably will if you've never kept one), just substitute the term "technical diary," because that's all a lab notebook is. Except that, as you'll see, unlike a regular diary, which is kept private and is not signed, this diary should be signed, dated, and witnessed frequently.

What type of notebook should be used? Preferably one with a stiff cover with the pages bound in permanently, e.g., by sewing or gluing. Also, the pages should be consecutively numbered. Lab notebooks of this type are available at engineering supply stores, and generally have crosshatched, prenumbered pages with special lines at the bottom of each page for signatures and signature dates of the inventor and the witnesses. If you don't have or can't get a formal lab notebook like this, a standard bound 8½-by-11-inch, crackle-finish school copybook will serve almost as well. Just number all of the pages consecutively yourself, and don't forget the dating, signing, and witnessing, even though there won't be special spaces for this.

As should be apparent, the use of a bound, paginated notebook that is faithfully kept up provides a formidable piece of evidence if your inventorship or date of invention is ever called into question, for instance, in an interference or lawsuit. A bound notebook with consecutively dated, signed, and witnessed entries on sequential pages establishes you almost irrefutably as the inventor on the indicated date of the invention since a bound book can't have later-completed pages inserted, and since the consecutively completed pages provide a logical, sequential record which would be very difficult to fabricate later.

How Should the Technical Information Be Entered in the Notebook?

The writing, sketches, and diagrams should be in ink to preclude erasures and later-substituted entries. For the same reason, no large blank spaces should be left on a page—it should be filled from top to bottom. If you do need to leave a blank space to separate entries or at the bottom of a page where you have insufficient space to start a new entry, you should draw a large cross over the blank space to preclude any subsequent entries, or, more accurately, to make it appear that no subsequent entries could have been made in your notebook.

If you make a mistake in an entry, don't attempt to eradicate it; merely line it out neatly and make a dated note why it was incorrect. The notation of error can be made in the margin adjacent to the correct entry, or can be made several pages later, provided the error is referred to by page and date. Don't make cumulative changes to a single entry. If more than one change is required, enter them later with all necessary cross-references to the earlier material they supplement. Refer back by page and date.

If possible, all entries should be made directly in the notebook, or transferred there from rough notes on the day the notes were made. If this is not possible, make them as soon as practicable with a notation explaining when the actual work was done, when the entries were made, and why the delay occurred.

How Should Large or Formal Sketches, Photos, and Charts or Graphs Drawn on Special Paper Be Treated?

If possible, items that by their nature can't be entered directly in the notebook by hand should be made on separate sheets. These, too, should be signed, dated, and witnessed, and then pasted or affixed in the notebook in proper chronological order. The inserted sheet should be referred to by entries made directly in the notebook tying them in with the other material in it. Photos or other entries which cannot be signed or written should be pasted in the notebook and referenced by legends made directly in the notebook, preferably with lead lines which extend from the notebook page over onto the photo, so as to preclude a charge of substituting subsequently made photos. The page the photo is pasted on should be signed, dated, and witnessed in the usual manner. See Fig. 1 for an example of a notebook page with an affixed photo.

```
Today I conceived of a better way to. . . .

I propose to do this by. . . .

The materials and procedures I used are. . . .

Here is a photo of my completed device, which I

    took today:


                    ┌─────────────┐ ◄─────────  Hinge
                    │  (Photo of  │
                    │             │
                    │  Apparatus) │ ◄─────────  Pedestal
                    └─────────────┘             (Etc.)


I tested the device and found it to work as follows

with the following result values:

_____

_____

_____

Jane Inventor  31 Dec. 1976
   Witnessed and Understood by

Robert Witness          31 Dec. 1976
Albert Attester         31 Dec. 1976
```

figure 1 An example of a properly completed notebook page.

If an item covers an entire page, it can be referred to on an adjacent page. It is important to affix the items to the notebook page with a permanent adhesive, such as white glue or nonyellowing transparent tape.

What Should Be Entered in the Notebook?

Generally, you should record all of your ideas, all of the ways you devise to implement these ideas (including sketches), all procedures contemplated or followed, and all results obtained, including all test results. It is important to record as much factual data as possible; conclusions should be kept to a minimum and should appear only if supported by factual data. Thus if a mousetrap operated successfully, describe its operation in enough detail to convince the reader that it works. Only then should you put in a conclusion, and it should be kept brief and nonopinionated, for example, "Thus this mousetrap works faster and more reliably than the Ajax brand." Sweeping, opinionated, laudatory statements tend to give an impartial reader a negative opinion of you or your invention.

The entries should be worded to be complete and clear in themselves so that anyone can duplicate your work without further explanation. While the lab notebook should not be used as a scratch pad to record every calculation and stray concept or note you make or think about, it should not be so brief as to be of no value should the need for using it as proof occur. If you are in doubt as to whether to make an entry, make it; it's better to have too much than too little.

If you build a model or prototype, it is very important that you record this fact, plus any tests which you make on it. It is very helpful and convincing to attach photos of your constructions in the notebook, and be sure the photos are fully identified, including the date they were taken.

It's also very helpful to save all of your "other paperwork" involved with the conception, making, or testing of an invention. Such paperwork includes correspondence, purchase receipts, etc. These papers are highly probative since they are very difficult to falsify. For example, if you buy a thermometer or have a machine shop make a part for you in January 1977, receipts from these purchases should be saved since they'll tie in directly with your notebook work.

How Should the Notebook Be Witnessed?

It is important that the notebook be witnessed since an inventor's own testimony, even if supported by a properly completed notebook, will rarely be sufficient to prove a date or inventorship.

The witnesses chosen should be as impartial and competent as possible; they should not be close relatives or people who have been working so closely with you as to be possible coinventors. A knowledgeable friend, business associate, or professional will make an excellent witness, given the necessary technical ability or background to understand the invention. If the invention is a very simple mechanical device, practically anyone will have the technical qualifications to be a witness, but if it involves advanced chemical or electronic concepts, obviously a person with an adequate background in the field will have to be used. The witness should also be available later; obviously a person visiting from abroad or one who is seriously ill or of very advanced age would not be suitable.

One witness normally is sufficient, but having two is better since it enhances the likelihood of at least one of them being available at a later date; if both are available, your case will be very strong. It is suggested that for very important work, two witnesses be used.

The witnesses should indicate that they have witnessed and understood the material by writing "witnessed and understood" below your signature and date. Follow these words with their signatures and dates. Remember that a bare signature is not enough. If called upon later, the witnesses should be able to testify of their own knowledge that the physical and/or chemical facts of the entry are correct. Thus they should not be witnesses to your signature (as a witness is when you write a will), but to the actual technical

```
                        JOHN INVENTOR

                      1919 Main Street

                   Anytown, State 99999


                   INVENTION DISCLOSURE

Title: . . . .

Purpose: . . . .

Detailed Description, including Sketches and Photos:

_____

_____


_____
```

John Inventor   31 Dec. 1976

Witnessed and understood by

Robert Witness   31 Dec. 1976
Albert Attestor   31 Dec. 1976

figure 2 An example of a properly completed invention disclosure.

subject matter in the notebook. Obviously, then, you should call in your witnesses to observe your final tests and measurements so that they can later testify that they did witness them. Fig. 1 shows a properly witnessed notebook page.

ANOTHER WAY TO RECORD THE INVENTION—THE DISCLOSURE

If keeping a notebook or technical diary is too difficult for you, or if you make or have made inventions only at very isolated points in time so that your activities would not justify keeping a notebook, then a second, albeit somewhat inferior, way for you to record your invention is by a document called an invention disclosure.

Despite its high-sounding, formidable name, an invention disclosure is hardly different from a properly completed notebook entry of an invention. It should be a complete record of your invention, including a title, its purpose(s), a detailed description of it, and results obtained, if any. These entries should be made on a separate sheet of paper which has no other information on it except details of your invention and you. A sheet of professional personal letterhead is suitable for an invention disclosure document. Business letterhead is good if the invention is to be owned by your business. As before, the description of your invention should be signed and dated by you and marked "witnessed and understood," preferably by two witnesses, who, as before, are technically competent to understand your invention and who have actually understood and witnessed the subject matter you have entered on your invention disclosure. It is desirable to include your address.

If the disclosure runs to more than one page, you should write the title of your invention on the second and each succeeding page, followed by the word "continued," numbering each page and indicating the total number of pages of the entire disclosure, for example, "Page 1 of 3." Each page should be signed and dated by both the inventor and the witnesses. Fig. 2 shows an example of a properly completed disclosure.

If you conceive of an invention on one date, and build and test the invention later, you should make two separate invention disclosures, one to record conception and the second to record the building and testing. The second should refer to the first and both should be signed and dated by you and the witnesses.

Should You Have Your Disclosure Notarized?

Or to be technically correct, should you have your signature on the disclosure notarized? The answer is no! Why? Because the notarization only means that the notary saw you sign the document on the date indicated. A witness's signature proves the same thing; moreover, a witness will be available personally to testify to the factual content of the disclosure, having seen your invention work or understood the concept as you explained it on the date indicated. This constitutes a far more valuable piece of proof. It is my opinion that notaries are a just about useless appendage to our society, and that their duties, functions, and purposes could easily be eliminated by a few deft strokes of the legislative knife.

Should You Mail a Copy of Your Disclosure to Yourself by Registered or Certified Mail?

This is another procedure frequently used by inventors and authors, but it serves little use and is far inferior for proving dates and inventorship than one or two witnesses. The disadvantage with self-mailings is that they cannot testify as a witness can; for use as proof they must be introduced by the inventor, whose testimony is always suspect as self-serving. Also, the envelope will not be unsealed in front of any judge if an interference proceeding occurs. Papers and similar evidence are not nearly as probative, in the American system of jurisprudence, as is the direct testimony of an actual witness, who can be cross-examined.

Of course, there may be situations where you cannot get anyone to witness your invention disclosure. If you choose not to use the PTO's disclosure document program, a notary's services, or a self-mailing are much better than just the inventor's signature. For self-mailings, it is best not to put the disclosure in an envelope, but rather to fold the disclosure itself to envelope size, forming a flap with the final fold so that the postage stamp and postmark "seal" the flap. (The side with the flap is the front of the "envelope.") The self-mailer should be mailed to you, certified, return receipt requested. The mailer and the receipt should both be kept, mailer unopened, in a safe place in case it is ever needed.

THE PTO'S DISCLOSURE DOCUMENT PROGRAM— "THE PTO IS YOUR WITNESS"

What It Is

Several years ago the Patent and Trademark Office started a program whereby it accepts invention disclosures and preserves them for two years, or longer if a patent application is filed which refers to the invention disclosure. The purpose of this service, for which the PTO charges $10, is to provide very creditable evidence of conception date and inventorship for inventors who, for some reason, do not wish to rely on witnesses, notaries, or self-mailings. There is no doubt that, in case of an interference or other proceeding where the date of invention or inventorship itself is at issue, the PTO's receipt of a Disclosure Document will be one of the best forms of evidence available. However, its use is not generally recommended because of the price; at $10 per invention, the costs could become substantial, and while it is desirable to have the PTO as your witness, a live witness can often be much more useful, being able to testify to additional facts surrounding conception and also to the building, testing, and operation of your invention, which the PTO cannot do. Thus the PTO's Disclosure Document Program is not recommended if witnesses are available.

It should be noted well, and cannot be emphasized too strongly, that the PTO's Disclosure Document Program exists and operates solely for one purpose: To provide inventors with a very creditable witness to their disclosures. The program is no substitute for filing a patent application or for building and testing the invention. Also, filing a disclosure under the program will not provide the inventor with any "grace period" or any other justification for delaying the filing of a patent application. Moreover, even if you use the PTO's Disclosure Document Program to record your disclosures, you still should use a lab notebook or separate sheets with proper witnessing, to record all the pertinent facts if you build and test your invention.

How to Participate

If you wish to file a disclosure with the PTO under its Disclosure Document Program, it is merely necessary to send the following four items to The Commissioner of Patents and Trademarks, Washington, DC 20231:

1. A letter, in duplicate, requesting that the attached disclosure be accepted under the Disclosure Document Program

2. A check for $10 payable to The Commissioner of Patents and Trademarks

3. Your invention disclosure

4. A stamped envelope addressed to you

A suitable request letter can be found as Form 1 at the end of this book.

The invention disclosure should be in the form stated earlier in this chapter. Although there is no requirement that the disclosure be witnessed, or even signed and dated, it is strongly recommended that it be signed, dated, and witnessed, as stated earlier. The disclosure, as stated by the PTO, should "contain a clear and complete explanation of the manner and process of making and using the invention in sufficient detail to enable a person having ordinary knowledge in the field of the invention to make and use the invention." Drawings, sketches, or photos of the invention should be included and the use of the invention should be stated, especially in chemical inventions.

The size of the sheets should not exceed $8\frac{1}{2}$ by 13 inches, but larger sheets can be folded to this size. Each sheet should be numbered. It is suggested that a photocopy of your original signed and witnessed disclosure be submitted and your original disclosure be retained.

What Happens to Your Disclosure Papers?

The PTO will stamp all of the papers with the date of receipt and an identifying number, and will return the duplicate of your request letter in your envelope. The date and number on the returned duplicate is important; it should be carefully preserved.

If you file a Disclosure Document with the PTO and then do nothing else, the PTO will keep the original of your request letter and your disclosure for two years and then destroy them. However, if you later file a patent application on the invention described in your disclosure, you should do so within two years of filing the disclosure. You should also file a separate reference letter in the application referring to the disclosure (Form 2). The PTO will then retain the disclosure indefinitely in case you ever need to rely on it in connection with your patent application. Be sure to file the reference letter within two years of filing the disclosure document; otherwise the disclosure will have already been destroyed by the PTO, even if you have filed a patent application.

A FINAL CAVEAT

I hope you'll be able to keep a properly witnessed notebook since it's the best, most reliable way to record conception, building and testing of your inventions. But no matter which method—lab notebook, disclosure, or the PTO's Disclosure Document Program—you choose, remember that *these methods are only the initial steps to proper protection of your invention.* You should not regard them as a substitute for filing a proper patent application on your invention, or even as an excuse or justification to relax or delay the filing of a patent application, no matter how carefully or fully you record your invention. So continue on after you record your invention: You should search the invention and must file a patent application on it to be fully protected.

CHAPTER THREE

Will It Sell?

WHY EVALUATE YOUR INVENTION FOR SALABILITY?

Now that you've made an invention (Chapter 1) and recorded it properly (Chapter 2), it's time to pause, step back, and make a very critical evaluation of it for commercial salability before proceeding further.

Why? Because the next step you take will involve an expenditure of money, or effort, or both. Specifically, your next step is to search the invention and/or build and test it for feasibility and cost, and then to file a patent application on the invention. Naturally, you won't want to spend money or do a lot of work before you know whether it is likely to be justified. So at this stage it is judicious to make a preliminary evaluation.

If your invention is simple enough that you've already been able to build and test it, so much the better: Your commercial evaluation will be much easier. But if you haven't yet built and tested it, and if the building and testing will involve significant work and/or cost, it's best to take some time to evaluate it commercially before going any further. If your commercial evaluation does look favorable, and you later are able to build and test the invention, it's best to make another commercial evaluation in light of your construction work.

It's hard to make rules as to when and in what order to build and test an invention, evaluate it commercially, and search it, but I favor doing the easiest things first. Most inventors will find building and testing an invention relatively difficult or expensive, as they will a patentability search, so I recommend that your next step after proper recordation be commercial evaluation. The commercial evaluation steps which I'll outline in this chapter will not involve significant expenditure or time, and the information you gather will be very valuable when you do build and test your invention, offer it for sale or license, and search it for patentability.

DO YOUR COMMERCIAL EVALUATION CAREFULLY AND METHODICALLY

The go or no-go decisions which you make at this stage will be crucial, so it's best to do your commercial evaluation carefully, completely, and objectively. Be sure to cover all the criteria outlined in this chapter religiously, and don't neglect to ask trusted advisors or friends to assist and work with you, if possible. Always try to be as objective and dispassionate as you can; it should help to pretend that you're evaluating someone else's invention.

Say you've evaluated all of the commercial criteria carefully, and your idea looks like it has great commercial potential, but some other factor such as patentability or operability doesn't look too promising. Don't make any hasty decision to drop it. Continue to explore the negative areas. On the other hand, if you are truly convinced that it really won't be a success, don't waste any further time on it, but move on to bigger and better things.

DON'T NECESSARILY BE DISCOURAGED BY NEGATIVE OPINIONS

If your evaluation brings forth a lot of negative opinions, but *you* still believe in the invention, don't get discouraged and drop it. Remember that many great inventions (and books) were at first rejected or given the cold shoulder, but because their inventors (or authors) believed in them, they persevered, and success was ultimately achieved. The publishing industry in particular abounds with stories of successive rejections of a book by many publishers, but the author, believing in it, kept trying, eventually found a publisher, and came up with a best-seller. The best example of a persevering inventor's success after fighting almost universal opposition for many years is told in the Wright Brothers' story in *One Day at Kitty Hawk*.

Remember that the greatest ideas by nature must be quite different from everything we already know and have done. But since inherent resistance to all new ideas is greatest when they are least like something already known, the most novel ones require the most effort to promote before people are convinced of their true value.

In short, be objective, but never drop something you truly believe in.

THE CRITERIA FOR COMMERCIAL EVALUATION

There is only one question you need to answer in commercially evaluating your invention: If this invention is manufactured and sold, or otherwise commercially implemented (for example, as a process that is put into use), will it be profitable?

No one can answer this question with complete certainty. The answer will always depend on how the invention is promoted, how well it is designed, the mood of the market, the timing, and hundreds of other intangible factors. Still, a fairly scientific approach is possible if you break the problem down into separate factors. In other words, you can make a relatively highly educated decision, rather than a visceral reaction or a guess, by carefully considering the factors which I list below.

The key to commercial evaluation is to recognize that every invention has its positive and negative factors. To evaluate the invention objectively, it is important to list as many of each as you can possibly think of. The way to do it is to make an "invention evaluation sheet," which is a table with two columns, listing the positive and negative factors separately as follows.

```
Invention_____

Inventor_____


Positive Factors              Negative Factors
                     |
                     |
                     |
                     |
                     |
                     |
                     |
                     |
Signed_____         Date_____
```

figure 3 Invention evaluation sheet.

Such a table should be made part of your notebook (if you use one) since it will provide added proof of diligence and inventorship, if needed. However, if you don't use a notebook, it can also be put on a separate sheet, or sheets, which should be signed and dated in case an additional bit of proof is ever needed.

If you fill out such a table and later think of additional factors, simply write them down at the end of the table, and date and initial each one, as of the date you wrote it down.

Positive Factors

One or more positive factors or benefits of your invention will usually be immediately obvious. For example, if you have invented a new can opener, it might be easier and faster to use, or if you had invented the new ring magnet for releasing police pistols, it would have been obvious that its main advantage was safety. But since most inventions have one or more secondary advantages or benefits, it's best to check out every factor on the following list carefully to make sure you've noted them all:

1. *Cost.* Is your invention cheaper to build or use than what is already known?

2. *Weight.* Is your invention lighter (or heavier) in weight than what is already known, and is such change in weight a benefit? For example, if you have invented a new automobile or airplane engine, obviously if it's lighter, the reduction in weight is a great benefit. But if you invented a new safe or ballast material, obviously an increase in weight (provided it does not come at too great a cost in money or bulk) is a benefit.

3. *Size.* Is your invention smaller or larger in size or capacity than what is already known and is such change in size a benefit?

4. *Safety/Health Factors.* Is your invention safer or healthier to use than what is already known? There is currently a very strong trend in government and industry to improve the safety and reduce the possible chances for injury or harm in most products and processes, and this trend has given birth to many new inventions. Often a greater increase in cost and weight can be tolerated if certain safety and health benefits accrue.

5. *Speed.* Is your invention able to do a job faster (or slower) than its previous counterpart and is such change in speed a benefit?

6. *Use.* Is your invention easier (or harder) to use or learn to use than its previously known counterpart? An example of a case where an increase in difficulty of use would be a benefit is a combination lock.

7. *Production.* Is your invention easier or cheaper (or harder or more expensive) to manufacture than previously known counterparts? Or can it be mass-produced whereas previously known counterparts had to be made by hand? An example where making a device more difficult to manufacture would be of benefit is an identification or credit card, which would be more difficult to forge if it were harder to make.

8. *Durability.* Does your invention last longer (or shorter) than previously known counterparts? While built-in obsolescence is nothing to be admired, the stark economic reality remains that many products, such as disposable razors, have earned their manufacturers millions by lasting shorter than previously known counterparts.

9. *Repairability.* Is it easier to repair than previously known counterparts?

10. *Novelty.* Is your invention at all different from all previously known counterparts? Merely making an invention different may not appear to be an advantage per se. But it usually *is* a great advantage: It provides an alternate method or device for doing a job in case the first method or device ever encounters difficulties, for example from governmental regulation, or in case the first device or method infringes a patent that you want to avoid infringing. In addition, merely offering something that is different can often be lauded in advertising and can be made to appear an advantage even though your product is no better than the competition. For example, how often have you ever heard a claim like "The only widget with slide lever action!" Even though the "slide lever action" (or some other feature which offers a physical difference but no advantage) is in reality not worth one iota more than the previous rotary action

device, you probably were impelled to buy the new widget because it sounded better.

11. *Convenience/Social Benefit.* Does your invention make living easier or more convenient? Many inventions with a new function provide this advantage, and although many may question the ultimate wisdom and value of such gadgets as the electric knife, the remote-control TV, the digital-readout clock, etc., again the reality remains that in our relatively affluent society, millions of dollars have been made and are being made by devices which save labor and time, even though the time required to earn the after-tax money to buy the gadget is often greater than the time saved by using it.

12. *Reliability.* Is your invention apt to fail less or need repairs less often than previously known devices?

13. *Ecology.* Does your invention either make use of what previously were thought to be waste products? Does it reduce the use of limited natural resources? Does it produce less waste products, such as smoke, waste water, etc.? If so, you have an advantage which is very important and which should be emphasized strongly.

14. *Salability.* Is your invention easier to sell or market than existing counterparts?

15. *Appearance.* Does your invention provide a better-appearing design than existing counterparts?

16. *Viewability.* If your invention relates to eye use, does it present a brighter, clearer, or more viewable image? For example, a color TV with a brighter picture or photochromic eyeglasses, which automatically darken in sunlight, are valuable inventions.

17. *Precision.* Does your invention operate or provide greater precision or more accuracy than existing counterparts?

18. *Noise.* Does your invention operate more quietly?

19. *Odor.* Does your invention emanate less fumes or odor?

20. *Taste.* If your invention is edible or comes into contact with the taste buds (for example, a pill or a pipe stem) does it taste better?

21. *Market Size.* Is your invention salable to a larger market than previously known devices? Because of climatic or legal restrictions, for example, certain inventions are only usable in small geographical areas; because of economic factors, certain inventions may be limited to the relatively affluent. If your invention can obviate these restrictions, your potential market may be greatly increased, and this can be a significant advantage.

22. *Trend of Demand.* Is the trend of demand for your device increasing? For example if your device is an integrated circuit, or a solar energy converter, obviously, the trend of demand is positive and this can be a significant advantage.

23. *Seasonal Demand.* Is your invention useful no matter what the season of the year? If so, it will have a greater demand than a seasonal (for instance, summertime) invention such as a sailboat.

24. *Difficulty of Market Penetration.* Is your device an improvement of a previously accepted device? If so, it will have an easier time penetrating the market than a device which provides a completely new function.

25. *Potential Competition.* Is your invention so simple, popular, or easy to manufacture that many imitators and copiers are likely to attempt to design around your patent, or break your patent, as soon as it is brought out? Or is it a relatively complex, less popular, hard-to-manufacture device, which others would not be likely to produce in competition with you because of the large capital outlay required for tooling, etc.?

26. *Obviation of Specific Disadvantages of Existing Devices.* This is a catchall to cover anything we may have missed in the previous twenty-five categories. Often the specific disadvantages which your invention overcomes will be quite obvious; they should be included here, nonetheless.

Negative Factors

Alas, every invention, no matter how great and disadvantage-free it seems, has one or more negative factors, even if the negative factor is merely the need to change or design and produce new tooling. I have seen inventions and developments which are better in every way than existing developments, but which were not used or implemented solely because their advantages were not sufficiently great to justify the cost of replacing existing tooling and the manufacturing and promoting of a new device. This is especially true nowadays, when the cost of capital is very great.

The negative factors of your invention are generally more important and require more consideration than the positive factors, since one or more of the negative factors are always the reason inventions are rejected. So consider the negative factors very carefully and make sure you have included all of them so you won't be surprised by a potential purchaser or developer who asks you about a negative factor you haven't yet considered.

Since all the positive factors listed above can be disadvantages when viewed in reverse, they should be carefully reconsidered but will not be reproduced here.

1.–26. *See positive factors above.*

27. *Legality.* Does your invention fail to comply with or will its use fail to comply with existing laws, regulations, and product and manufacturing requirements, or are administrative approvals required? If it does not comply, it is not likely to be acceptable, no matter how great its positive advantages are, and if ecological or safety approvals are required (for example, for drugs and automobiles), there is a distinct disadvantage.

28. *Operability.* Is it likely to work or will significant additional design or technical development be required to make it practicable and workable?

29. *Development.* Is the product already designed for the market or will additional engineering, material selection, appearance work, etc., be required?

30. *Profitability.* Because of possible requirements for exotic materials, difficult machining steps, great size, etc., is your invention likely to be difficult to sell at a profit?

31. *Obsolescence.* Is the field in which your invention is used likely to die out soon? If so, most manufacturers will not be willing to invest money in tooling and production.

32. *Incompatibility.* Is your invention likely to be incompatible with existing patterns of use, customs, etc.?

33. *Product Liability Risk.* Is your invention in an area (such as drugs, automobiles, etc.) where the risks of lawsuits against the manufacturer, due to product malfunction or injury from use, are likely to be greater than average?

34. *Market Dependence.* Is the sale of your invention dependent on a market for other goods, or is it useful in its own right? For example, an improved television tuner depends upon the sale of televisions for its success, so that if the television market goes into a slump, the sales of your tuner certainly will slump also.

35. *Difficulty of Distribution.* Is your invention so large, fragile, perishable, etc. that it will be difficult or costly to distribute?

36. *Service Requirements.* Does your invention require frequent servicing and adjustment? If so, this is a distinct disadvantage. But consider the first commercial color TVs, which by any reasonable standard were a service nightmare, but which made millions for their manufacturers.

CONSULTATION AND RESEARCH

How to Go About It

It is very unlikely that you will be able to make a complete evaluation of all of the positive and negative factors above on your own. It is best to do a little bit of evaluation, and, if the invention still looks promising, to deepen your investigation by consultation and research. If it continues to look promising, deepen your search until you have learned all you can about the field of your invention. This knowledge will also be of great benefit when you make your patentability search.

The areas of consultation and research which you can investigate are three: (1) Nonprofessionals, (2) experts, and (3) literature. As you use each of these, keep in mind and ask about all of the positive and negative factors listed above.

1. Nonprofessionals can often be an excellent source of information and advice because they are the ones who will be likely to be purchasing your invention if it ever is mass-produced or used. Consult your lay friends and associates, those who have no special expertise in the field in

which you are interested, but whose opinion you trust and feel will be objective. Often it may be valuable not to tell them that you are the inventor but to ask their opinion generally so you will get a more objective evaluation. An excellent use of lay consultants is to put an estimated price on your invention (see Chapter 8) and ask your lay consultants if they would buy it at this price.

2. Experts in the field you can consult are salespeople in stores with similar devices to yours; engineers, managers, or technicians in companies in the field of your invention; and scholars, educators, professors, friends who are "in the business," etc. Naturally, you may not know these experts, so it's best to gain an entree by first flattering them with a request for their expert advice. Usually they'll be very glad and pleased to help you. With marketing-type experts, such as salespeople, you should obviously focus on the marketing factors, such as salability, while with technical experts, you should concentrate on technical factors such as operability, reliability, etc.

3. For your literature search, the best place to start is your librarian, who is trained to assist researchers and who is familiar with the library's research materials. It is generally most useful to consult a reference professional or librarian with an M.L.S. (Master's in Library Science) rather than a lay clerk, who may be trained only to check out books.

The library literature which you should investigate includes product directories, how-to-do-it books, catalogs, general reference books, patents (if available), etc.

Remember that the purpose of the literature search is not to determine whether your invention is new or patentable, but rather to give you additional background in the field so you can evaluate the positive and negative factors listed above. While you're doing your literature search you may find an anticipation of your invention; this is especially likely to occur if you search patent literature. If so, you'll either have to drop the invention right there, since you'll know you aren't the first inventor, or try to make a new invention by improving your first effort.

You'll be surprised how much better a feel you'll have for your invention once you've done some research and become familiar with the field.

When you do your actual novelty search, or when you have your novelty search made for you (see next chapter), you'll get additional background in the field which will help you evaluate and formulate additional positive and negative factors.

If you work for or have access to a large company, visit their purchasing department and ask permission to look through their product catalogs. Most companies have an extensive library of such catalogs and you'll often find much relevant and valuable information there that you won't find in even the biggest and best public libraries.

PRECAUTIONS DURING CONSULTATION

If you do show or discuss your invention, a degree of care to prevent theft, or to prove it in case it occurs, is mandatory. The best protection is to have all of your disclosees sign a receipt or log book entry indicating that they have seen your invention. The log book entry can be simply a page in your notebook which says at the top, "The undersigned have seen and understood Tom Brown's (name of invention) as described on pages —— of this book on the dates indicated"; you should also add a "Comments" column to flatter your consultants and indicate that you value their opinion. This column will also indicate that you are asking your consultants to sign your receipt page or log notebook in order to obtain their opinion, and not because you don't trust them.

If you use a separate receipt-sheet type of consultant's log, it can be appended to a copy of your disclosure; it should read similarly, for example: "The undersigned has seen and understood Martha Brown's (name of invention) as described in the foregoing disclosure on the dates indicated."

Another excellent way to protect your invention is to ask those to whom you show your invention to sign and date your disclosure as witnesses; witnesses can hardly ever claim that they invented independently of you if they are on record as having witnessed your invention. Bear in mind that the number of consultants you can use as witnesses is limited before you start interviewing a lot of them.

Another, albeit inferior, way to protect yourself is to send a confirming or thank-you letter before or after your consultation so you'll have a written record that you showed your invention to the person on a specific date.

Another way to protect yourself is to discuss your invention in vague terms only, reviewing only its functions and purposes and keeping the details confidential. In this way it is extremely unlikely that your invention can ever be stolen; on the other hand this method cannot be used with all inventions and you're not as likely to get as complete and useful an evaluation as if you showed actual drawings or a working model of your invention.

THE DECISION

Once you've gotten all your input, filled out your balance sheet with the positive and negative factors, etc., it's time to make a decision whether to go ahead or not. If your decision is that, even considering the negative factors, it would most likely be profitable to make and sell your invention, it's time to get to the legal area to determine whether it is novel enough to be patentable. Since the patentability search will generally require more money or time (unless you live near Arlington, Va.), it is again important to stress that you first complete a careful commercial evaluation so as not to waste your valuable money or time.

If your commercial evaluation and list of all the positive and negative factors you can think of still leaves you uncertain, though you feel there is good potential, wait a while before proceeding. The passage of time will often give you a new perspective that can make your decision easier. If after a couple of weeks you still can't make up your mind, it's best to go ahead and make the search. If the search discloses that your invention is already known, your decision will be obvious, but if the search shows that you have a new invention, you should attempt to patent and market the invention rather than let a potentially valuable and profitable idea die without being given its day in court.

CHAPTER FOUR

Search and You May Find

THE PATENTABILITY SEARCH VIS-À-VIS COMMERCIAL EVALUATION

Assuming your invention has received a passing grade on the commercial scorecard (Chapter 3), it's time to investigate its patentability. Although commercial evaluation is treated in a separate chapter, and although it should be done first since it is generally easier and cheaper (unless you live near the Patent and Trademark Office in Arlington, Virginia), it is important to remember not to spend too much effort on it before you investigate patentability to some degree. This is because both criteria—good commercial potential and patentability—are generally necessary for success. Therefore, it doesn't make sense to put an exhaustive amount of energy into evaluating the commercial potential of your invention since you may discover after five minutes of searching that the idea was old fifty years ago.

My advice would be to play it by ear to a great extent, but to start by making a fair to good investigation of commercial potential; if things look promising, make your patentability search; if things still look promising, and if you still have any doubts or second thoughts about commercial potential, investigate this aspect more exhaustively. It all depends on the facilities available to you, the amount of money and time you are willing to invest in the enterprise, and how energetic and thorough you are.

WHY MAKE A PATENTABILITY SEARCH?

The main reason for making a patentability search of your invention is just what you thought: To discover if you are likely to get a patent on your invention. If you can, manufacturers will want to buy it because it will give them what the Boston Consulting Group terms a "privileged position," that is, a monopoly in the field of the invention so that they can be "kings of the road" (if only for a limited number of years), which will enable them to charge more, to derive income from licensing, and not to worry about competition so much, etc.

Also, it's a lot easier (and cheaper) to make a patentability search than to prepare a patent application with its specification, drawing, claims, filing fees, etc. So it makes sense to do a relatively small amount of work or make a relatively small expenditure in order to avoid wasting a large amount of time or making a relatively large and needless expenditure.

In addition, you will find it far easier to prepare a patent application on your invention if you have made a patentability search first. This is because a search will bring out references in the field of your invention. After reading these, you will be very familiar with the field. You will understand its terminology and know the format of similar patent applications. Thus the writing of your patent application will be more approachable, far easier, and go much faster. Also, by familiarizing yourself with the prior art, you'll be able to tailor your patent application so as to avoid such prior art, thus saving yourself work later on during the "prosecution" stage.

If your patentability search indicates that your invention isn't patentable, you will not be able to obtain any real protection and most manufacturers will not want to invest the money in tooling, producing, and marketing something their competition can copy at much lower cost with little risk. However, as we will see later, even if your invention is not patentable, it still may be possible to market it—indeed fortunes sometimes have been made on unpatentable inventions—but the road is relatively difficult, particularly if you do not do the manufacturing yourself.

PATENTABLE AND NONPATENTABLE SUBJECT MATTER

Before you make a search for patentability, you must be sure that your invention comprises *patentable subject matter*, that is, something upon which the Patent and Trademark Office will be able to grant a patent, assuming you're the first to come up with it. The patent laws do not allow the PTO to grant patents on everything that is new; only certain categories of inventions can be patented; everything else is considered nonpatentable subject matter.

The categories of patentable subject matter, although only five, are pretty comprehensive. They are:

1. Processes

2. Machines

3. Manufactures

4. Compositions of matter

5. New uses of any of the above four

1. *Processes*, sometimes termed "methods," are ways of doing or making things. Processes always have one or more steps, each of which expresses some activity. Examples are heat treatment processes, chemical

reactions or processes, material treatment processes, ways of making products or chemicals, ways of changing things, etc.

2. *Machines* are devices or things for accomplishing a task; like processes, they usually involve some activity or motion that is performed by working parts. Examples of machines are cigarette lighters, sewage treatment plants, clocks, all electric circuits, automobiles, boats, rockets, telephones, TVs, computers, etc.

3. *Manufactures*, sometimes termed "articles of manufacture," are things which are relatively simple and which don't have working or moving parts as prime features. There is some overlap between the machine and the manufacture categories. Many devices, such as mechanical pencils, can be classified in either; the distinction isn't important so long as the device can be assigned to at least one category. Examples of manufactures are erasers, desks, houses, wires, tires, books, cloth, chairs, containers, transistors, dolls, hairpieces, ladders, envelopes, buildings, etc.

4. *Compositions of matter* are chemical compositions, conglomerates, aggregates, or other chemically significant substances which are usually supplied in bulk, in liquid, gas, or solid form. Examples are road-building compositions, gasoline, fuel gas, glue, paper, etc. One inventor even obtained a patent on a new element he discovered.

5. *New uses of any of the above four* are rare, but if you discover a new, unobvious *(unrelated)* use of any old invention or thing, you can get a patent on the new use. For example suppose you discover that your venetian-blind cleaner can also be used as a seed planter: You obviously can't get a patent on the venetian-blind cleaner per se since someone already patented, invented, and/or designed it first, but you can get a patent on the specific new use (seed planting) you've invented. One inventor obtained a patent on a new use for aspirin: Feeding it to swine to increase their rate of growth.

If you've invented something and you can't reasonably assign it taxonomically to one of the five classes above, your invention can't be patented, no matter how new it is. Examples of inventions which can't be patented are processes that must be performed solely by hand, or by hand with only simple implements, such as a method of styling hair with a comb and brush; methods of doing business, printed matter; naturally occurring articles, even if modified somewhat, such as a shrimp with its head and digestive tract removed; and abstract scientific principles.

Computer programs per se, that is, naked algorithms not tied in with any machine, are still not patentable. However, most patent lawyers will agree that it is possible effectively to patent an algorithm if it can be claimed as a machine or as a method which utilizes a machine; the important thing is to recite plenty of hardware in the claims (Chapter 7) and not to wave a red flag in the examiner's face by using the words "program" or "algorithm" in your claims.

Ideas per se, that is, thoughts or goals not expressed in hardware form or usage, are obviously not assignable to any of the five categories above. If you have an idea, you must express it in tangible form, if only on paper, before the PTO will accept it. Often the act of expressing an abstract idea in tangible form will be more significant than the idea.

To be patentable, inventions must fulfill two other requirements in addition to those listed above. Problems are seldom encountered with these, but I include them for the sake of completeness. The invention must be useful, and it must not be an atomic weapon.

Regarding the requirement of usefulness, it's hard to think of an invention which couldn't be used for some purpose, if only for amusement, but occasionally a totally chimerical invention might be filed that the PTO will have to reject. For example, I have heard a story, perhaps apocryphal, that an application was once filed on a rear windshield (with wiper) for a horse, and that the PTO rejected it for lack of utility.

A more important requirement, which the legislature hasn't mentioned, but which the PTO and courts have brought in on their own initiative (by stretching the definition of "useful"), is *legality*. If the invention is useful solely for an illegal purpose, for example, to disable burglar alarms, aid in safecracking, copy currency, etc., the PTO won't allow it. (The PTO in the past had also—again on its own initiative—included *morality* in its requirements, but in recent years, with increased sexual liberality, the requirement is no longer extant: The PTO now regularly issues patents on sexual aids and stimulants.)

Another more important requirement, which the PTO has also brought in under the usefulness requirement, again probably stretching the definition of the term, is operability. The invention must work for it to be patentable. Thus if your invention is a true perpetual-motion machine, or a metaphysical-energy converter, or, more realistically, a very esoteric invention which looks technically questionable, which is to say, like it might not work, the PTO will ask you to bring it in for a demonstration to prove its operability before they'll issue you a patent. And remember that patent examiners all have technical degrees (some are even Ph.D.s), so expect a very stringent test if the operability of your invention is ever questioned.

Regarding the bomb, inventions devoted to or usable exclusively as atomic or nuclear weaponry are not patentable because of a special statute. However, if you have invented that doomsday machine, don't be discouraged. You can be rewarded directly by making an application with the Energy Research and Development Agency, formerly the AEC.

NOVELTY AND NONOBVIOUSNESS: TWO INDISPENSABLE ELEMENTS OF PATENTABILITY

Novelty

Rarely will a patentability search produce a reference (a prior patent or other publication) that is a dead ringer for your invention; usually your invention will have one or more differences from the "prior art" your search uncovers. Of course, if your search does produce a dead-ringer reference for your invention, that is, a reference showing all the features of your invention and operating in the same way for the same purpose, obviously your patentability decision can be made immediately: Your invention lacks *novelty* over the prior art, or is *anticipated* by the prior art, and is thus definitely unpatentable.

Thus as you have gathered by now, for your invention to have novelty, an essential requisite to patentability, it must differ in some way, however minor, from the prior art. But as you will see in the next part, novelty is not enough and can be effectively disregarded since it is inherent in the requirement for nonobviousness.

Nonobviousness

Most of the time a patentability search will produce one or more references similar to your invention, or which show several, but not all, of the features of your invention. That is, you will find that your invention has one or more features or differences that aren't shown in the prior art. A little reflection will convince you that even though your invention is different from the prior art, this is not enough. If any difference could get you a patent, there could be tens of thousands of patents issued each week to everyone who "invented" something that was at all, however slightly, different from the prior art, for example, something that had a different color, a different size, a different arrangement of parts, etc.

Thus to say your invention is different from the prior art is definitely not enough; in order to obtain a patent, the differences must be substantial and significant. In the law, the crucial word is "nonobviousness." That is, the differences between your invention and the prior art must not be obvious to one with ordinary skill in the field. In the words of the statute [Section 103 of Title 35 (Patents) of the U.S. Code]:

A patent may not be obtained though the invention is not identically disclosed or described [in the prior art] if the differences between the subject matter sought to be patented and the prior art are such that the subject matter as a whole would have been obvious at the time the invention was made to a person having ordinary skill in the art to which said subject matter pertains.

While the language quoted may sound a bit heavy, legal, and confusing, remember that all it means is that you can't get a patent if all the differences between your invention and the prior art would have been obvious, at the time the invention was made, to a person having ordinary skill in the field of your invention.

The phrase "a person having ordinary skill in the art to which said subject matter pertains" can best be illustrated by examples. For example, if your invention has to do with electronics, say an improved flip-flop circuit, a person having ordinary skill in the art would be a computer-circuit engineer. If your invention has to do with chemistry, say a new photochemical process, a photochemical engineer would be our imaginary skilled artisan. If your invention is mechanical, such as an improved cigarette lighter or belt buckle, a hypothetical cigarette-lighter engineer or belt-buckle designer would have to be postulated.

Most of the trouble in interpreting Section 103 is encountered with the word "obvious." If after reading my explanation you still do not understand it, don't be dismayed. Most patent attorneys, patent examiners, and judges can't agree on the meaning of the term.

Many tests for obviousness have been used, and some have been rejected over the years. The courts have often referred to "a flash of genius," "a synergistic effect," or some other colorful term. The United States Court of Appeals for the Ninth Circuit (which covers all of the far western states) says that nonobviousness is manifested if the invention produces "unusual and surprising results." Most examiners in the PTO look for a new result that is not expected from a review of the prior art.

The illustration of an unexpected new result can best be illustrated by an example. Suppose you make a bicycle out of a new lightweight alloy that has recently been discovered, and as a result your bicycle is lighter than ever before. Is your invention "unobvious"? The answer is no, because such a result would be expected from the known prior art, which comprises existing bicycles and the new lightweight alloy. In other words, if a skilled bicycle engineer were to be shown the new, lightweight alloy, it would obviously occur to him to make a bicycle out of this alloy since bicycle engineers are always seeking to make lighter bicycles. In other words, the results (the lightweight bicycle) are entirely foreseeable.

However, if a chemist through experimentation combines several metals which cooperate in a new way to provide added strength without added density, and such a result is not reasonably foreseeable, the new alloy is almost certainly patentable.

For an example from electronics, consider an invention made by a current client of mine—a circuit that, when connected across a light switch, holds the light on for about twenty seconds after the light is switched off, and can be used repeatedly and always operates in the same manner. The prior art showed "delayed-off" circuits, but all of these could only be used once every several minutes, requiring a waiting period before they could be used again. By incorporating special discharging and reset circuits that had never before been used or anticipated, a new, improved, unexpected, and unsuggested result was produced, so that the circuit was patentable over the prior art.

For some mechanical examples, consider all the inventions listed in Chapter 1: The magnetic pistol guard, the buried plastic cable, the car-lift bag, the watch calendar sticker, and GRASSCRETE. All of these inventions produced new, unexpected results, which were probably not suggested or shown in the prior art.

Although generally you must make a significant physical change for your invention to be considered unobvious, often a very slight change in the shape, slope, size, or material can produce a very patentable invention that operates entirely differently and produces totally unexpected results. Consider a centrifugal vegetable juicer composed of a spinning perforated basket with a nonperforated grater bottom. When vegetables, such as carrots, were pushed into the grater bottom, they were grated into fine pieces and thrown against the side walls of the basket, adding weight to the basket and blocking the perforations, making the machine impossible to run and operate after a relatively small amount of vegetable was juiced. Someone conceived of making the basket with sloping sides so that (while the juice was still centrifugally extracted through the perforated sides of the basket) the pulp, instead of adhering to the vertical sides of the basket, was centrifugally forced up the sloped sides of the basket where it could be diverted to a separate receptacle. Thus the juicer could be operated continuously without the pulp having to be cleaned out. Obviously the result is entirely new and unexpected, and deserves patent protection.

I could go on writing pages and pages about obviousness, but I do not think this would help you understand the concept any better. The best advice I can give is the simplest: Ask yourself the question, Does my invention have one or more new features which are important, significant, and which produce valuable, unexpected new results? If it does, it probably will pass muster with the PTO and the courts. It does not have to be an earthshaking or outstanding development. It can be a relatively minor change, so long as the results are not anticipated or suggested by the prior art.

It is recommended that you note the test of the foregoing paragraph well, as it probably is the most important concept in patent law and will be referred to again and again.

WHAT IS PRIOR ART?

The term "prior art," which is used in the all-important Section 103, means generally the state of knowledge existing or available before your invention. It is what your invention must be significantly different from in order to be patentable.

While the above concepts may seem clear to you, in practice you will find they are of little use because of the specific problems that almost always arise. Fortunately we can be very precise here. Prior art comprises all of the following:

1. *Prior Publications.* Any publication, not written by you, from anywhere in the world in any language, that was made available to the public before you conceived of your invention. The word "publication" includes trade and professional journals, magazines, patents, and even unprinted theses, provided they were made publicly available. This is the most important category of prior art, and will generally constitute about 99 percent of all the prior art you will encounter.

2. *Your Publications.* Any publication written by you if it was published over a year before you filed your patent application. The "one-year rule" states, in effect, that if you publish details of (or offer to sell) anything which embodies your invention, you must file a patent application within one year, although, as you will see later, you would be wise to file your patent application *before* selling or publishing your invention to minimize theft and loss of foreign filing rights.

3. *Public Knowledge.* Public knowledge or use in the United States which, although not published, existed before you conceived of your invention.

4. *Prior U.S. Patents.* Any U.S. patent application filed by another before you conceived of your invention. This is one area in which you will not be able to make a complete search since it includes pending patent applications, which, by statute, are preserved in secrecy.

5. *Prior Public Use.* Any work done by anyone else in the United States, who, even though not attempting to patent the invention, did not abandon or conceal it from the public. This area is difficult to search, and the problem rarely occurs in practice, but it must be considered. For example, suppose you "invent" a metal heat-treating process which a blacksmith in a remote area has been using for twenty years before you thought of it, and the blacksmith never kept it secret but freely showed the "invention" to anyone in town; your right to a patent would be defeated by the blacksmith's earlier work.

THE PRELIMINARY LOOK

If you do not live near the PTO in Arlington, Virginia, it is sometimes wise to make a brief preliminary look before spending the money or time for a formal search. Sometimes you can "knock out" your invention and save yourself cost and effort. If you haven't made the preliminary look already as part of your commercial evaluation, do so now by looking in stores, catalogs, reference books, product directories, etc., for your invention. An hour or two in your library and perhaps a visit or two to likely stores or suppliers should be sufficient. If you do not find anything in your preliminary look, and if your invention does not fall into the category discussed under the next heading, you are ready to make the formal search.

WHEN NOT TO SEARCH

Generally almost all inventions should be searched for patentability, but there are occasionally inventions in such new or arcane fields, with which the inventor is so familiar, that a search would not be profitable. For example, if you are an inventor intimately familiar with semiconductors and with up-to-the-minute knowledge of all known transistor-diffusion processes, and you come up with a breakthrough transistor-diffusion process, it is extremely unlikely that a search will produce any reference showing your idea. Before deciding not to search, however, you should be reasonably certain that you or someone else with whom you are in contact knows all there is to know about the field in question, and that there is little likelihood of any obscure reference which shows your invention.

THE QUALITY OF A SEARCH CAN VARY

Like anything else, the quality of a search for patentability can vary from very bad to near perfect. It will never be quite perfect because, as stated before, there is no way to search pending patent applications filed before you made your invention. To apply a cliché, what you get out of a search will depend on what you put into it—it depends on where you search, who searches, for how long, and how much imagination goes into the search.

There are two main ways to go about searching: Hiring someone else to do the job for you, or doing it yourself. If you can afford it, and if you do not live near the PTO, obviously it is best to hire someone, but if you can't afford the expense, or don't live far from Arlington, you will probably want to do it yourself, so go right on to the section of this chapter called *Do-It-Yourself Searching.*

If you are going to make the search yourself, it is recommended that you do it well and thoroughly. If a valuable reference is missed, a lot of time will have been wasted on the search and preparation of your patent application. It is better to spend a few more dollars or hours searching than to miss an important reference that can make all of your hours and money expended worthless.

If you want to hire a searcher, at the low-quality end of the scale, there are searchers who advertise in science or hobby journals, offering to make a search of your invention for $6. No one can make a decent search without spending several hours on the job, so a moment's reflection shows you that anyone who professes to maintain an office in the Washington, D.C. area, advertise services, and search your invention for $6 is putting you on.

At the high-quality end of the scale, there are many very competent attorneys and former examiners who work near the PTO, who search all the time, and who will do an excellent job for $125 to $150. Again, at the high end of the scale, if you are a very thorough, scientific, methodical person, and you go to the PTO yourself and spend a day or two at it, your own search will probably equal the best that money can buy.

But remember again that no search, no matter how long and how careful, can cover pending patent applications or all the sometimes obscure foreign references and patents, which may not even be available.

HIRING SOMEONE TO SEARCH

If you do hire someone to search, the only one whom I would choose is an individual who will make the search at the PTO in Arlington. If you pay for a search anywhere in the United States other than the PTO, I believe you are wasting your money: The PTO is the only place in the country where all patents are available and where patents are classified by subclasses.

A patent searcher does not have to be licensed; therefore practically anyone can get set up in this business and take the title of "patent searcher." Thus it is advisable to be careful to select a searcher who you can be sure is competent, honest, and diligent.

You can avail yourself of two classes of searchers: (1) Lay searchers, (most of whom advertise,) and (2) patent attorneys and patent agents; these are now permitted to advertise but few do so yet.

Many searchers can be located in the Yellow Pages of local telephone directories under the heading "Patent Searchers." Others advertise in periodicals such as *The Journal of the Patent Office Society,* a publication for patent professionals edited and published by a private association of patent examiners. I have had success with lay searchers, but before hiring any, I found out about the searcher's charges, technical background, on-the-job experience, and usual amount of time spent on a search. I would also ask for the names of some clients, preferably local, so as to call and check with them. The response you receive from such an inquiry, together with the comments of any previous clients you contact, should give you a reasonably good idea of the searcher's honesty, competency, and diligence. If, after receiving and checking all this information, you still have any doubts about a lay searcher, try someone else.

As for attorneys or agents, it is definitely a problem to obtain one since generally they do not advertise yet, although this may change in the future. Your best chance for success in finding an attorney or agent to perform a search for you is to get a referral from someone you know or are associated with in some manner.

For example, if you work for a large company which has its own patent attorney or which uses independent patent attorneys, you should ask that patent attorney for the name of a competent patent searcher in the Washington area. All patent attorneys not located in the Washington area are associated or have a relationship with a patent attorney in the Washington area who performs searches and other functions in the PTO for them.

If you have no access to a patent attorney, you may have access to a general attorney who knows a patent attorney and who can obtain for you the name of the patent attorney's Washington area associate.

If you cannot get a referral to a Washington area patent attorney, your best bet is to refer to the Government publication, *Attorneys and Agents Registered to Practice Before the U.S. Patent and Trademark Office*, which is available at Government book stores and many libraries. This soft-cover book contains the names of virtually all the patent attorneys and agents in the United States. It has two parts: The first lists all the patent attorneys and agents alphabetically; the second lists them geographically, by state and zip code. Most patent attorneys and agents who do searching in the PTO can be found in the District of Columbia section, or the Virginia section under zip code 22202. Pick any one of these; then call or write to say you want a search made in a particular field. Ask about fees and terms for services, and find out whether this attorney or agent has done searches in your field before. If this person is not able to handle the job for you, ask for a referral to someone else. I suggest spending a few dollars and rapping for a few minutes to see if you've found someone who is right for you; if you get bad vibes, feel condescended to, or think that personality is being emphasized over substance, spend your money elsewhere. Most searchers who do not know you will probably require some sort of retainer in advance, which I feel is reasonable.

Be sure to send the searcher you engage a clear and complete description of your invention, together with clear and easily understandable drawings. Test your disclosure on a friend first to make sure it is completely clear and understandable. If you wish any type of particular emphasis applied to any aspect of your search, be sure to tell the searcher so.

After you send out the search request, it will generally take the searcher several weeks to perform the search and report to you. Most search reports are issued in four parts:

1. A description of your invention provided by the searcher to assure to you that your invention has been understood correctly, and to indicate exactly what has been searched.

2. A citation list of the patents and other references discovered during the search.

3. A brief discussion of the cited patents and other references, pointing out the relevant parts of each.

4. A list of the classes and subclasses searched and the examiners consulted, if any.

The searcher will enclose copies of the references cited in the search report and enclose a bill. Most searchers charge separately for the search, the references obtained, and the postage. If you have paid the searcher a retainer, you should be sent a refund unless it was insufficient, in which case you will receive a bill for the balance you owe.

It is now up to you to read the search report and the references carefully, and to determine whether your invention is patentable over the references obtained in the search. Use the criteria given above under "non-obviousness."

You will note that the four-part list above does not include an opinion on patentability. This is for two reasons: First, most searchers are used to working for patent attorneys who like to form their own opinions on patentability for their clients. Second, if the searcher's opinion on patentability is negative, a negative opinion on the record might be damaging to your case if you do get a patent and sue on it. However, a negative opinion on the record is not all that bad, and if you want the searcher's opinion on patentability in addition to the search, all searchers will be glad to give it to you without extra charge or for a slight additional cost of probably not more than $25 or $50. Do not hesitate to ask in advance and to specify exactly what you want in your search: It is your money and you are entitled to specify what you are paying for before you make any contract with a searcher.

One final word on hiring searchers. A third possibility is to use a local patent attorney or agent. However, this is a very inefficient and costly way to do the job. The local patent attorney or agent will either have to hire an associate in Washington to make the search for you, whereby you will have to pay two patent professionals for the search, or will have to travel to Arlington to make the search, whereby you will have to pay the travel expenses. Thus I do not recommend the use of a local patent attorney or agent to do searching unless you are willing to pay the extra intermediary's charges involved.

DO-IT-YOURSELF SEARCHING

In the PTO in Arlington

As you have gathered by now, the best place to make a patent search is in the PTO in Arlington* since it has all of the patents arranged into subclasses, and also has foreign patents and literature classified in the subclasses in the examiner search areas. If you do go to the PTO in Arlington, it may be to your advantage to make several searches at once to make the trip worthwhile; your travel expenses will be tax-deductible.

---

* Some large companies maintain their own search files in certain fields; if you can get access to one of these in your field, you're probably even better off than if you go to the PTO.

Once in the PTO, there are two places you can make the search: The public search room and the examiners' search files in the actual examining divisions. Most searchers make their search in the public search room because it is more convenient—there are search tables, and it is large and well-lighted—but I recommend putting up with a little inconvenience and going to the examiners' search files. The examiners will be there to assist you, and foreign patents and literature are also available. If you do go to an actual examining division, you must ask permission from a primary examiner or clerk before commencing your search. If you want to use the search room, you must first obtain a user's pass from a clerk outside the search room (security is omnipresent today).

It is perfectly safe to ask any of the assistants in the public search room or the examiners about your search and to give them all the details of your invention. They see dozens of new inventions every week and they are perfectly used to helping searchers and others. I have never heard of an examiner or search assistant stealing an invention. Besides, employees of the PTO are not allowed to file patent applications.

If you do make your search in the examiners' files, it will first be necessary to make a stop in the public search room to find out exactly where to search, that is, what classes and subclasses to search. Once you have found the pertinent classes and subclasses, ask in the search room or look in the appropriate index to find which examining division these classes and search classes are to be found in. Then go to the examining division and make your search. Do not hesitate to ask the clerk or the examiners to refer you to the examiner who makes searches in those classes and subclasses to assist you in your search.

The procedure for making a search on your own can be broken into four parts:

1. Write down all the features of your invention in a brief, concise format. This is done to simplify your invention so that you will know exactly what to look for when searching. For example, if you are searching a bicycle with a new type of sprocket wheel, write down "bicycle, sprocket wheel" and add briefly the details. If you are searching an electronic circuit, write down in a series of phrases like the foregoing or in a very brief sentence the quintessence of your invention, such as "flip-flop circuit with unijunction transistors" or some other very brief and concise description. Ditto for chemical inventions. Take this brief description, a drawing of your invention, the full description of it, and a log book with you.

2. Find the relevant classes and subclasses in which to search. Patents are classified by subject matter into over 300 main classifications, each of which has an average of about 220 subclasses, giving a total of about 66,000 subclasses! To find the subclasses into which prior art on your invention may be classified, look into the *Index of Classification*, which has all the subclasses and their synonymies arranged alphabetically. Look carefully into the index, observe the cross-references, and spend enough time to be sure you are very familiar with it and have obtained the right subclasses. When you find one or more subclasses which you

feel may be relevant, check these in the *Class Definitions* manual to be sure that you have obtained the right subclasses; this manual will also give you valuable searching hints and cross-references. Usually two or more subclasses will be appropriate. Also refer to your subclasses in the *Manual of Classification* (which is arranged by classes and subclasses) to see if there are any other relevant subclasses near your selected subclasses.

For example, if you have invented a bicycle with a new sprocket wheel, one particular subclass you may want to search may be under the "Bicycles" classifications. Another subclass may be under the "Gears" classifications. Refer to *Class Definitions* and the *Manual of Classification* to be sure you obtain all the appropriate subclasses.*

An excellent article on how to search in the PTO is "The Patent System—A Source of Information for the Engineer," by Joseph K. Campbell, Assistant Professor, Agricultural Engineering Department, Cornell University, Ithaca, New York, which was presented at the 1969 Annual Meeting of the American Society of Agricultural Engineers, North Atlantic Region. The ASAE's address, if you can't find the article in your library, is P.O. Box 229, St. Joseph, MI 49085.

Professor Campbell gives a good example of class and subclass selection. He postulates a hypothetical search of a machine that encapsulates or pelletizes small seeds (such as for petunias or lettuce) so they may be planted accurately by a mechanical planter.

To find the appropriate subclasses, look in the *Index of Classification*, which indicates that Class 47, Plant Husbandry, contains a subclass 1 entitled, "Seed Containing Compositions." Thus a first search would be in Class 47, subclass 1. Using his imagination, Professor Campbell also notes that some candy, such as chocolate-covered peanuts, consists of encapsulated seeds, and comes up with several subclasses under Class 107, "Bread, Pastry, and Confection Making," namely subclass 1.25, "Composite Pills (with core)"; subclass 1.7, "Feeding Solid Centers into Confectionery"; and subclass 11, "Pills." Thus he adds Class 107, subclasses 1.25, 1.7, and 11 to his search.

3. Review the patents (and foreign patents and literature) in the selected subclasses.

After obtaining a list of the classes and subclasses to search, find the appropriate examining division or location in the search room† and look

---

* You can get a free, informal mail-order classification of your invention for search purposes by sending a copy of your invention disclosure with a request for suggestions of one or more search subclasses to Search Room, Patent and Trademark Office, Washington DC 20231. However, unless you're really stuck in obtaining subclasses, I do not recommend using this method since you have the interest and familiarity with your invention to do a far better job if only you put a little effort into it.

† The PTO recently implemented the following automated search systems: (1) A computer-controlled microfiche system to search inventions in digital processors and A-D converters (class 340, subs 172.5 and 347); (2) a punch card system to search inventions in electrolysis, organometallics, and steroids; (3) a notched-edge card system to search inventions in fluid devices; and (4) a TERMATREX search system to search inventions in automatic fluid controls, boots and shoes, chemical testing, combined fasteners, electrical contact materials, and surface bonding using critical metals. If your invention is in any of these fields, you're lucky; ask for assistance and information.

through all the patents in your selected subclasses. In the search room, you will have physically to remove bundles of patents from slotlike shelves, bring them to a table in the main search area, and search them by placing the patents in a packet holder and flipping through the patents. In the examiners' search room, the patents are found in small drawers, called "shoes" by the examiners, and you will have to remove the drawer of patents, hold it in your lap and flip through the patents while you are seated in a chair, generally without a table being available to you.

As you flip through the patents, it may first seem very difficult to understand the patents and to make your search. This is especially so with old patents which have several sheets of unlabeled drawings and a closely printed description, termed a "specification," after the drawings. Newer patents will be easier since they have an abstract page up front that contains a brief summary of the patent and the most relevant figure or drawing. However, even with older patents, you can get a brief summary of the patent by referring to the summary of the invention, which is usually found in the first or second column of the specification, or by referring to the claims at the end of the patent. These usually contain a good summary of the invention.

After flipping through several patents for an hour or so, you will find you are able to understand the patents much more easily and can learn the gist of each patent after just a few seconds or minutes. If, after searching through some of the patents in your subclass, you find that they definitely are not relevant, you can either go to another one of your selected subclasses and, keeping in mind the main features of your invention as you have written them down, look for them in the patents you are flipping through.

If you find relevant patents, write down their numbers, and order copies later. If you do find a good reference, don't stop; continue your search to the end. Be sure to keep a careful record of all patents you have searched, writing down the most relevant features of each. Also write down a list of all the classes and subclasses you have searched. For each patent you select, write down not only the patent number, but the name of the patentee, and the date of the patent as a means of double-checking in case you have written down a wrong number.

In each subclass you will find a first group of patents, which are directly classified there, and a second group, termed cross-references (XRs), which are primarily classified in another subclass, but are also classified in your subclass because they have a feature which makes the cross-reference appropriate. Be sure to review the XR patents in each subclass.

The public search room has facilities for making copies of patents for 15 cents per page, but you can buy complete patents at 50 cents each. Purchase an adequate supply of 50-cent coupons from the PTO's cashier; then write down the numbers of the patents you select on these coupons and deposit them in the appropriate box in the search room. Your patents will be mailed to you, generally in several weeks to a month.

4. After you have obtained your patents and other references, study them all carefully to see if the concepts of your invention are really shown and described in the references you have selected. It's a good idea to write down a brief summary of each patent on the face of the patent if it doesn't have an abstract or if the abstract is inadequate. Always bear in mind that if your invention has several features in combination, it is perfectly legitimate to combine several of your selected references, but it has to be obvious how to combine the references, that is, there must be some reason for one skilled in the art to combine the indicated references in the manner you intend.

In the example we have given above, if you have invented a new lightweight bicycle out of a lightweight alloy, and if you found a reference showing a bicycle, and another reference showing the lightweight alloy, it would be perfectly obvious to combine these two references to come up with a bicycle made of the lightweight alloy. As you read through the patents and other references to make a determination of patentability, keep in mind the criteria given above under *Obviousness* in order to make your decision.

Patent Depository Library

If you can't search in the Patent and Trademark Office, the next possibility, although decidedly inferior—and one I don't recommend—is to search your invention in one of the twenty-nine depository libraries listed below, all of which currently receive all patents issued by the PTO:

State	City	Library
Alabama	Birmingham	* Public
California	Los Angeles	* Public
	Sunnyvale	* Public
Colorado	Denver	* Public
Georgia	Atlanta	* Georgia Institute of Technology
Illinois	Chicago	* Public
Massachusetts	Boston	* Public
Michigan	Detroit	* Public
Missouri	Kansas City	* Linda Hall
	St. Louis	* Public
Nebraska	Lincoln	* University of Nebraska
New Jersey	Newark	* Public
New York	Albany	* New York State
	Buffalo	* Buffalo and Erie County Public
	New York	* Public
North Carolina	Raleigh	* North Carolina State University
Ohio	Cincinnati	* Cincinnati and Hamilton County Public
	Cleveland	* Public
	Columbus	* Ohio State University
	Toledo	* Lucas County Public
Oklahoma	Stillwater	* Oklahoma State University
Pennsylvania	Philadelphia	* Franklin Institute
	Pittsburgh	* Carnegie

State	City	Library
Rhode Island	Providence	* Public
Texas	Dallas	Public
	Houston	Fondren, Rice University
Washington	Seattle	Engineering, University of Washington
Wisconsin	Madison	* Engineering, University of Wisconsin
	Milwaukee	* Public

All those libraries marked with an asterisk (*) have all the patents issued from No. 1 to the present, but they are not physically separated into any type of classification. The Sunnyvale library has patents issued since 1962 physically separated into the 300 main classes, and the other libraries have only recently started receiving patents.

If you do have access to a patent depository library and wish to make a search there, you should go through the four steps given above. After you have found the relevant classes and subclasses, however, you have to get a list of patents in those selected classes and subclasses. Many of these libraries have lists of patents in each class and subclass on microfilm, but if your depository library does not have such a list, you will have to order one from the PTO in Arlington, which may take several weeks to arrive. (The depository library staff will show you how to order.) Once you have obtained a list of the patents in your selected classes and subclasses, you have to select each patent individually and examine it. As the patents will probably be in separate bound volumes, it will be much more difficult and time-consuming than if you were in the PTO in Arlington, where all the patents are physically arranged by subclasses. You will have to decide whether your time is worth more than the $125 or so you would spend for a professional searcher.

Official Gazette Search

This type of search is decidedly inferior even to the depository library search and I would not include it, except for the fact that I have known several inventors who made an adequate *Official Gazette* search on their own, although it takes a very dedicated and diligent individual to do so.

Most libraries around the country subscribe to the *Official Gazette*, which is published by the PTO each week (see Chapter 14), and which contains an abstract or claim and single figure of drawing of each of the patents issued that week. The entries in the *Official Gazette* are classified by patent number, and also by class and subclass under the headings "General and Mechanical," "Chemical," and "Electrical."

If your library subscribes to the *Official Gazette* and has an *Index of Classification*, you can make a search, provided you do the four steps listed in the PTO search, plus the additional step of obtaining a list of the patents in your selected subclasses, as outlined in the depository library search. When you have obtained a list of the patents in each selected class and subclass, then review each of these patents in the copies of the *Official Gazette*. Each patent entry you find will contain only a single claim or abstract and a single figure of drawing of the patent, so that you will not have all of the information on the patent at hand, but if the drawing and claim look relevant, order a copy of the patent and study it at your leisure.

Some libraries may also have the *National Catalog of Patents*, which lists abstracts of patents by subject matter for each year, and you may search into this directly, but I believe the *National Catalog* was discontinued in 1963—at least that is the latest date of this publication in the San Francisco Public Library.

THE FINAL DECISION

After you have made your search, obtained all your references, and looked them over, you should have a pretty good idea of the patentability of your invention. If you are in doubt, it probably isn't patentable, or if patentable, it would be easy to design around. One possibility, if you can't make a decision, is to pay at this stage for a patent professional's opinion. If you found nothing like your invention in your search, congratulations. You probably have a very broad invention, since, of the 4-million-plus patents which have been issued thus far, one or more of the features of most inventions are likely to be shown in the prior art.

CHAPTER FIVE

What Do I Do Now?

Now that you've evaluated the commercial potential and patentability of your invention you may well ask, Why the need for a chapter at this point to tell me what to do? Why can't I just start preparing a patent application or selling my invention?

Well, if your invention has commercial potential and patentability, generally you should prepare a patent application and then market it (I'll explain the reason for this order later), but there are quite a few fine points and other choices to consider before you go forging ahead. Moreover, there still is plenty of hope even if your invention isn't patentable, as you will soon see.

INVENTION DECISION CHART

Because the choices are somewhat numerous, I have provided an Invention Decision Chart (Fig. 4) to simplify and organize things. The chart is organized like a computer programmer's flowchart, and you will find it very easy and simple to use even if you have never used a flowchart before. One word of caution, however: Because of size limitations, the chart is necessarily oversimplified, so don't rely on it exclusively. Read the text carefully and use the chart merely as an aid to understanding the text and organizing your thoughts as you proceed.

The Invention Decision Chart consists of twenty-three blocks with interconnecting lead lines. The numbered blocks (even numbers from 10 to 40) represent various tasks and decisions on your route to a final decision, and the lettered blocks (A to F and X) represent the various final actions which

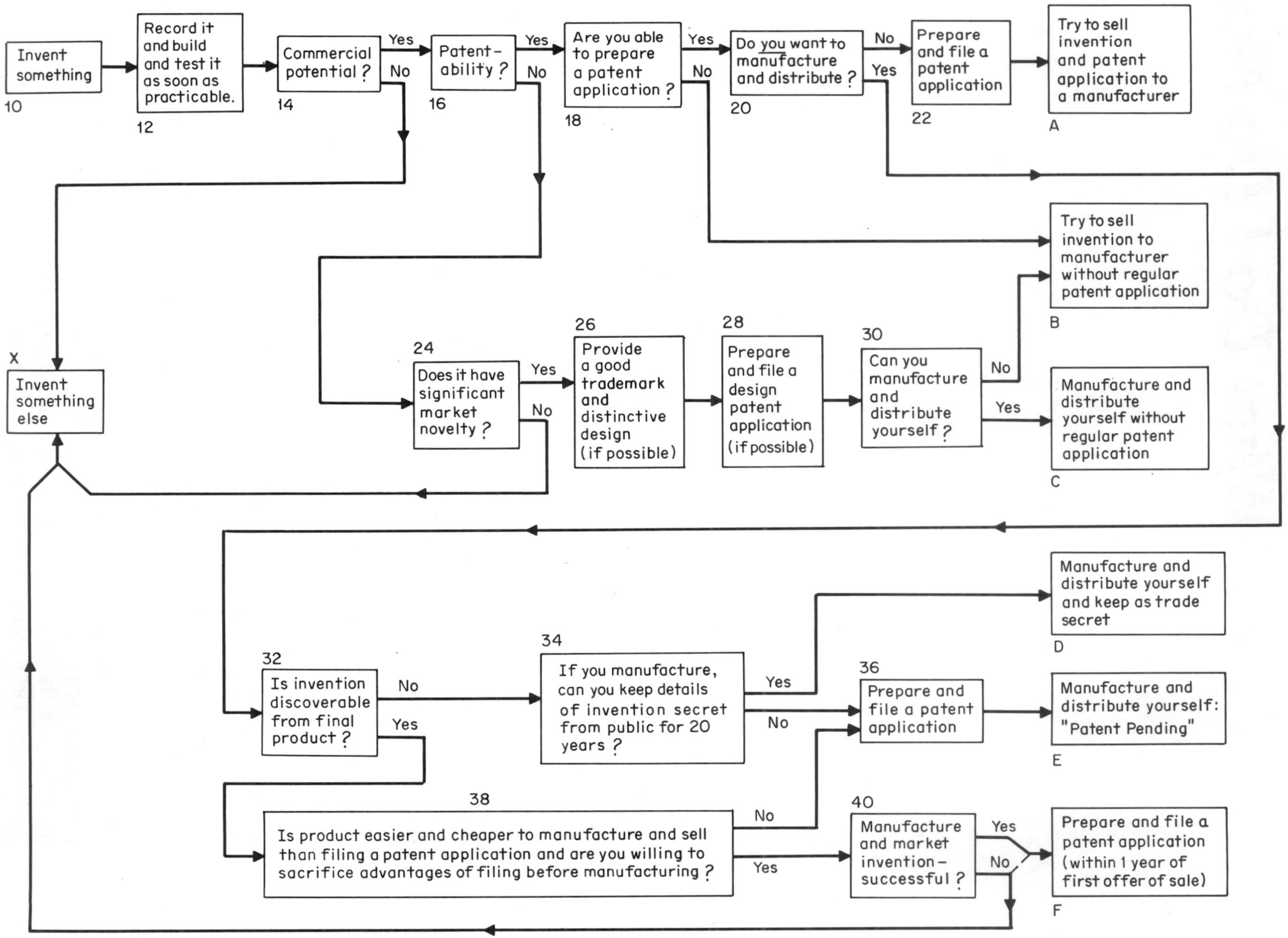

Invent something
10

Record it and build and test it as soon as practicable.
12

Commercial potential ?
14
Yes
No

Patent - ability ?
16
Yes
No

Are you able to prepare a patent application ?
18
Yes
No

Do you want to manufacture and distribute ?
20
Yes
No

Prepare and file a patent application
22
No
Yes

Try to sell invention and patent application to a manufacturer
A

Try to sell invention to manufacturer without regular patent application
B

Does it have significant market novelty ?
24
Yes
No

Provide a good trademark and distinctive design (if possible)
26

Prepare and file a design patent application (if possible)
28

Can you manufacture and distribute yourself ?
30
No
Yes

Manufacture and distribute yourself without regular patent application
C

Is invention discoverable from final product ?
32
No
Yes

If you manufacture, can you keep details of invention secret from public for 20 years ?
34
Yes
No

Is product easier and cheaper to manufacture and sell than filing a patent application and are you willing to sacrifice advantages of filing before manufacturing ?
38
No
Yes

Manufacture and distribute yourself and keep as trade secret
D

Prepare and file a patent application
36

Manufacture and distribute yourself: "Patent Pending"
E

Manufacture and market invention — successful ?
40
Yes
No

Prepare and file a patent application (within 1 year of first offer of sale)
F

Invent something else
X

figure 4 Invention decision chart.

can be taken. The numbers in parentheses in the following discussion are block numbers. While there are seven final choices of action (one negative and six positive), several of these can be reached by different routes so that there are more than seven sections to the following discussion of your choices.

No Commercial Potential (Chart Route 10–12–14–X)

This route has already been covered in the previous chapter, but in order to acquaint you with the use of the chart I'll review it again.

Referring to the chart, assume that you invented something (block 10) and then have recorded properly (block 12), you should proceed to build and test it as soon as practicable. If it is simple, build and test it right away, but if it's more complex, you should wait until after commercial potential, or even patentability, is evaluated. But always keep the building and testing as a goal since it will help you evaluate commercial potential and be vital in an interference. What is more, as you will see in Chapter 9, a working model is extremely valuable when you show the invention to a manufacturer. Of course, if the invention is too complex, exotic, or expensive for you to build or have someone build for you, you aren't expected to do the impossible.

Your next step is block 14, that is, investigating commercial potential, using the criteria of Chapter 3.

Assuming you have made a final decision that your invention has no commercial potential, that is, that it would not be possible to market and sell it profitably, your answer to the commercial question is no, and thus you would follow the "No" line from the right-hand side of block 14. You will find that it leads you to the ultimate decision box X which says "Invent something else," as already covered in Chapter 3. See how easy it is?

Selling Invention and Patent Application to Manufacturer (Chart Route 14–16–18–20–22–A)

This probably will be the usual route for most inventors with a patentable invention since most inventors do not have the capability to manufacture and distribute an invention although they *are* able to prepare a patent application.

Assuming your decision on patentability (16) is favorable, that you are able to prepare a patent application (18), and that you do not want to manufacture and distribute your product or process yourself (20), your next step is to prepare a patent application (22). (I will show you how in Chapters 6 to 8.) After you prepare the patent application you should then try to market your invention and the patent application to a manufacturer (A).

Why file a patent application before offering the invention to a manufacturer? A good question, which has four good answers:

1. By preparing and filing a patent application, you have defined your invention and its ramifications in very precise terms, made formal drawings of it, and recorded it in the Patent and Trademark Office, so that if anyone who sees the invention after you have filed the patent applica-

tion wants to steal or adopt it, it will be virtually impossible without the most elaborate back-dating and forging exercises. Even then the would-be thief will have to file after you. Thus, once you file the application, you may publish details of your invention freely and show it to anyone you think may have an interest in it.

2. A manufacturer to whom you show the invention, seeing that you have thought enough of your invention to take the trouble to prepare and file a patent application on it, will treat it and you with far more respect and give it much more serious consideration than if you offered an unfiled invention.

3. As you'll see in Chapter 9, most manufacturers to whom you offer an invention will ask you to sign a waiver under which you release all your rights, *except* your rights under the patent laws. If you have a patent application, you are still protected: Once the patent issues, you'll have a very powerful and important tool with which to protect your invention. Without a patent application, once you sign the manufacturer's waiver, you will have no bargaining power left, and you will be at the mercy of the manufacturer. Moreover, even the most generous and reputable manufacturers will not offer you as much if you do not already have a patent application.

4. Most manufacturers want a proprietary or privileged position, so that if you have a patent application already covering your invention, they will be far more likely to buy it than if you offered them a "naked" invention on which they have to take the time and trouble to file a patent application. Moreover, if you do make an agreement to sell your invention to a manufacturer, the patent application itself will provide a tangible consideration for the manufacturer to purchase; most lower-echelon executives will have a far easier time justifying the purchase of your rights to their superiors if they can state that they're purchasing a pending patent application as well as an invention.

Selling an Unpatentable Invention without a Regular Patent Application to a Manufacturer (Chart Route 16–24–26–28–30–B)

If your invention is not patentable (decision in block 16 is negative), don't give up; there's still hope. You must now decide, on the basis of your research in evaluating commercial potential and patentability, whether your invention still has "significant market novelty" (24). If it does, it means that although it's not different enough to be patentable, it is different enough to be considered a new and possibly profitable product or process if introduced to the market. In other words, your patentability search hasn't produced a dead ringer, indicating that no one has tried your particular idea before (although someone has come close enough to block you from getting a patent). There are thousands of examples of new products introduced every year which, although not patentable because their differences from the prior art are minor, have sufficient market novelty to be successes, sometimes outstanding successes. Examples are the previously mentioned Salton products, such as the peanut-butter maker, the warming tray, and the yogurt maker; also slow cookers and the broad idea of an electric knife. (With the electric knife, although the broad idea was not patentable, note that there were probably many patentable inventions applicable to the actual marketed product, such as the use of interconnected blades, the motor, the blade release mechanism, etc.) Also consider our hypothetical example of the first manufacturer of a bicycle made of a new lightweight alloy: Although the contribution isn't great enough to get a patent (it's "obvious" in the legal sense), it still has significant market novelty.

On the other hand, if your invention seems to be completely old, or you feel, looking back on your commercial-potential and patentability evaluations, that for some other reason it doesn't have significant market novelty, there isn't much hope and you'll have to try again (block X).

Assuming your invention does have significant market novelty (24), even though it isn't patentable, there still are several tricks which you can use to get some proprietary rights on your invention and make it more attractive, which will eliminate the need to "go naked" and will bring you a better price if a manufacturer does decide to buy your invention.

The first trick is to provide a clever trademark for your invention (26). A trademark is a brand name for a product. The type of brand name you should choose for an invention you are trying to market is one which suggests the function of the product in a very clever way. Such a trademark can be a powerful marketing tool, which will greatly enhance the value of your invention and give your added proprietary rights to sell to a manufacturer. Examples of clever suggestive trademarks are CROCK POT for the slow crockery cooker, HULA HOOP for a hip exerciser or game hoop, WATER PIC for an oral irrigation device, and FACIAL SAUNA for a facial steaming machine. These clever trademarks provided a very important marketing tool, tremendously enhancing the values of their respective inventions.

Of course it's not always possible to pick a clever trademark for every invention since there are some processes or products which are not meant to be offered to the public or which are internal components that improve an existing product on process. But sometimes choosing a clever slogan just for the purpose of selling an invention to a manufacturer will be of great benefit.

If you can pick a clever trademark, record it in your notebook or on a subsequent disclosure form, with witnesses, in the same manner as you recorded your invention. With a trademark, it is also desirable to either have a notary public attest to your signature on your "disclosure" of a trademark; or use a self-mailing as outlined in Chapter 2 to have an extra bit of proof that you thought of the trademark as of a certain date. Unfortunately there is no way to register a trademark in the PTO until it is actually used on goods which are sold, so you will have to rely on your own records in case of a dispute. Therefore it behooves you to have these records witnessed well and to make them as convincing and detailed as possible in case anyone ever tries to steal your mark.

If the unpatentable invention is a product, the second trick to obtain proprietary rights is to provide a distinctive design for the product (26). By distinctive design I mean a shape or appearance that is unique and different from anything you've seen so far. The "design" in this case doesn't mean the function or internal structure of the product, but only its outward appearance. It will not be possible to provide such a design too often since you will find that most products which don't already have a distinctive design can't be changed that much to give them one. In addition, providing a distinctive design requires artistic creativity, which not everyone has. But if you can provide a distinctive design for your product, it will be of great help. You should, of course, record your design in the same manner as you recorded your invention, and as with your invention, you should build a prototype or model as soon as practicable.

If you can come up with a distinctive design you should prepare and file a design-patent application (28) on the ornamental appearance (not workings) of your invention. Unless you live across the street from the PTO, it doesn't pay to search a new design beyond the most cursory look in product catalogs since the cost of the search will greatly exceed the cost and effort to prepare and file a design-patent application. As you'll see in Chapter 8, a design-patent application consists simply of a drawing and a form that is filled out; it is very easy and economical to prepare.

Frankly, design patents do not provide that much protection and are not very difficult for others to avoid infringing, but I believe that if you can provide a distinctive design, it is worth the effort when marketing an invention or product.

Once you file your design-patent application (28), and assuming you can't manufacture and distribute it yourself (30), you should try to sell the invention to a manufacturer without a regular patent application (B), as outlined in Chapter 9. You will find that, although you do not have a regular patent application, you will have significant leverage and some protection if you have a good trademark and /or distinctive design.

Selling a Patentable Invention without a Regular Patent Application (Chart Route 30-C)

Assuming again that you have an unpatentable invention, if you can manufacture and distribute it yourself (30), it is better to do so (C) than to try to sell it to the manufacturer without a regular patent application. This is because if you have only a trademark (even a good one) and a design patent application to bargain with, and no regular patent application, a manufacturer does not get a really good privileged position and so will generally not be inclined to buy your invention. However, if you manufacture it yourself, even if you do not have a regular patent application to give you a strong privileged position, you will be the first on the market with the product, which will give you a significant marketing advantage. Also, since you are the manufacturer, you will make a much larger profit per item than if you received royalties from a manufacturer.

If you decide to manufacture your invention yourself, and you already are a manufacturer, you know what is involved. But if you are not a manufacturer, be forewarned that manufacturing and marketing any product are very difficult tasks, which are compounded when the product is novel. It demands a lot of time and money. You have to come up with a good, workable design that can be readily manufactured, either by you or by a job shop. You must also consider materials, packaging, machinery (including tooling and molds), plant facilities, labor, accounting, business licenses, taxes, insurance, distribution, and advertising. Sometimes a small manufacturing run with local test marketing can be very helpful. You will find that the Small Business Administration of the U.S. government probably has a local office near you that can give you much free and valuable literature to aid your effort and point out pitfalls. Financing for your manufacturing efforts will be difficult for a nonpatented invention, especially if you have never manufactured before, but the *Guide to Venture Capital Sources* (see Bibliography) can provide you with much assistance and valuable suggestions.

Another problem a manufacturer of a new product must deal with is pricing. One rule of thumb is to price a thing at three times what it costs you to make it, that is, three times the cost of labor and materials. This will allow you to receive one-third for labor and materials, one-third for overhead, and one-third for profit. However, all pricing should be calculated so that your price won't be so high that it deters purchasers, nor so low as to give an unrealistic market test or leave you with an inadequate or no profit. If you sell directly to the public, you may be able to increase the price somewhat, but if you're in a highly competitive area, you will have to lower your price.

Manufacture and Distribute Invention Yourself and Keep It as a Trade Secret (Chart Route 20–32–34–D)

Even though your invention may be commercially feasible and patentable, it is not always in your best interest to patent it. The alternative, when possible, is to keep an invention a trade secret. As you've guessed, you can't have your cake and eat it too, since if you try to patent a trade secret, the trade secret will be published when the patent issues. And if you don't put the essence of your trade secret in your patent application, the patent will be held invalid.

A trade secret is any design, process, composition, device, technique, or any unique thing that only you, or a limited group of people, are aware of and that is commercially valuable. Trade secrets are almost always limited to manufacturing processes, production machines, or chemical formulae. Almost every factory has one or more trade secrets, but the most familiar and very valuable ones are the composition of COCA-COLA and the compositions of various cosmetics. The method of manufacturing certain sewing needles is also a trade secret.

Trade secrets have significant advantages over their patent counterparts:

1. The main advantage of a trade secret is the possibility of perpetual protection. While a patent is limited by statute to 17 years and is renewable, a trade secret theoretically lasts perpetually if not discovered.

2. A trade secret can be "obtained" without the cost or effort involved in patenting.

3. There is no need to disclose details of your invention to the public (as you have to do with a patented invention) if you have a trade secret.

4. With a trade secret you have definite, already existing protection and do not have to worry about whether your patent application will be allowed.

5. Since a trade secret is not distributed to the public as a patent is, no one can look at your trade secret and try to design around it, as they can with the claims of your patent.

Although trade secrets do have disadvantages, I don't believe they overshadow their important advantages. The disadvantages are:

1. Trade secrets can't be kept on inventions which could be discovered by the public from an inspection, dissection, or analysis of the product. Thus, mechanical things that are sold can't be kept as trade secrets. However, certain chemical compositions sold to the public, like COCA-COLA and cosmetics, supposedly can't be discovered. Nevertheless, very sophisticated tools of analysis are now available, such as chromatographs, Auger analyzers, spectroscopes, spectrophotometers, scanning electron microscopes, etc., so that most things can be copied, no matter how sophisticated or small they are. And the law generally allows anyone to copy and make anything freely, unless it's patented or unless its shape is its trademark.

2. If your trade secret is discovered legitimately or by any other method, it is generally lost forever, although you do have rights against anyone who purloins your trade secret by illegal means.

3. Strict precautions must always be taken to maintain the confidentiality of a trade secret.

4. A trade secret is harder to sue on and enforce than a patent. A patent must be initially presumed valid by the court, but a trade secret must be proven to exist before the suit may proceed.

5. A trade secret is not respected like a patent, that is, it is generally considered fair game for all potential copiers.

Because of the great advantage of perpetual protection and because infringement of patents or "trade-secretable" inventions is difficult to discover, I feel that if you have an invention which can be kept as a trade secret, it is far better to do so than to patent it. Thus if your invention is *not* discoverable from your final product (32), and if you feel you can keep the invention secret from the public for at least 20 years (34) in order to significantly outlive the term of a patent (17 years), you should manufacture and distribute your invention yourself and keep it as a trade secret (D).

However, if you do manufacture an invention you wish to keep as a trade secret, you must institute and maintain strict and rigid controls throughout the life of the trade secret. This involves having all employees who have access to it sign a special agreement whereby they acknowledge your trade secret and agree to respect and maintain it. You must also label and lock up all papers which contain your trade secret. You must take and maintain adequate safeguards to keep the public and employees who should not have access to your trade secret out of the section of the plant where it is used. If you do not take all of these precautions and if you cannot document all of the precautions that you have taken, a court will not enforce your right to a trade secret.

Although not specifically covered on the chart, there is another possibility in the trade secret category. That is that you may sell your invention to a manufacturer who may choose to keep it as a trade secret. This may occur with either unpatentable or patentable inventions (chart routings 16–24–26–28–30–B or 16–18–20–22–A, but you do not have to worry about this alternative since it is the manufacturer's choice, not yours. If you have already filed a patent application and a manufacturer buys the patent application with a view to using your invention as a trade secret, the manufacturer will allow the patent application to go abandoned so it won't be published, thereby maintaining the trade secret. While you may lose a possible patent, you will have been adequately compensated.

File Patent Application and Manufacture and Distribute Invention Yourself (Trade-Secretable Invention) (Chart Route 20–32–34–36–E)

Suppose your invention is not discoverable from your final product (32) so that it can be kept as a trade secret, but you don't feel that you can keep the details of your invention from the public for 20 years (34), or, after evaluating the advantages and disadvantages of a trade secret under the criteria above, you do not wish to choose the trade-secret route and prefer to patent your invention. You should then prepare and file a patent application (36; see Chapters 6 to 8) and then manufacture and distribute the invention yourself with the notice "patent-pending" affixed to the invention (E). While the patent application is pending you should *not* publish any details of your invention since, if the patent application is disallowed for any reason, you can allow it to go abandoned and still maintain your invention as a trade secret.

The patent-pending notice on your product does not confer any legal rights, but it is used by most manufacturers who have a patent pending in order to deter potential competitors from copying the invention. The notice effectively warns them that you may get a patent on the product so that if they do invest the money and effort in tooling to copy the invention, they could be enjoined from manufacturing so that all their investment will have been wasted. (It is a criminal offense to associate a patent-pending notice with a product which is not actually covered by a pending application.)

File Patent Application and Manufacture and Distribute Invention Yourself (Non-Trade-Secretable Invention) (Chart Route 20–32–38–36–E)

This will be the most common route most inventors who wish to manufacture their own invention will follow.

Assuming that your invention, like most, is discoverable from the final product (32), and assuming your product is not easier and cheaper to manufacture and sell than filing a patent application (38), or that you do not want to sacrifice the advantages of filing before manufacturing, you should prepare and file a patent application (36) and then manufacture and distribute the invention yourself with the patent-pending notice (E).

Test Market Before Filing (Chart Route 20–32–38–40–F)

Sometimes it is advantageous to manufacture your invention before filing a patent application on it, but the instances when this occurs are very rare, and I generally do not recommend it. The disadvantages of test marketing before filing are three:

1. If you do manufacture before filing, you have only a limited time to make the test; you *must* file your patent application within one year of first offering your invention for sale or first using it commercially to make a product which is offered for sale. (You actually have less than a year because you need time to prepare your patent application.)

2. If you market your invention and it isn't successful, you probably will be too discouraged to file a patent application and therefore you will lose all rights on the invention forever. (If you don't file the patent application within a year of first selling the invention in a product, you can never do it again.) Thus, because a market test failed, you will have given up all your rights forever on a patentable invention which at one time you thought to be commercially promising.

3. On the other hand if you file a patent application first, you have a very long time— about 19 years (2 years during pendency and 17 years during the term of your patent protection)—to test market your invention. Remember you have already decided (block 4) that your invention has good commerciality.

So assuming your invention is discoverable from the final product (32), ask yourself whether it is easier and cheaper to manufacture and test market it than to file a patent application. If it is, and if you also are willing to sacrifice the above three advantages of filing before manufacturing (38), you should manufacture and market your invention (40) before filing. If you discover within about 9 months of the date you first introduce your product that it is a successful invention and likely to have good commercial success, begin immediately to prepare your patent application (F) so that you will be able to get it on file within 1 year of the date you first offered it for sale or used it to make a commercial product.

If your manufacture and market test (40) are not successful, you should generally drop the invention and concentrate on something else (X), although you still have the right to get a patent on your invention. Thus if the market test is unsuccessful, but you feel that you do not want to give the invention up forever and that at some time within the next 20 years market conditions may change and become more favorable, by all means follow the line, and prepare and file the patent application within 1 year of the first offer of sale (F). If you do manufacture and market your invention, and then later file a patent application on it, be sure to retain all of your records and paperwork regarding the manufacture of your invention since these will be helpful if you ever get into an interference with someone else.

Now that we've covered all possible routes on the chart, I hope you have found one which will meet your needs and bring you success, fame, and fortune. If your choice is to file a patent application, move on to Chapters 6 to 8; if you want to try to market your invention first, skip over to Chapter 9.

CHAPTER SIX

How to Write and Draw It for Uncle Sam

In this and the next two chapters I'll cover the writing and transmittal of your patent application to the Patent and Trademark Office. This chapter deals with the specification and drawings; Chapter 7 deals with the claims, and Chapter 8 first, with the "finaled" application and its transmittal to the PTO, and second, design patent applications.

WHAT IS ACTUALLY SENT TO THE PTO?

To demystify the concept of a patent application, I'll start by listing all the parts of a patent application that must be sent to the PTO:

1. Self-addressed receipt postcard

2. Transmittal letter (Form 3)

3. Check for the filing fee

4. Formal drawing(s) on bristol board in India ink

5. Specification containing the following sections:

   a. Title
   b. Cross reference to corresponding applications, if any
   c. Field of invention
   d. Discussion of prior art
   e. Objects of your invention
   f. Brief description of drawings

  g. Description of invention
  h. Operation of invention
  i. Broadening paragraph

6. Claims (Chapter 7)

7. Abstract

8. Completed declaration form (Form 4)

9. Statement of Prior Art (Form 5)

  The Statement of Prior Art can be submitted up to 3 months after the other parts of the application are filed.

  The specification, claims, and abstract should be typewritten to form one document, which as a whole is sometimes referred to as the "specification," but to avoid confusion, I will consider the claims separately.

  The specification, claims, and other parts of the application are sent to:

Commissioner of Patents and Trademarks
Washington, District of Columbia 20231

(This address is misleading; the Commissioner will never personally see your application, and the PTO is actually in Arlington, Virginia, rather than in Washington, D.C., but for statutory and postal reasons, everything must be addressed to the Commissioner in Washington.)

  Once in the PTO, your papers are put in a folder, assigned a serial number, and sent to an appropriate examining division.

  When its turn is reached (within a few months to a year), the application will be reviewed by a patent examiner, who will correspond with you, most likely requiring you to make changes, additions, or deletions in the specification and claims. If the examiner eventually decides to allow the application, you'll be asked to pay a base-issue fee. Your specification and claims, along with certain other information (your name, address, and all prior art cited by the examiner), will then be sent to the U.S. Government Printing Office, where they will be printed verbatim as your patent.

PRELIMINARY WORK

Before you begin the actual writing of the patent application or preparation of any of the forms that go along with it to the PTO, it's important to make complete preparations. Having prepared many patent applications, I, as well as most patent attorneys, find that, if adequate preparations are made beforehand, the actual writing of the application rarely takes more than several hours to a half a day, or, in rare instances, a day. So if you do all of the following carefully and thoroughly, you'll be very grateful when you begin to write the application.

1. *Review the prior art.* Assemble all your prior-art references, including any references to textbooks, magazines, or journals you have searched or discovered relating to your invention or the field of your invention. Read each of these references carefully, noting the terms used for the parts or

steps that are similar to those of your invention. Write down the terms of the more unusual parts and if necessary look them up so that you will be familiar with them and their precise meaning. Also note the way the drawings in these prior art references are arranged and laid out, paying particular attention to what parts are shown in detail, and what parts need be shown only very roughly or generally because they are well-known or are not essential to the invention.

2. *Review your disclosure.* Reread and review your own disclosure well. Be sure that you have all of the details of your invention drawn or sketched in understandable form and that the description of your invention is complete. If you don't have good sketches and a complete description, do them now, referring to Chapter 2 to find out how to do them and record them properly.

3. *Ramifications.* Write down all of the known ramifications and embodiments of the invention. That is, record all other materials that will work for each part of your invention, all other possible uses your application can be put to, all other possible modifications of your invention, all ways in which its size or shape can be altered, and all parts or steps that can be eliminated. The more ramifications you can think of, the broader your invention will be, and the more you will be able to block others from getting patents on improvements of your invention.

4. *Sources of supply.* If your invention contemplates the use of any exotic or uncommon materials, components, or steps, obtain the names and addresses of suppliers for any unusual materials, or a textbook or other reference describing how any unusual component or step is made or performed. If any dimension, material, or component values of your invention are at all critical or unusual, describe them in detail. With an electrical circuit, it is not generally necessary to write down the values of components, but if the operation of the circuit is at all unusual, or if any component values are critical, write down the names or identifications of the components. With a chemical invention, write down the source or full identification of how to make any unusual components or reactions. With a mechanical invention, if any unusual part or assembly steps are required, be sure you provide a full reference as to where to obtain or how to perform them.

5. *Advantages/disadvantages.* Write down and list all disadvantages of the prior art that your invention overcomes, referring to the list in Chapter 3 to make sure your list is complete. Then list all the advantages of your invention over the prior art and also all the general disadvantages of your invention.

YOUR SPECIFICATION MUST BE AS COMPLETE AS POSSIBLE

In writing the specification of a patent application, the main thing is to disclose clearly everything you can think of about your invention. In case of doubt as to whether or not to include an item of information, put it in! If you don't put enough information in about your invention, your entire application can be rejected on the grounds of "incomplete disclosure," and there is nothing you can do about a valid rejection on this ground because you are not allowed to add any new matter to a pending application. Moreover, once your patent issues, if you ever sue under it, the party you sue has a right to attack your patent on grounds of incomplete disclosure, even if the PTO did not reject it on this ground. To forestall any such attack, and to win if any such attack is made, it is imperative that you include as much detailed information about your invention as possible.

The statutory provision that mandates the inclusion of all this information in your patent application is Section 112 of the patent laws, paragraph 1, which reads as follows:

The specification shall contain a written description of the invention, and of the manner and process of making and using it, in such full, clear, concise and exact terms as to enable any person skilled in the art to which it pertains, or with which it is most nearly connected, to make and use the same, and shall set forth the best mode contemplated by the inventor of carrying out his invention.

This paragraph means that you must provide enough information in your patent application to enable anyone working in the field of your invention to be able to build a working model of your invention from the information contained in your patent application. However, to comply with this section, it is not ordinarily necessary to put in dimensions and values of components because the skilled artisan is expected to have a working knowledge of dimensions and component identification. But if any dimensions or components are critical to the performance of your invention, or if they are at all unusual, or if you have any doubt at all, you should include the values of components and their identifications.

Regarding the last part of this statutory paragraph, which refers to the best "mode" contemplated by the inventor (you) of carrying out the invention, if you have several different embodiments of your invention, identify the one you presently prefer, that is, the one which operates the best. If you can't decide which embodiment is the best, it is OK to list each embodiment and tell its relative advantages and disadvantages.

When writing a patent specification, it is well to keep in mind the "exchange" theory of patents. Under this theory, the government grants an inventor a patent (that is, a monopoly on the invention) for a limited term of years *in exchange for* the inventor's disclosing to the public the full details of the invention. Unless they want patents, inventors do not have to disclose any details of their inventions to the public, but they are encouraged to do so by the enticement of a limited (17-year) monopoly on their inventions. Naturally, any such disclosures from inventors should be full and complete, or else they won't have properly complied with the terms of the bargain.

Another reason for disclosing as much as you can about your invention is, as stated, to block others from getting a subsequent improvement patent on your invention. If you invent something and disclose one embodiment of it or one way to do it, and get a patent only on that one embodiment, later on someone may see your patent and think of another embodiment or another way to do it that may be better than yours. This person will then be able to file a new patent application on the improvement of your invention and thus, if it is allowed, obtain a monopoly on the improvement. You won't be able to make, use, or sell the improvement without a license from the person who invented the improvement even though you have a patent on the basic invention. To forestall and block anyone from getting an improvement patent, it is important that you include as many ramifications and embodiments of your invention in your patent application as you can think up, so that once your application is published, your patent will become "prior art," which will prevent anyone else from getting a patent on any of these ramifications or embodiments.

THE PENCILED DRAWINGS

The drawings which you send to the PTO must be drawn carefully and clearly on strong, white, smooth paper, preferably in India ink on the stiff, thick, calendared paper called bristol board, available in most art-supply stores. Before making the formal or bristol-board drawings, you should first make pencil drawings or rough sketches so as to lay out your drawings properly for the inked versions.

The drawings must be done in separate, unconnected figures, each one labeled (Fig. 1, Fig. 2, etc.) so that all possible different views and embodiments of your invention will be shown. The drawings can be done on the old larger-size sheets (8½ by 14 inches), which are useable for U.S. applications only, but preferably should be done on the new smaller-size international sheets (21 by 29.7 centimeters), which can be used for both domestic and international applications (see Chapter 11). On the old sheets there should be a 2-inch top margin and ¼-inch side and bottom margins, so as to provide a borderless drawing area of 8 by 11.75 inches. On the new international sheets there should be top and left-side margins of 2.5 centimeters, a bottom margin of 1 centimeter, and a right side margin of 1.5 centimeters, so as to provide a borderless drawing area of 17 by 26.2 centimeters. You can use as many sheets as necessary, and each sheet can have several figures, but the figures should not be crowded too close together nor spaced too far apart. Look at the prior-art patents to get an idea as to how it's done. Note that the views should generally be perspective or isometric views, rather than front, side, and top, engineering-type views. For complicated machines, exploded views are desirable. Phantom parts should be shown in broken lines.

If your invention is a machine or an article of manufacture, your drawings should contain enough views to show every feature of the invention, but they should not show every feature that is old and known in the prior art. For example, if you've invented a new type of pedal arrangement for a bicycle, one view can show your pedal arrangement in gross view without detail. Other views can show your pedal arrangement in detail, but you do not have to include any views showing the bicycle itself in detail, since it is not part of your invention. If one figure of your drawing shows a sectional or side view of another figure, it is customary to provide cross-section lines in the latter figure; these lines should bear the number of the former figure. Look at prior-art patents to see how this is done.

If your invention is a chemical composition, drawings are generally not required unless your invention is a material which has a nonhomogeneous composition, in which case you should show it in cross-sectional detail. Benzene rings and other molecular diagrams can usually be presented in the specification.

If your invention is a process, either chemical or mechanical, it is desirable to provide a flowchart showing the separate steps involved, each described succinctly in a different block. If your blocks are connected, they should all be labeled as one figure; if disconnected they should be labeled as separate figures. As before, each figure should be labeled, for example, Fig. 1, Fig. 2, Fig. 3, etc. If you desire, you can put a title after each figure giving a general description of the part of your invention shown in the figure, just as you would do if you were writing a scientific article for an engineering magazine or textbook.

If you believe it will help in understanding your invention, it is permissible to include a drawing of the prior art as one figure of your drawings. This figure should be labeled "prior art" to indicate that it is not part of your invention.

One figure of your drawing should be fairly comprehensive so as to be suitable for inclusion in the *Official Gazette*.

If you're like me and can't draw too well, it may be necessary to have an artist or professional draftsman make your final (inked) drawings and even your penciled drawings. A regular patent draftsman will merely need to be shown your invention and be told what you want, and can take it from there. Having provided pencil sketches on bristol board for you to review, and having received your approval, the draftsman will ink them in. The disadvantage is that patent draftsmen charge about $50 per sheet. If you're working with an artist who has never done patent drawings before, it will be necessary for you to work with the artist to indicate exactly what is required. An artist who feels competent enough can make pencil sketches right on bristol board, but less experienced artists should probably make them on separate paper first. Note that the standards for formal drawings are reproduced in their entirety in Chapter 8.

Remember that it is important to provide a complete disclosure of your invention in the drawings as well as in the specification, so be sure to include every detail of your invention in the drawings. Remember: In case of doubt, put it in! And don't rely entirely on the standards of drawing completeness of prior-art patents since these, while adequate to have passed PTO muster, are sometimes inadequate to pass court scrutiny.

THE DRAFT OF THE APPLICATION

Now that you have the sketches of your drawings as you want them to appear in your final version, it's time to begin the draft of your patent application. Review the prior-art patents to find out how they're written, noting the respective parts of the application, which I've listed in the section *What is Actually Sent to the PTO?* (above).

When writing your application, it is generally best to write it in pencil on letter- or legal-size sheets, double-spaced. However, if you are used to composing with a typewriter, or you have a dictating machine and a secretary, all the better. Your specification and claims should be written as one continuous document with separate sections, each with a heading as in the following sections, (except that "Title" and "Broadening Paragraphs" should not be headings).

1. *Title.* Make a title that gives the essence of your invention, but is not so long or so specific that it is narrower than the full scope of your invention. On the other hand don't pick a title so broad—such as "Electrical Apparatus"—that it will be meaningless. A look at some recently issued patents in your field should give you a good idea of how specific to make your title.

2. *Field of Invention.* This can be a brief, one-sentence paragraph stating the general and specific fields to which your invention relates. The sentence might simply read, for example, "This invention relates to bicycles and specifically to an improved pedal mechanism for a bicycle."

3. *Cross-Reference to Related Applications.* If you have filed any other patent applications that are related to your present application, include this section and identify these applications here. If, as will likely be the case, you have no such corresponding applications, omit this section and heading entirely.

4. *Discussion of Prior Art.* Discuss how the problem to which your invention is directed was solved before, and then list all the disadvantages of the old ways of doing it. You can start this section out with the word "Heretofore," for example, "Heretofore, bicycle pedal mechanisms had . . ." and then list the constructions which were used in the past and their disadvantages. Again look at prior-art patents to get an idea of what was done.

   Occasionally you may have such a completely unique invention that there really is no prior art directly germane to your invention. In such case, you can completely omit this section and its heading.

5. *Objects.* List all the advantages of your invention over the prior art. You can start out this section as follows: "Accordingly several objects of my invention are . . ." And then include the objects or advantages of your invention. You already know these from your commercial evaluation (Chapter 3). At the end of this section add a catchall paragraph reading as follows: "Further objects and advantages of my invention will become apparent from a consideration of the drawings and ensuing description thereof."

6. *Drawings.* Here provide a series of separate paragraphs, each briefly describing a respective figure of your drawing, for example, "Fig. 1 is a perspective [or plan, side, exploded, or rear] view of my invention" or, "Fig. 2 is a view in detail of the portion indicated by the section lines 2–2 in Fig. 1."

7. *Description.* Here describe in great detail the *physical structure* (not operation or function) of your invention or the machinery involved in your invention if it is a process. Refer to the figures or drawings by number and provide a separate reference number for each element or component in your drawings. Where several figures show different views of an embodiment of your invention, it is permissible to refer to several figures at once. Be sure to cover every part of your drawings and be sure to use consistent terminology and nomenclature for parts of the drawing. Also be sure to detail the interconnections or mountings between parts. If any special or exotic parts are used, include detailed descriptions of these and sources of supply, if applicable, in this section. Although it may seem senseless and unduly laborious to describe every part of your invention in detail, especially if everything is shown clearly in the drawing, it is desirable to do so in order to provide support for the claims and to comply with Section 112, quoted above.

8. *Operation.* Here describe in extensive detail the operation or function of the parts covered in your description. Be sure to include the working or function of every part.

   Your invention may be of such a nature that it may not be possible to include a physical description and an operational description in separate sections, but you will find that this mode of description works generally for most inventions, and you should try to adhere to it since it will force you to be complete and comprehensive in your description of the invention.

   If your invention includes several embodiments, you can describe each embodiment separately in your description, or you can describe the structure and the operation of each embodiment together.

   If you choose the latter course, several sets of description/operation sections would be indicated, for example, "Description of Motor/ Operation of Motor," "Description of Mounting/Operation of Mounting," etc. Any way that you arrange these sections is satisfactory, so long as you include a very, very detailed description of each and every part of your invention, together with a very, very detailed description of the operation of each part and its relation to the other parts.

   If you are not an experienced writer, it is best to write your description in short, simple sentences, with short, simple paragraphs, each paragraph relating to one part or subpart of your invention. Don't worry about the style of writing or the beauty of your language, so long as you include all points of substance of your invention and your description is clear and understandable. If your sentences are too long and complex, break them up into several sentences. If you get stuck and don't know how to phrase a description of a part or an operation, simply pretend that you are talking to a close friend, recite it aloud, remember what you said (or make an audio recording), and write it down. Then go back and polish the language a bit.

9. *Broadening paragraphs.* After you finish your detailed description of the operation, add a "Broadening paragraph", such as the following:

While the above description contains many specificities, these should not be construed as limitations on the scope of the invention, but rather as an exemplification of one preferred embodiment thereof. Many other variations are possible, for example [then continue with brief description of possible variations]. Accordingly, the scope of the invention should be determined not by the embodiment illustrated, but by the appended claims and their legal equivalents.

In the "for example" portion of the above paragraph, include a brief description of any alternative embodiments you can think of and which you didn't consider important enough to show in the drawings and describe in detail in your description.

10. *Claims.* The claims, which are discussed in the next chapter, should be provided here as a series of separate, numbered sentence fragments. For reasons discussed in the next chapter, although the claims are quite important and indicate the scope of your invention, it is not necessary to by overly concerned about the claims at this stage.

11. *Abstract.* Write one or two brief paragraphs providing a concise summary of your invention in about 250 words or several sentences. Generally you should spend a good deal of time writing the abstract to make it concise, complete, and clear, since the abstract is usually the part of an application that is read first and most frequently consulted. Look at the abstracts of several of the prior-art patents to get an idea of what is involved. To be concise, your abstract should *not* include phrases like "This invention relates to" but rather should get right into it and state, for example, "An improved bicycle pedal mechanism having . . ., etc." (Abstracts formerly were required at the beginning of an application, but now are to be provided on a separate sheet, after the claims.)

REVIEWING THE APPLICATION

After you have completed your draft, be sure to review it and the drawing very carefully to be sure you have included everything about your invention you can think of and that there is no possible ground for anyone to say that you haven't included enough to teach one skilled in the art how to make and use your invention. If your invention has any nonapparent disadvantages, these should be included; it's best to phrase them in a fleeting, positive manner so as to minimize them, for example, "Although a special alloy is required for sprocket 18, it eliminates three previously used components." Be sure to compare your specification with those of other patents in the field so that yours is *at least* as complete as theirs. Many prior-art patents are actually inadequate legally, especially under today's more demanding standards, so don't rely on them as a standard; rather follow the guidelines of this chapter to be sure you'll comply with Section 112. It may be necessary to write several drafts of your application before you're satisfied with it. A good suggestion is to have a friend review the draft for you to make sure it is clear, complete, and entirely understandable.

Now for the Legalese: The Claims

CHAPTER SEVEN

WHAT ARE CLAIMS?

If you don't yet know what patent claims are, or have never read any, you're in for a surprise because the word "claim," in the patent context, is a word of art, that is, it has a very special meaning and doesn't mean what you think it would. A "claim" is *not* what the common dictionary definitions recite: It's not a demand for something due, a title to something in the possession of another, or that which one seeks or asks for. Rather, a "claim," in this context, is a very formally worded sentence fragment at the end of a patent application or patent. It recites and defines the structure or acts of an invention in very precise, logical, and exact terms, and it serves as a measuring tool in determining whether or not a patent is infringed.

If all of that sounds a bit formidable, don't let it throw you; it will become quite clear as we progress and after you see some examples.

It helps to remember that just as there are five statutory classes of inventions, there are five corresponding types of claims: (1) Process or method claims; (2) machine claims; (3) article or article of manufacture claims; (4) composition of matter claims; and (5) claims directed to a new use of any of (1) to (4). As with the classes of inventions, the line between (2) and (3) is blurred.

Claims, unfortunately, give patent examiners, patent attorneys and agents, judges, and inventors—that is, just about everyone who has to deal with them—a good deal of trouble. This is because claims are concatenations of very troublesome, imprecise elements called words, which, in the hands of poets and other creative writers are readily used with free license to stimulate images, illusions, and other emotional manifestations, but which patent attorneys must use only according to the most precise and strict rules so as to affect solely our most logical and rational senses. Moreover claims must meet standards of substance as well as form: While defining the invention narrowly enough to clear the prior art and broadly enough to preclude easily designing around the invention, they must simultaneously be logical, precise, concise, and distinct.

Therefore, I won't kid you into thinking claims are easy or simple to write, but at the same time I wouldn't be writing this book and this chapter if I didn't think most amateurs could learn to do a very passable job. Moreover, even if you are as far from being a wordsmith as I am from being Michelangelo, I'll tell you later about a powerful, but little-known tool you can employ to get perfectly acceptable claims written by an expert for free.

THE LAWS REGARDING CLAIMS

As difficult as claims are, the laws and rules concerning them are unfortunately written in only the most general and vague terms and don't even make a respectable attempt to define them. The real definitions of claims and precise rules concerning them are found in everyday practice, court decisions, and books. Nevertheless since the statutes and rules concerning claims are quoted and referred to quite often in patent practice, we'll begin by quoting and explaining them.

The only pertinent statute is the last two paragraphs of Section 112 of the patent laws (Title 35 of the U.S. Code), which state:

The specification shall conclude with one or more claims particularly pointing out and distinctly claiming the subject matter which the applicant regards as his invention. A claim may be written in independent or dependent form, and if in dependent form, it shall be construed to include all the limitations of the claim incorporated by reference into the dependent claim.

An element in a claim for a combination may be expressed as a means or step for performing a specified function without the recital of structure, material, or acts in support thereof, and such claim shall be construed to cover the corresponding structure, material, or acts described in the specification and equivalents thereof.

The first sentence is the one that mandates the use of claims in patents. It also means that the claims should be specific enough to define the invention over the prior art ("particularly pointing out") and also should be clear, logical, and precise ("distinctly claiming"). This sentence is the most important part of Section 112 and moreover probably is the best-known sentence in patent law. It is referred to by patent examiners almost daily because of the frequency with which they reject claims for lack of clarity or for some other similar reason.

The second sentence, a relative newcomer to patent law, was added to make it clear that a dependent claim—one which refers back to and narrows a preceding claim—includes all the limitations of the preceding claim.

The third sentence was added specifically to overrule a famous Supreme

Court decision that held certain claims invalid for "functionality at the point of novelty" because these claims expressed the essence of an invention as a "means" for performing the novel function of the invention, rather than reciting the specific structure of the invention that performed the novel function. It will be apparent that a means clause in a claim is far more desirable than a specific-structure clause since the means clause will cover all possible structures that can perform the function, whereas the specific-structure clause is essentially limited to the specific structure it recites. Therefore, patent attorneys are quite fond of means clauses, and you should use them in your claims whenever possible.

In addition to the statutes, in the Rules of Practice which are promulgated by the PTO, parts (b), (d)(1), and (e) of Rule 75 add additional requirements regarding claims:

(b) More than one claim may be presented provided they differ substantially from each other and are not unduly multiplied.

(d)(1) The claim or claims must conform to the invention as set forth in the remainder of the specification and the terms and phrases used in the claims must find clear support or antecedent basis in the description so that the meaning of the terms in the claims may be ascertainable by reference to the description.

(e) Where the nature of the case admits, as in the case of an improvement, any independent claim should contain in the following order, (1) a preamble comprising a general description of all the elements or steps of the claimed combination which are conventional or known, (2) a phrase such as 'wherein the improvement comprises,' and (3) those elements, steps, and/or relationships which constitute that portion of the claimed combination which the applicant considers as the new or improved portion.

Part (b) requires that the claims differ substantially from each other and not be too numerous. In practice, minimal differences will suffice; the rule prohibiting numerous claims is more strictly enforced. If more than about twenty claims are presented, there should be some justification, such as a very complex invention.

Part (d)(1), enforced only sporadically, requires that the terms in the claims should correspond to those in the specification. It has often been said that the specification should serve as a dictionary for the claims.

Part (e), a newcomer, was introduced to make claims read, insofar as practicable, as in W. German or "Jepson" style (from a famous decision of that name). The German- or Jepson-type claim is very easy for examiners to read and understand; it puts the essence of the invention into sharp focus by placing it in the second part or body of the claim. In practice this part is hardly ever enforced, however.

SOME SAMPLE CLAIMS

A claim is generally written as an Aristotelian definition, that is, as a genus or title, which orients and gives the reader a broad idea of the subject matter involved, and a species or detailed description, which tells the reader what specifically is involved.

Claims also express the true essence of an invention: While the specification can be a rambling discourse, which can and should discuss almost everything you know about the invention and how to make and use it, a claim must be a definition which boils everything down into a fragment of one sentence.

Consider some examples of simple claims in the five respective statutory classes of invention. (The first four of these claims would now be invalid since the "inventions" they define are obviously old and in the public domain; the fifth—to a new use—is from an in-force patent.)

Note that each claim is a sentence fragment; it does not contain the usual subject, predicate, and object a sentence contains.

1. PROCESS OR METHOD CLAIM: SEWING FABRIC

A method for joining two pieces of cloth together at their edges comprising the steps of:
   a. positioning said two pieces of cloth together so that an edge portion of one piece overlaps an adjacent edge portion of the other piece, and
   b. passing a thread repeatedly through and along the length of the overlapping portions in sequentially opposite directions and through sequentially spaced holes in said overlapping adjacent portions.

Note that the first part of this claim contains a title, preamble, or genus, which states the purpose of the method but doesn't use the term "sewing" because sewing is the invention and is assumed to be new at the time the claim is drafted. The claim contains two steps, (a) and (b), which state in sequence the acts one would perform in sewing two pieces of cloth.

2. MACHINE CLAIM: AUTOMOBILE

A self-propelled vehicle comprising:
   a. a body carriage having rotatable wheels mounted thereunder for enabling said body carriage to roll along a surface,
   b. an engine mounted in said carriage for producing rotational energy,
   c. means for controllably coupling rotational energy from said engine to at least one of said wheels so as to propel said carriage along said surface.

This claim again contains a title in the first part. The second part or body contains three elements, the carriage, the engine, and the transmission. These elements are defined as connected or interrelated by the statement that the engine is mounted in the carriage and the transmission (defined broadly as "means for controllably coupling . . .") couples the engine to at least one wheel of the carriage.

3. ARTICLE OF MANUFACTURE CLAIM: PENCIL

A hand-held writing instrument comprising:
   a. an elongated core-element means that will leave a marking line if moved across paper or other similar surface, and
   b. an elongated holder surrounding and encasing said elongated core-element means, one portion of said holder being removable from an

end thereof to expose an end of said core-element means so as to enable said core-element means to be usable for writing, whereby said holder protects said core-element means from breakage and provides a means of holding said core-element means conveniently.

This claim, like the machine claim, contains a preamble and a body with two elements: (a) The "lead" and (b) the wood. As before, the elements of the body are associated; here the wood ("elongated holder") is said to surround and encase the lead ("elongated core"). Since the purposes of the holder are not readily apparent, a "whereby" clause has been added at the end of the claim to state these. Such clauses are optional, but they are useful since they provide someone who only reads the claim with an explanation of otherwise unexplained elements.

4. COMPOSITION OF MATTER CLAIM: CONCRETE

A rigid building and paving material comprising a mixture of sand and stones, and a hardened cement binder filling the volume between and adhering to said sand and stones.

This claim, although not in subparagraph form, still contains a preamble and a body containing a recitation of the elements of the composition (sand, stones, and cement binder), plus an association of the elements. (Sand and stones are mixed and binder fills volume between and adheres to sand and stones.)

5. NEW-USE CLAIM: ASPIRIN TO SPEED GROWTH OF SWINE

A method of stimulating the growth of swine comprising feeding such swine aspirin in an amount effective to increase their rate of growth.

This claim recites the newly discovered use of aspirin and the purpose of the new use in a manner which defines over and avoids the known, old use of aspirin (analgesic).

Now that you've read a few claims, you should begin to get the idea. I suggest you try writing a practice claim or two of your own to become more familiar with the process. Try a simple article or machine with which you are very familiar. Write the preamble and then the body. To write the body, first list the elements or parts of the article or machine, and then associate or interconnect them. Don't worry too much about grammar or style but try to make the claim clear and understandable.

A CLAIM SHOULD BE AS BROAD AS POSSIBLE

A patent attorney's main job in writing and prosecuting a patent application is to get the broadest possible claims allowed for his client. The broader the claims of a patent, the harder they are to design around and the more the patent will be worth. Paradoxically, the shorter the claim, the broader it is (in the legal sense).

There are two ways to make a claim broader: (1) Eliminate elements; and (2) recite the existing elements more broadly.

To understand why eliminating elements from a claim will make it broader, it's necessary to understand how infringement of claims is determined. To infringe a claim, a device must have at least all of the elements of the claim. If it has more elements than are in the claim, it still infringes; but if it has less, it doesn't infringe.

For example, take our machine claim which recites three elements, A, B, and C, that is, the wheeled carriage, the engine, and the transmission. If an accused machine contains just these three elements it will of course infringe. If it has these three plus a fourth, for example a radio, which we'll label D, it will still infringe. But if our accused machine contains only elements A and B, the carriage and engine, it won't infringe since it doesn't contain all of the claimed elements, A, B, and C.

If a claim contains many, many elements, say A to M, only devices with all of the elements A to M will infringe. If just one element, say G, is eliminated, infringement will be avoided. But if a claim contains only two elements, A and B, any device with these two elements will infringe, no matter how many other elements it has. And the only way to avoid infringement is to eliminate either element A or element B, which would be very difficult to do.

It will, therefore, be apparent that the fewer the elements in a claim, the harder the claim will be to avoid, that is, the broader it will be and the more devices it will cover. And that is why it's the general rule that the shorter a claim, the fewer the elements it will have, and the broader it will be. Therefore, when drafting a claim to your invention, it will behoove you to put in as *few* elements of your invention as possible.

With regard to the second way of broadening a claim, that is, reciting existing elements more broadly, consider a few examples. Suppose an invention involves a chair, and the chair element can be drafted broadly as "seating means" or narrowly as a four-legged maple chair with a vinyl-covered padded seat and a curved plywood back. Obviously, a three-legged plastic stool would be "seating means," and it would infringe the broadly recited element, but would miss the narrowly recited maple chair by a country mile. In electronics, a controllable electron valve is broader than a vacuum tube or transistor. In machinery, rotational energy connecting element is broader than helically cut gear or V-belt.

The best way of reciting elements broadly, however, is to take advantage of the last sentence of Section 112 by reciting an element, wherever possible, as a "means" plus a specified function. In this way, any device or means which performs the function will infringe. For example, "means for conveying rotational energy" is broader than and covers gears, belts and pulleys, drive shafts, etc. "Amplifying means" is broader than and covers transistor amplifiers, tube amplifiers, masers, etc.

BUT THE PRIOR ART'S THE RUB

Now that you've learned how to make your claims as broad as possible, it's time for the bad news: You can't really do it. Although it's desirable to make your claims broad, you'll find you'll rarely be able to get claims allowed as broadly as you'd like and you'll often have to make your claims much, much narrower than you'd like. This is because each claim *must* define an invention that is patentable over the prior art. Remember Section 103 and the problem of nonobviousness? Well it's an ever-present factor, which must *always* be considered in claim drafting.

To make the matter very simple to start, let's go back further than Section 103, namely to Section 102, which deals with novelty. A claim must first define an invention which is novel in view of the prior art, that is, it must recite something the prior art doesn't show. Just as a claim can be made broader by eliminating elements and reciting the existing elements more broadly, it can be made narrower to define over the prior art (1) by adding elements or (2) by reciting the existing elements more narrowly.

For an example of adding elements, suppose a prior art reference shows a machine having three elements A, B, and C, and your claim recites these three elements A, B, and C. Your claim would be said to lack novelty over the prior art and would be rejectable or invalid under Section 102. But if you added a fourth element, D, to the claim it would clear the prior art and would recite a novel (but not necessarily patentable) invention.

For an example of reciting existing elements more narrowly, suppose the prior art shows a machine having the same three elements A, B, and C. You could also clear this prior art and claim a novel invention by reciting in your claim elements A, B, and C', where C' would be the prior-art element C with any change whatever that is not shown in the prior art. For example, if the prior art shows element C as a steam engine and you recite a gasoline engine (C'), you've obviated any question of lack of novelty, though probably not obviousness.

In sum, although you'd like to be able to eliminate as many elements as possible and recite all of your elements as broadly as possible, you will usually settle for less because there will always be some prior art there to make you toe the line of novelty.

Moreover, as I've mentioned, novelty isn't enough; the claims must define an invention which would be *unobvious* to one having ordinary skill in the art. Or to use the paraphrase of the law from Chapter 4, the invention defined by each claim must have one or more new features that are important, significant, and produce valuable, unexpected new results.

Thus when you have to narrow a claim to define over the prior art, you must do so by adding one or more elements or reciting existing elements more narrowly, and you must be sure that the added or narrowed elements define a structure or step which is sufficiently different from the prior art to be considered unobvious. More on this in Chapter 10.

TECHNICAL REQUIREMENTS OF CLAIMS

As stated, in addition to defining adequately over the prior art, each claim must also be worded in a clear, concise, precise, and rational way. If the wording of a claim is poor, the examiner will make a "technical" (non-art) rejection under Section 112. It's easiest to understand how to word claims correctly by reviewing how not to word them. The main technical errors which arise in claims are as follows:

1. *Vagueness and Indefiniteness.* Wording is unclear or imprecise. For example, if "said lever" is used in a claim and no lever has previously

been mentioned, a non sequitur is said to occur and a rejection for vagueness and indefiniteness will be made by the PTO. Or if the same element is positively recited twice, e.g., "a lever" . . . "a lever," the claim is unclear. The solution is to change the second "a lever" to —said lever—.

2. *Functionality.* Elements of the claim are recited in terms of their function or result rather than in terms of their structure. This rejection often occurs when applications are prepared by inventors without an attorney. The remedy is to recite the elements of the claim as "means" for performing the function or achieving the result.

3. *Incompleteness.* Claim doesn't recite enough elements to make a working, complete invention. Remedy is to add the needed elements, either separately or by rewording other elements to cover any missing function. Examiners and attorneys frequently disagree as to whether a claim is incomplete, the examiner wanting the claim narrowed by the addition of elements and the attorney wanting it to remain broad, that is, not to add any more elements.

4. *Prolixity.* Claim is too chatty or wordy. Another frequent error committed by beginners. Remedy is to reword the claim in more compact language.

5. *Aggregation.* Elements of invention don't cooperate. This is a more substantive type of rejection since it's almost always directed at the underlying invention rather than the claim. For example, if you've invented a combination waffle iron and tape recorder, these elements don't cooperate and hence constitute an aggregation. But the elements don't have to work at the same time to cooperate; in a typewriter, for example, the parts work at different times but cooperate toward a unitary result.

6. *Old Combination.* Claims are directed to a well-known combination of elements, such as a carburetor and an automobile when the invention is only in the carburetor. Remedy is to remove the automobile from the claim: Carburetors have a recognized status of their own.

7. *Improper Negative Limitation.* In the past all negative limitations were *verboten,* but now only those which make the claim unclear or awkward are proscribed. Examiners still wince when they see negative limitations in claims (such as "noncircular"), so it's best to avoid them by reciting what the invention is, rather than what it isn't, although this is often difficult to do without unduly narrowing the claim. So don't hesitate to use a negative limitation if you can't think of another way to state your claim.

8. *Improper Alternative Expressions.* Like negative limitations, disjunctive expressions—that is, those using "or" or the like—were also a no-no, but now they are permissible so long as the two expressions are just different ways of reciting the same thing. If two different things are meant, try to find a generic term to cover both, or use two separate claims.

9. *Multiplicity.* If you've put in too many claims, even though you've paid for them, you'll have to eliminate some to make the examiner's job easier. If you ever have more than twenty claims, the invention should be complex enough to justify them.

10. *Lack of Correspondence with Disclosure.* The terms or words of the claims must be present in the specification. If they are not, the remedy is to amend the specification by adding the terms used in your claims, or to amend the claims by eliminating the terms which aren't in the specification.

11. *Lack of Support in Drawing.* Nothing is really wrong with the claim here, but remember that the drawings must show every feature recited in the claims. If they do not, drawing amendments or claim amendments are indicated.

DRAFTING YOUR CLAIMS

To draft a claim, the easiest and most direct way to do it is to follow these three basic steps:

1. Write a preamble giving the name or title of the invention.

2. List the elements (or steps) of the claim.

3. Interconnect the elements or steps.

The claim can be structured so that the elements of the claim appear together, followed by the interconnections; or each element can appear in conjunction with its interconnection(s) to adjacent element(s). Most patent attorneys use the latter method—see claims (2), (3), and (4) above for examples—but beginners will find it easier to recite the interconnections separately, except with process claims, where it will be easier directly to associate each step with its predecessor.

Draft your broadest claim first. Start by writing a claim for your invention as you understand it without regard to breadth. Then see how many elements (or steps) you can eliminate and how many remaining elements you can broaden without leaving something which treads on the prior art, and still maintains sufficient structure to define something that is unobvious over the prior art. Remember that the broadest way of defining any element is by using "means-plus-a-function" language. Don't forget to refer to your prior-art patents for examples.

When you're satisfied with your first, basic, and broadest claim, write as many dependent claims as you can think of. Each dependent claim should begin by referring to your basic claim, or a previous dependent claim, for example, "The bicycle of claim 1 wherein . . ." and then continue by reciting an additional feature of your invention.* The additional features can be

---

* Dependent claims can be dependent on other dependent claims, but I recommend that, unless you're experienced in claim drafting, you make each dependent claim refer back to *one* preceeding claim only (preferably independent), since multiple dependent claiming is confusing, does not save any claim fees, and in reality eliminates only the typing of separate claims.

those you eliminated in broadening your basic claim and all other subsidiary features of your invention you can think of. The features added by the dependent claims can be specific parameters (materials, temperatures, etc.) or other specifics of your invention (specific shapes, additional elements, specific modes of operation, etc.). Be sure to refer to your prior-art patents for examples and ideas.

After you've written your first basic claim and all the dependent claims you can think of (all numbered sequentially), consider writing another independent claim if you can think of a substantially different way to claim your invention. See the prior-art patents for examples of different independent claims on the same invention. Then write another set of dependent claims, similar to your first set. Writing more claims will not give your invention broader coverage, but will provide alternative weapons to use against an infringer.

It is permissible to put the drawing's reference numerals in your claims after the appropriate elements, but this is seldom done unless the elements of the claim aren't clear.

If your invention has an opening, hole, or recess in its structure, it is permissible to recite the hole directly as such, even though it isn't tangible. For example, the recitation "said member having a hole near its upper end" is permissible.

Sometimes instead of using the preamble-elements-interconnections approach, it is desirable to omit the preamble, especially if you feel the preamble will be restrictive, that is, if the elements of the body of the claim can be used for another function. In this case simply start the claim, "In combination:" or "A process comprising:" and then recite the elements or steps and their interconnections.

"Whereby" or "thereby" clauses at the end of a claim, as in claim (3) above, do not generally help to define over the prior art, but they do help to clarify and illuminate the claim and thus are often helpful in getting the claim allowed.

With regard to Rule 75 (e) (quoted above) requiring the use of Jepson- or German-style claims (with a preamble containing old elements and body of claim containing improvements of your invention): Most patent attorneys recommend that claims *not* be cast in this style unless the examiner requires it or unless the examiner is having trouble understanding exactly what your inventive contribution is. The reason for this recommendation is that a Jepson claim isolates and hence minimizes your improvement and thus may be easier to invalidate. To write a claim in the Jepson format, draft your preamble so that it includes all the elements or steps and their interconnections that are already known from the prior art, then add a "cleavage" clause such as "the improvement comprising," or "characterized in that," and then recite the elements of your invention and their interconnections.

Lastly, many patent attorneys recommend that a claim not *appear* too short. A claim that is short will be viewed adversely (as possibly overly-broad) by many examiners, regardless of how much substance it contains. Thus many patent attorneys like to pad short claims by adding whereby clauses, providing long preambles, adding long functional descriptions to their means clauses, etc.

As with the specification, be sure to review your claims very carefully after you've written them.

WHERE TO GET HELP IF YOU NEED IT

If all you've read so far about claims has frightened or intimidated you, don't despair. I've included a good deal just to be sure all the important points are covered. Claim writing really won't be that hard if you first study the sample claims above plus those of a few patents to get the basic idea, use the three-step method (preamble—elements—interconnections) to write the claims, and are conversant with the appropriate terminology of the elements of your invention.

Moreover, it isn't that important that you write perfect claims when you file the application because if you have a patentable invention, you can have the examiner write them for you. A provision of the *Manual of Patent Examining Procedure*, Section 707.07(j), states:

When, during the examination of a pro se [no attorney] case, it becomes apparent to the examiner that there is patentable subject matter disclosed in the application, [the examiner] shall draft one or more claims for the applicant and indicate in office action that such claims would be allowed if incorporated in the application by amendment.

This practice will expedite prosecution and offer a service to individual inventors not represented by a registered patent attorney or agent.

Although this practice may be desirable and is permissible in any case where deemed appropriate by the examiner, it will be expected to be applied in all cases where it is apparent that the applicant is unfamiliar with the proper preparation and prosecution of patent applications.

You can ask the examiner to write claims for you pursuant to this section if you feel yours aren't adequate. The examiner is bound to do so if your invention is patentable. But if you do choose this option, be sure the claims are made broad enough since it isn't in the examiner's own interest to write broad claims for you. As with any other claim, ask yourself if any elements of the examiner's claim can be eliminated or recited more broadly, and still distinguish adequately over the prior art.

Another excellent source of help is the book, *The Mechanics of Patent Claim Drafting* by Landis (see Bibliography), which will tell you practically everything you may want to know about this subject. Although it's expensive, compared to the average patent attorney's hourly charge, it's actually very inexpensive.

Lastly, help is available from patent attorneys and agents, most of whom will be willing to review or draft your claims at their regular hourly rates. But use this as a last alternative since most patent attorneys in private practice charge $60 to $100 per hour. If possible, you should choose a company-employed or retired patent attorney who works at home since such attorneys' rates will usually be one-half to one-third of those charged by their downtown counterparts. To find the company-employed patent attorneys in your area, look in the latest edition of *Attorneys and Agents Registered to Practice Before the U.S. Patent and Trademark Office.*

CHAPTER EIGHT

Putting It All Together for Uncle Sam — Designs Are Easy

MAKE THE FINAL DRAWING

After you have completed your final drafts of the specification, claims, and drawing, you are now ready to begin the "finaling" process. So that you will know what is required for formal drawings, the following reproduces the PTO's Rules 81 and 83 to 85, which state the applicable standards. These should be reviewed very carefully before you ink your drawings.

81 *Drawings required.*

(a) The applicant for patent is required by statute to furnish a drawing of his invention where necessary for the understanding of the subject matter sought to be patented; this drawing must be filed with the application.

(b) Illustrations facilitating an understanding of the invention (for example, flow sheets in cases of processes, and diagrammatic views) may also be furnished in the same manner as drawings.

(c) When a drawing or illustration is not necessary for, but would facilitate, the understanding of the subject matter sought to be patented and the applicant has not furnished such a drawing or illustration, the Office may require its submission within a time period of not less than two months from the sending of a notice thereof.

83 *Content of drawing.*

(a) The drawing should preferably show every feature of the invention specified in the claims. Conventional features disclosed in the description and claims, where their detailed illustration is not essential for a proper understanding of the invention, should be illustrated in the drawing in the form of a graphical drawing symbol or a labeled representation (e.g., a labeled rectangular box).

(b) When the invention consists of an improvement on an old machine the drawing should when possible exhibit, in one or more views, the improved portion itself, disconnected from the old structure, and also in another view, so much only of the old structure as will suffice to show the connection of the invention therewith.

84 *Standards for drawings.*

(a) *Paper and ink.* Drawings must be made upon paper which is flexible, strong, white, smooth, non-shiny and durable.

Two-ply or three-ply bristol-board is preferred. The surface of the paper should be calendered and of a quality which will permit erasure and correction with India ink. India ink, or its equivalent in quality, is preferred for pen drawings to secure perfectly black solid lines. The use of white pigment to cover lines is not normally acceptable.

(b) *Size of sheet and margins.* The size of the sheets on which drawings are made may either be exactly 8½ by 14 inches (21.6 by 35.6 cm.) or exactly 21.0 by 29.7 cm. (DIN size A4). All drawing sheets in a particular application must be the same size. One of the shorter sides of the sheet is regarded as its top.

(1) On 8½ by 14 inch drawing sheets, the drawing must include a top margin of 2 inches (5.1 cm.) and bottom and side margins of one-quarter inch (6.4 mm.) from the edges, thereby leaving a "sight" precisely 8 by 11¾ inches (20.3 by 29.8 cm.). Margin border lines are not permitted. All work must be included within the "sight." The sheets may be provided with two one-quarter inch (6.4 mm.) diameter holes having their centerlines spaced eleven-sixteenths inch (17.5 mm.) below the top edge and 2¾ inches (7.0 cm.) apart, said holes being equally spaced from the respective side edges.

(2) On 21.0 by 29.7 cm. drawing sheets, the drawing must include a top margin of at least 2.5 cm., a left side margin of 2.5 cm., a right side margin of 1.5 cm., and a bottom margin of 1.0 cm. Margin border lines are not permitted. All work must be contained within a sight size not to exceed 17 by 26.2 cm.

(c) *Character of lines.* All drawings must be made with drafting instruments or by a process which will give them satisfactory reproduction characteristics. Every line and letter must be durable, black, sufficiently dense and dark, uniformly thick and well defined; the weight of all lines and letters must be heavy enough to permit adequate reproduction. This direction applies to all lines however fine, to shading, and to lines representing cut surfaces in sectional views. All lines must be clean, sharp, and solid. Fine or crowded lines should be avoided. Solid black should not be used for sectional or surface shading. Freehand work should be avoided wherever it is possible to do so.

(d) *Hatching and shading.* (1) Hatching should be made by oblique parallel lines spaced sufficiently apart to enable the lines to be distinguished without difficulty.

(2) Heavy lines on the shade side of objects should preferably be used except where they tend to thicken the work and obscure reference characters. The light should come from the upper left hand corner at an angle of 45°. Surface delineations should preferably be shown by proper shading, which should be open.

(e) *Scale.* The scale to which a drawing is made ought to be large enough to show the mechanism without crowding when the drawing is reduced in size to two-thirds in reproduction, and views of portions of the mechanism on a larger scale should be used when necessary to show details clearly; two or more sheets should be used if one does not give sufficient room to accomplish this end, but the number of sheets should not be more than is necessary.

(f) *Reference characters.* The different views should be consecutively numbered figures. Reference numerals (and letters, but numerals are preferred) must be plain, legible and carefully formed, and not be encircled. They should, if possible, measure at least one-eighth of an inch (3.2 mm.) in height so that they may bear reduction to one twenty-fourth of an inch (1.1 mm.); and they may be slightly larger when there is sufficient room. They should not be so placed in the close and complex parts of the drawing as to interfere with a thorough comprehension of the same, and therefore should rarely cross or mingle with the lines. When necessarily grouped around a certain part, they should be placed at a little distance, at the closest point where there is available space, and connected by lines with the parts to which they refer. They should not be placed upon hatched or shaded surfaces but when necessary, a blank space may be left in the hatching or shading where the character occurs so that it shall appear perfectly distinct and separate from the work. The same part of an invention appearing in more than one view of the drawing must always be designated by the same character, and the same character must never be used to designate different parts. Reference signs not mentioned in the description shall not appear in the drawing, and vice versa.

(g) *Symbols, legends.* Graphical drawing symbols and other labeled representations may be used for conventional elements when appropriate, subject to approval by the Office. The elements for which such symbols and labeled representations are used must be adequately identified in the specification. While descriptive matter on drawings is not permitted, suitable legends may be used, or may be required, in proper cases, as in diagrammatic views and flowsheets or to show materials or where labeled representations are employed to illustrate conventional elements. Arrows may be required, in proper cases, to show direction of movement. The lettering should be as large as, or larger than, the reference characters.

(h) [Reserved]

(i) *Views.* The drawing must contain as many figures as may be necessary to show the invention; the figures should be consecutively numbered if possible in the order in which they appear. The figures may be plain, elevation, section, or perspective views, and detail views of portions or elements, on a larger scale if necessary, may also be used. Exploded views, with the separated parts of the same figure embraced by a bracket, to show the relationship or order of assembly of various parts are permissible. When necessary, a view of a large machine or device in its entirety may be broken and extended over several sheets if there is no loss in facility of understanding the view. Where figures on two or more sheets form in effect a single complete figure, the figures on the several sheets should be so arranged that the complete figure can be understood by laying the drawing sheets adjacent to one another. The arrangement should be such that no part of any of the figures appearing on the various sheets are concealed and that the complete figure can be understood even though spaces will occur in the complete figure because of the margins on the drawing sheets. The plane upon which a sectional view is taken should be indicated on the general view by a broken line, the ends of which should be designated by numerals corresponding to the figure number of the sectional view and have arrows applied to indicate the direction in which the view is taken. A moved position may be shown by a broken line superimposed upon a suitable figure if this can be done without crowding, otherwise a separate figure must be used for this purpose. Modified forms of construction can only be shown in separate figures. Views should not be connected by projection lines nor should center lines be used.

(j) *Arrangement of views.* All views on the same sheet should stand in the same direction and if possible, stand so that they can be read with the sheet held in an upright position. If views longer than the width of the sheet are necessary for the clearest illustration of the invention, the sheet may be turned on its side so that the top of the sheet with the appropriate top margin is on the right hand side. One figure must not be placed upon another or within the outline of another.

(k) *Figure for Official Gazette.* The drawing should, as far as possible, be so planned that one of the views will be suitable for publication in the Official Gazette as the illustration of the invention.

(l) *Extraneous matter.* Identifying indicia (such as the attorney's docket number, inventor's name, number of sheets, etc.) not to exceed $2\frac{3}{4}$ inches (7.0 cm.) in width may be placed in a centered location between the side edges within three-fourths inch (19.1 mm.) of the top edge. Authorized security markings may be placed on the drawings provided they are outside the illustrations and are removed when the material is declassified. Other extraneous matter will not be permitted upon the face of a drawing.

(m) *Transmission of drawings.* Drawings transmitted to the Office should be sent flat, protected by a sheet of heavy binder's board, or may be rolled for transmission in a suitable mailing tube; but must never be folded. If received creased or mutilated, new drawings will be required.

85 Informal drawings

The requirements of Rule 84 relating to drawings will be strictly enforced. A drawing not executed in conformity thereto, if suitable for reproduction, may be admitted but in such case the drawing must be corrected or a new one furnished, as required. The necessary corrections or mounting will be made by the Office upon applicant's request or permission and at his expense.

The main drawing rules to remember are: (1) Use paper of the right size; (2) keep your drawings in the right-size drawing area with invisible margins; (3) all lines must be solid, black, and sharp; (4) keep the figures unconnected and uncrowded; (5) use proper shading (that is, all right-hand and bottom lines must be heavier than upper and left-hand lines, and shade lines must be used to indicate curved surfaces); (6) hatch all cross-section areas with parallel lines (crisscross hatching and solid-black areas are not permitted).

You will find that it is difficult to work with ink because it tends to smear and is hard to erase. If you do intend to make your own drawings, you should practice a good deal to attain proficiency in the use of ink. A Rapidograph or other brand of tube pen is much easier to use than the old-fashioned double-nib pen. If you need to erase a previously drawn line, an electric eraser is best, and the trick is to hold the eraser lightly and take a long, long time to erase the line; otherwise you'll burn or tear the paper.

Be sure to study the drawings of other patents to get an idea of what is involved and the standards required. If you feel you won't be able to do it adequately, don't hesitate to hire a professional artist, art student, or patent draftsperson.

PREPARING THE APPLICATION

The paper on which your application is typed should be 8 to 8½ inches wide and 10½ to 13 inches long, with at least a 1-inch left-hand margin and at least a ¾-inch top margin. But if you think you may later want to file corresponding foreign applications, you should type your application on paper that meets the new international format requirements, that is, the sheets should be 21 by 29.7 centimeters in size, with top margins of 8 to 9 centimeters on the first sheet and 2 to 4 centimeters thereafter, left margins of 2½ to 4 centimeters, and bottom and right margins of 2 to 3 centimeters, with sheets numbered consecutively at the top and lines typed one-and-one-half spaces apart. (For applications limited exclusively to the United States, you can use double spacing and number the sheets at the bottom.)

You should start your claims and abstract on new pages. The title should go on the first page and the last page which should contain the abstract.

Do not submit an application on easily erasable paper, or on paper which has white pigment covering any typewritten lines, since these are not considered permanent, unaltered records. If you're not that good a typist, one solution is to type your application on easily erasable paper or regular paper, cover errors with white pigment, type in the corrections, and then make bond paper photocopies of your typewritten original for submission to the PTO.

If after drawing up your application you find you must make a few minor changes in it, it is OK to do so, provided you make these changes neatly in ink, in handwriting, and date and initial the margin adjacent to each change, *before* you sign the application.

PROPER INVENTORS

If you have conceived, built, and tested the invention entirely on your own, of course there's no problem about who is the proper inventor to be named on your application. But if you've invented it with someone else, both of you should be named as "joint" inventors. But be sure that both of you actually are joint inventors. If one of you came up with the concept of the invention, while the other merely built and tested it, not contributing any inventive concepts but merely acting as any skilled artisan or model maker might, the second person is not a coinventor. On the other hand, if you came up with the idea for your invention and your model maker came up with valuable suggestions and contributions that made the invention work and went beyond the skill of an ordinary model maker or machinist, you both should be named as coinventors.

The rule is that each inventor should have contributed something to every claim of the application. With regard to the dependent claims, consider these as incorporating all the limitations of the parent claim and be sure that each inventor contributed something that was in either the dependent claim or parent claim that it incorporates.

It is important to include in your application all the inventors who are true inventors and not to include those who aren't inventors. If your inventorship is later discovered to be incorrect, and you did it with bad faith, your patent can be held invalid.

TRANSMITTAL LETTER, CHECK, AND POSTCARD

The transmittal letter is provided in Form 3 at the back of this book. The letter should be dated as of the date the entire patent application is mailed. The names of the inventor(s), the title, the total number of pages of specification claims, and the number of sheets of drawing should be indicated in the appropriate spaces on this form. The date the application was signed should also be indicated in the space provided; normally the date when the application was signed and the date when the application is mailed to the PTO should be close.

The basic filing fee for an application is $65, which entitles you to file one independent claim and nine dependent claims, assuming that each dependent claim refers back to only one preceding claim (dependent or independent). If any one of your dependent claims refers directly to plural preceding claims, that claim counts as plural dependent claims, equal to the number of claims it directly refers to.

For each independent or dependent claim in excess of ten an additional fee of $2 is charged; and for each independent claim in excess of one, an additional fee of $10 is charged. Thus, you should insert the total number of claims (both dependent and independent) after "Total Claims," subtract 10 from this figure, indicate the result, multiply it by 2 and indicate the resulting amount in the first space under "$65." Next, enter the total number of independent claims where indicated; subtract 1; enter the results where indicated; multiply by 10; and enter the product in the space indicated. Finally, add all three figures to get your total filing fee. Make a check out for this amount, payable to the Commissioner of Patents and Trademarks, and attach it to the letter. Be absolutely sure you have enough money in your checking account to cover the check; if the check bounces, you will lose the filing date of your application.

If there are two inventors, both should sign the letter and their respective addresses should be provided. If there are more than two inventors, retype the form with additional spaces for the additional inventors. Whenever there is more than one inventor, all inventors must sign every communication to the PTO.

Whenever you send anything to the PTO, you should include a receipt postcard. The PTO will stamp and mail it back to you as soon as they open your letter. Postcards are used because the PTO receives many, many thousands of pieces of mail each day and occasionally loses some. It may be months before you receive any reply to a paper you have sent to the PTO, so you'll want to be assured it arrived safely.

The front of the postcard should be addressed to you. The back should read as follows:

```
Application papers of [name of inventor(s)] for
[title of invention] consisting of_____pages
of specification and claims,_____sheets of
drawings, check for $_____, and declaration
received for filing today:
```

figure 5

DECLARATION

The declaration form appears as Form 4 at the end of this book, and the manner of completing it is straightforward. The title goes in the space at the top; the name, residence, citizenship, and post-office address of each inventor (if there are more than one) go in the appropriate spaces at 201, 202, and 203. Your residence (city and state) will normally be the same as the city and state of your post-office address, unless you have a post-office box or a postal address in a city other than the one in which you actually reside. In the box in the middle of the form, enter your name, address to which correspondence is to be sent, and telephone number; if there are more inventors than one, enter the name, address, and telephone number of the inventor you select to receive any correspondence and telephone calls.

Each inventor should sign and date the appropriate spaces at the bottom of the form.

The declaration should not be treated in a light or cavalier manner, or as a formality; it should be read and reviewed very carefully before it is signed. By statute, it lists all the conditions required for your patent application to be valid. If anyone can prove that you signed the declaration knowing that any of its statements were false, your patent can be held invalid.

The wording of the declaration will not be reviewed here since it essentially repeats the criteria of "prior art" listed in Chapter 4. Note, however, the last sentence of the declaration, which states that you acknowledge a duty to disclose information of which you are aware and which is material to the examination of the application. This provision, which is relatively new, has been added to impress upon inventors that they have a duty to disclose to the PTO any information which could affect the examination or validity of the application. This means that you must disclose to the PTO all relevant prior art which you uncovered in your search; any disadvantages of your invention of which you are aware; or any other fact you think the examiner would want to be aware of when examining your application. Normally all of this information will be provided in the Statement of Prior Art.

STATEMENT OF PRIOR ART

The Statement of Prior Art, Form 5, is a relatively new development. It is now required because, in several suits involving patents, it was held that where the inventor or the inventor's attorney knew of relevant prior art, it should have been revealed to the examiner. The court decisions have now been incorporated in the PTO's rules. Rules 97 to 99 require that each inventor submit a statement of prior art at the time of filing the application or within the following three months.

The Statement of Prior Art must list all prior references known to the inventors that are relevant to the patentability of the application. In addition, the inventor must send to the PTO a copy of each cited reference and discuss its relevance to the invention.

You may well ask why, if the prior art you discover consists of patents, you have to send patents to the PTO. Isn't this carrying coals to Newcastle? Well, yes; but the PTO is such a large and complex organization that it would involve administrative difficulties and additional time for examiners to dig out all of the patents you cite, so it's easier for them if you send them the references directly.

If you send the Statement of Prior Art (Form 5) in with your application, the names of the inventors and title of your invention are the only information you need to put at the top of the form. If you send it in after your application is filed, you will know the serial number, filing date, and group art unit, and can insert them. You normally will not know the examiner's name unless you have received a first "office action" from the PTO.

After the first paragraph on this form, list each prior-art reference of which you are aware, and, briefly, its relevance. For example, "Patent 3,731,670 to Loe, 8 May 1973: Shows a magnetically operated bistable gas valve" is a suitable citation and discussion. Optionally, you can add a second sentence stating briefly how your invention differs from each reference. Then add a closing salutation, for example, "Very respectfully"; type your name and address below this and sign your name. (If there are more inventors than one, each inventor should sign.)

If you send in the Statement of Prior Art with the application, you should list it on the postcard that you send with your application. If you

```
Statement of Prior Art in application of
[name(s) of inventor(s)], Serial No._____
Filed_____, Title:_____received for
filing today:
```

figure 6

send it in after the application is filed, you should send in a separate post-card. Again the front of the card should be addressed to you; the back should read as in Fig. 6.

MAILING

Congratulations. You are now ready to mail your patent application to the PTO. Assemble your postcard; your check and transmittal letter (stapled together), your drawing(s); the specification and claims; the declaration; and the Statement of Prior Art (if you are sending it in with the application). The pages of the application, including the declaration, should all be stapled together. All the papers should then be fastened together by a paper clip or other temporary device. The papers can be transmitted in a large envelope with one or two sheets of stiff cardboard to protect the drawing from bending; or, if they are thin enough, they all can be rolled and mailed in a mailing tube.

It is important to keep an identical, line-for-line copy of every page of your application (including the drawing), in your own file. It is suggested that you file a photocopy and keep the original of your application, or make and keep several extra copies of the application, so that you can send them to manufacturers when you market your invention. As you must file the original of the drawing and declaration, you should make several extra copies for your file.

The application should be sent to the PTO by first-class mail; you may want to register the parcel to cover the expense of making a new drawing in case it is lost. However, registering your mail will not cover you for loss of any legal rights in case your application is lost in the mail on the way to the PTO.

About one to two weeks after you send your application to the PTO, you will get your postcard back, stamped to indicate the filing date of your application, and also stamped with a six-digit serial number that has been assigned to your application. Within about a week to a month after that, you should get a small blue filing receipt back from the PTO indicating that your application has been officially filed in the PTO. If for any reason your application is incomplete or deficient, it will not be officially "filed" but will be regarded as "deposited." The application branch of the PTO will send you a letter stating the deficiency in your application, and you should promptly remedy it. However, if you follow all the instructions in this chapter carefully, you should get the blue filing receipt in due course.

Once you get the blue filing receipt, your application is officially "patent pending," and unless you want to keep your invention a trade secret in case your patent application is ever disallowed, you are free to publish details of your invention or market it to whomever you choose. If you manufacture anything embodying your invention, you should mark it "patent pending."

DESIGN PATENT APPLICATIONS

As I've indicated, a design patent covers the *ornamental appearance*, rather than the internal structure, function, composition, or steps of an invention.

It is possible to have both a design-patent application and a regular patent application pending on the same device, but, of course, they should not cover the same features of the device. The regular patent application should cover only the structure, function, or operation of the device, and the design-patent application should cover an entirely separate "invention," namely, the ornamental (aesthetic) appearance of the device.

You'll be relieved to know that design patents are very easy to file. A design-patent application can consist simply of the "application" itself (Form 6) plus the drawing(s).

If you believe that your invention has a unique ornamental appearance that is significantly different from anything heretofore designed, you can prepare a design-patent application on it.

The first step in a design-patent application is to prepare drawings in the same format as for a regular patent application. However, the drawings for the design-patent application should show only the exterior appearance of your invention; no interior parts or workings need be shown or indicated. But it is important to remember that drawings of your design-patent application should show all of the details of the external surface of your design. A company I once worked for had an important design-patent application on a TV set held invalid because the design patent failed to show the rear side of the TV set.

Once you have made your penciled sketches and had them inked, fill out Form 6 as indicated. The title of your design can be very simple, and need not be specifically directed toward your invention. For example, "Bicycle" is sufficient. Each view of the drawing should be separately indicated, for example, "Fig. 1 is front perspective view, Fig. 2 is a side view, etc."

You will note that the design-patent application has one claim only, and to write the claim you need merely fill in the blank with the title of your design.

A design-patent application with the drawings and the receipt postcard should be sent to the PTO in the same manner as your regular patent application. Be sure to keep an identical copy of your design patent application and the drawing(s). The filing fee is only $20.

You'll receive your receipt postcard back in a week or two and you'll receive a blue filing receipt a week to a month thereafter.

CHAPTER NINE

Now You Can Sell It

INTRODUCTION

Now that you've filed a patent application on your invention it is OK to relax and take a well-deserved rest. You may, then, if you wish, show your invention to practically whomever you want, write and publish material about it, and sell either the invention or the product embodying it or both. (If it's a process, you may put it into commercial use). It would be very difficult for anyone who sees your invention to defeat your right to a patent now, since to do so it would be necessary to file another application and win an interference with you. It would be very difficult to win such an interference because, first of all, the filing date on the application would be later than yours. Thus, to overcome your earlier filing date, a person would have to prove, in effect, having built and tested the invention before you filed your patent application, (or, if you built and tested your invention before you filed, a person would have to antedate your date of building and testing). Such proof would be very difficult without the most elaborate acts of forgery. Moreover, you would be able to make a strong showing that this person derived the invention from you since you would be able to prove that the later application was filed with knowledge of your invention; that is, you could raise a presumption that the other person "derived" the "invention" from you. Keep in mind, however, that although you are free to publicize, market, and sell products embodying the invention, you should continue to keep careful records, preferably in your notebook, in chronological order, of all the actions that you take so that you will be able to make a case for derivation in case you are so unfortunate as to cross paths with an invention pirate.

Although you now can take a breather, don't rest too long. There is still a good deal to do to make your invention pay off. Remember that neither a patent application nor a patent per se will make you any money; a product or process embodying or using the invention must almost always be marketed by someone in order for a patent application or patent to pay off. Note also that a pending application will not give you any protection whatever against infringers. So it's time to start your efforts to market the invention as the final phase in making your creativity bear fruit. Aside from your brief, well-deserved rest, you should continue to be diligent in your efforts since others may come up with your idea independently of you, and, even though you'll get the patent, they may beat you to the marketplace, and thus establish market leadership before your patent issues. Moreover, their idea may be a sufficiently different variation from yours that your patent may not cover it, they may decide to contest your patent, or they may have already filed an application of their own independently of you.

Your next goal is, therefore, to get the invention into a commercial product or process as soon as possible. The best way to do this is to get a company to take over your invention, manufacture, and sell it, giving you a lump sum or royalty payments for your contribution.

Under no circumstances should you wait until your patent issues to begin your marketing efforts, because the delay will only prejudice you, and, although a patent is prestigious, it is not valuable enough to justify waiting several years to market your invention.

SALES PRESENTATION AND MODEL

You will find that it is most advantageous, when showing your invention to manufacturers or others you want to invest in your invention, to demonstrate a working model, if at all possible. Pictures and diagrams may convey an idea and get a message across, but the working model is the thing that will make believers out of most people, and show them that your invention is real and fulfillable, and not just scratches on paper. So if you haven't made a model before, try your best to make one now, even if it has to be made of cardboard or wood. If you're not handy, hopefully you can afford to have a professional model maker or artisan make you one, or you may have a handy friend or relative.

If you do use a model maker and you disclose critical dimensions, materials, suppliers, or other information you consider to be proprietary, it is best to ask for a signed Proprietary Information Agreement (Form 7) before you turn over your drawings or other papers. To fill out the form, merely list the model maker's or machinist's name as "Recipient"; list the documents which you are turning over on line 2; put your name on line 3 and on the third line of subparagraph 1; and have the recipient sign and date the Agreement.

It is also desirable to add a proprietary legend to any drawings or descriptions you turn over to your model maker. Such a legend, which can be made in rubber-stamp form or can be typed on the drawings, can read as follows:

This drawing or description contains proprietary information of [your name] and is loaned for use only in evaluating or manufacturing an invention of [your name]. Reproduction or disclosure of any part hereof to others, or manufacture of matter described herein, or use for any other purpose is prohibited without express written consent of [your name]. This drawing or description is the property of [your name] and must be returned upon demand. By acceptance hereof, recipient agrees to all of the above conditions.

After you have made a working model, you should take at least one good photograph of it. The photograph should be of professional quality; if you are not a good photographer, have a professional do it, and order several views if necessary. Have at least fifty glossy prints made of the photo, possibly with several views on one sheet. Then write a descriptive blurb about your invention, stating the title or the trademark, what it is, how it works, its main advantages and selling points, plus your name, address, telephone number, and the legend "Patent Pending." Make your write-up snappy and convincing. Show it to a friend or someone who has experience in writing to be sure that it is as clear and convincing as possible. Then have it typed or printed and have at least fifty copies made to go with the photographs.

Since you will be distributing the photo and description of your invention to people in the field, it is best to learn the terminology and nomenclature of the field (if you haven't done so already) so that you will appear knowledgeable and confident when you show your invention around. Thus you should read appropriate trade journals, textbooks, patents, etc.

If your invention is of a nature that would make it difficult or impossible for you to make a working model, perhaps you can make a scaled-down, nonworking model. Failing this, you should at least make some good drawings and a description; you can use your patent drawings if they are clear and easily understandable.

FINDING PROSPECTIVE MANUFACTURERS

After you have made the photos and descriptions, the next step is to compile an initial listing of manufacturers who you believe could manufacture your invention profitably. Your initial list should comprise all the manufacturers who meet the following three criteria: (1) They are geographically close to you; (2) they already manufacture the same or a closely related product; and (3) they are not too large.

Nearby or local manufacturers are best; you will have low travel and telephone expenses and will be able to call and communicate with them freely whenever you want. If they manufacture your invention, you can monitor the progress and consult with them frequently. Lastly, local manufacturers, especially from small towns, will tend to have an inherent bias in favor of local inventors.

Manufacturers in a closely allied field are best because they have experience with the product line or devices similar to your invention, have the sales volume in the field to be aware of competitive pricing policies, can make it part of their existing product line in order to keep sales costs low, and want new models related to their existing products each year in order to keep ahead of the competition. If the manufacturer is not in a closely allied line, both the seller and the product will be on trial, so why start with two strikes against you?

To find a manufacturer in a closely allied field, look at products which are close physically or functionally to yours. For instance, if your invention is an improved carburetor, a carburetor manufacturer is your only obvious choice; but if your invention is a totally new idea, say a solar heat absorber, you would get the best physical approximation with a plumbing-parts or a plastic-parts manufacturer and the best functional approximation with a manufacturer of heat-absorbing swimming pools.

The reasons for avoiding giant manufacturers are these: Smaller manufacturers are more dependent on outside designers; you can contact the decision makers or the owners of the company directly or more easily; decisions are made more rapidly because the bureaucracies are smaller; smaller companies have constant or continuous owners who are very familiar with the field and have spent many years in it; and smaller companies are less likely to insist that you sign a waiver form (see *The Waiver* below). Of course, don't use companies that are so small that they won't have enough money to finance the manufacture of your invention or the marketing of it adequately. Companies with sales of about $5–50 million dollars are best. You should avoid giant companies like Ford, General Motors, and General Electric since they are so big and have such a complicated bureaucracy and a strong inbred NIH (Not Invented Here) syndrome that you will have great difficulty selling them your invention, unless you are extremely large and well established (like the owner of the Wankel-engine patents).

You can find companies meeting the above criteria by first looking in your local Yellow Pages under the appropriate subject headings. Also, a publisher in your state may publish a manufacturers' register (such as the California Manufacturers Register); if not, a national directory or register, such as the *Thomas Register*, The Duns Million Dollar Directory, etc., is best. Also get company names from ads in pertinent trade and hobby magazines, see your local chamber of commerce and your local library, especially if it has a business branch. Lastly, stock advisory services, such as *Value Line Investment Survey*, Standard & Poor's, and Moody's, supply excellent information about companies. Get the names of the company presidents, vice presidents, directors of engineering, marketing, etc. Find out all you can about each company you select; know its products, sales, corporate history, factory location(s), etc.

If you can't find any local, small, and closely allied companies, or if after trying, your invention is not accepted by the first set of companies you choose, branch out to larger, more distant ones, or to companies whose products are more remote from your invention. Another possibility is to use a local nonmanufacturing (marketing) company with access to U.S. or foreign manufacturers who can manufacture your invention cheaply for the marketing company.

If your invention is in the gadget category and you believe it would have an appeal to affluent taste, your first choice might be Hammacher Schlemmer, a specialty store and mail-order house at 147 East 57th Street, New

York NY 10022. As noted on the front page of *The Wall Street Journal* of May 2, 1977, H.S. develops and sells a wide variety of gadget exotica, both through its catalogs and over the counter. The company receives about 3000 ideas from inventors each year, accepts about 50 to 75 of these, and arranges to have them produced by manufacturers, usually with their own INVENTO trademark. Many items H.S. financed and had manufactured or first sold as strictly luxury gadgets have become commonplace in most American homes today. For example, the steam iron, the electric razor, the pressure cooker, the blender, the humidifier, the electric can opener, the high-intensity lamp, the microwave oven, and the automatic-drip coffee maker were first introduced by this unique and innovative retailer. Address your presentation to Mr. Dominic Tampone, the president.

THE NIH SYNDROME

Before presenting your invention to any manufacturer, two possible impediments should be kept in mind: The NIH (Not Invented Here) syndrome and the waiver. Generally, the larger the manufacturer, the greater the chances of encountering one or both of these impediments.

The NIH syndrome is an unwritten attitude which handicaps inventors submitting their ideas to a company, no matter how meritorious such ideas may be. Many companies have an attitude, especially prevalent in the engineering department, which manifests an inherent bias against any outside invention because it was "not invented here." This attitude prevails because of jealousy: The job of the corporate engineering department is to create new and profitable products for their company. If an engineering department were to recommend an outside invention, it would almost be a tacit admission that the engineering department had failed to do its job in solving the problem and coming up with the solution the outside inventor has found. For more on the NIH syndrome, read the front-page article in *The Wall Street Journal* of November 28, 1966.

How can you overcome the NIH syndrome? First, try to avoid larger companies, or companies with engineering departments. Second, when forced to deal with engineering departments or any department in a company where the NIH syndrome may be present, try to flatter them and validate their raison d'être by asking for their advice and review of your invention, tell them that they *may* (not "*will*") find it a profitable addition to their company's line, they *may* be able, *with their skills*, to adapt it to their company's line and make it a commercial success, etc.

THE WAIVER

The corporate waiver originated because many companies have been burned by suits brought by outside inventors who alleged that their ideas were stolen or publicized without permission, or that companies had failed to pay them under an implied contract for use of their ideas. Companies often lost these suits even though they had not used an inventor's idea, or had come up with the same idea independently, sometimes many years after the inventor's idea was submitted.

For example, one company I worked for received an idea from an inventor in the 1940s for a phonograph arm, which the company reviewed (without requiring the inventor to sign any waiver) but didn't find suitable for its product line. About twenty years later, the company independently came out with a phonograph arm which had some similarities, but in actuality was substantially different from the inventor's previous submission. When the inventor found out about the new phono arm, he filed suit against the company. The company eventually settled by making a token payment of about $1,000 rather than go to trial (even though they believed they had a certain chance of winning), because the cost of trial would have amounted to about $25,000.

As a result of these and similar experiences, most companies with good legal advice will ask you to sign a waiver before they will even look at your ideas. The usual procedure, if you send a letter mentioning your idea to the company, is for the company to route your letter to the patent or legal department, which will send you a form letter back stating their policy and asking you to sign the waiver before they can review your idea. Once you do so, the patent or legal department will approve your submission for review and send it to the appropriate engineering manager of the company. (For reasons explained below, if at all possible, you should *not* use this method of submitting your invention to a company.)

The waiver itself usually requires you to give up all your rights, except those which you may have under the patent laws. Specifically, the waiver asks you to agree, that (1) there is no implied contract that the company will pay you if they use your idea; (2) the company is not bound to keep your idea in confidence; (3) the company has no obligation to return any papers you submit; and (4) the company has no obligation whatever to you, except under the patent laws. Many companies add many other minor provisions, which are not significant enough to discuss here. The effect of the waiver is that you have no rights whatever against the company if they use your invention, except to sue them for patent infringement if and when you get a patent.

Since you may not get a patent, since the company may use a variation of your idea that may not be covered by any patent you do get, and since you would like to have the company keep your submission in confidence, it's best to avoid signing any waiver if at all possible. Ergo you should, at least initially, concentrate on smaller companies. The smaller the company, the less likely they are to make you sign a waiver.

In fact, the best sort of relation you can have with a company to which you submit your ideas is to *have them sign your agreement.* If you can swing it, have the company sign a proprietary submission agreement such as the following:

X Company agrees to review an invention from [your name] for a new and improved [describe invention], to keep such invention and all papers received in confidence, to return all papers submitted upon demand, and to pay [your name] a reasonable sum and royalty to be settled by future negotiation or arbitration if it uses or adopts such invention.

To get a company to sign such an agreement is extremely difficult because most companies are fairly sophisticated, but it has been done. If you're a good salesman and can give them an enticing story about how great your invention is, how much money they'll make from it, how they don't have to pay you unless they use it, how what you're asking is only reasonable, etc., you *may* be able to do it. (See advice below about timing the presentation of the agreement.)

If they won't sign the above agreement, you can make it a bit more palatable by eliminating the last clause (regarding the payment of a reasonable fee and royalty). Even with the last clause eliminated, you're in a very good position if you've gotten them to sign.

Even if the company refuses to sign any agreement submitted by you, you're still in a pretty good position legally if you can get them to review your invention without any agreements being signed by either side. If they later use the invention, or publicize it without your authorization, you can make a pretty good case against them in court, and most juries will go along with you anyway because you're a relatively small individual and your adversary is a relatively large company.

Even if the company has a firm policy of not reviewing any outside ideas unless a waiver is first signed, astounding as it seems, it still may be possible, if you're persistent enough, to get your idea reviewed without signing a waiver. One large company I worked for had a firm waiver policy, but one outside inventor contacted a particular executive, stating that he had a valuable invention, and asking the executive if he could meet with him to review it. The executive refused to meet with the inventor or review any papers until getting clearance from the patent department, that is, until the inventor signed the waiver. The inventor, a persistent fellow, and his patent attorney, equally persistent, were not put off by this policy in the least, but badgered and pleaded with the executive through a series of phone calls and letters until the executive, who was high enough to overrule the patent department and company policy, finally agreed to review the submission without a waiver. After review, he decided that the company wasn't interested in the invention, but as I warned him, if the company changed its mind and independently came up with the same idea several years later, they were sure to face a lawsuit from the aggressive inventor and his patent attorney. The moral is that if you are persistent enough, you may be able to bypass the waiver and the patent/legal department in almost any company.

If all else fails and you do have to sign a waiver before the company will look at your invention (this is what will usually happen), it's not all that bad since you do have a patent application—see why I told you to file your patent application before submitting your invention to any company? However you should read the waiver carefully to make sure you retain your full rights under the patent laws and that the waiver does not contain any extraordinary provisions.

If you are submitting an invention to a company without a regular patent application (block B of the Invention Decision Chart from Chapter 5), it's very important that you try to get the company to sign a Proprietary Information Agreement, or, failing that, try to submit it without signing their waiver. If all else fails and you have to sign their waiver, it's best to make sure the company is a reliable and fair one since you will be completely at their mercy once you sign the waiver. I believe most companies and most company executives will be honest and fair with you (even if they don't have to be) if you really contribute something which they can use and make a profit from.

THE BEST WAY TO PRESENT YOUR INVENTION TO A MANUFACTURER

The best and most effective way to sell your invention to a manufacturer is personally to visit and demonstrate your invention (or present drawings of it if you have no working model) to the decision maker in the company you select.

The best way to accomplish this is to write a brief personal letter to the president of the company, saying that you have a very valuable invention you believe would be very profitable for the company's business and that you would like to make an appointment to get together when convenient to demonstrate the invention briefly. Keep the initiative by stating that you will call in a few days. Follow through accordingly.

Besides the NIH syndrome, another drawback to be aware of at this stage is the secretarial shield—the tendency of most private secretaries to build a wall around their bosses to prevent outsiders from reaching them. If, when you call the president a few days after your letter is sent, you encounter a secretarial shield, you can usually pierce it by stressing the importance of your invention and how much the boss would like to see it, how valuable it will be to the company, and how much the boss will appreciate being notified about it. Flatter secretaries by asking their names, calling them by name, and telling them that you will appreciate it if they can help you to see whom you want to see.

When you call for an appointment, don't allow yourself to be shunted to the purchasing department—you're selling an invention, not a product—or the engineering department—your invention needs a decision from a person with vision and your invention is already substantially engineered. If the president or the president's secretary still tries to shunt you to a lower level, try your utmost to avoid this since underlings often don't have the power to commit the company to new product ventures, won't present your ideas in the right fashion or as enthusiastically as you would, and they may not have enough depth to appreciate your invention as the president would. Hold out for the boss. Be persistent. Remember, the squeaking wheel gets the grease. If you bug them enough, they will eventually give you a hearing, if only to get rid of you.

If you do get any rejections or rebuffs, don't let your ego or pride get in your way. If you keep at it long and hard enough, they'll believe you have something and probably give you a fair hearing.

When you get an appointment mention the Proprietary Submission Agreement if you think the company might be willing to sign one. If they at first refuse, try to sell them on it, using the arguments given above.

When you come to the demonstration, be prepared! Set up your presentation well in advance. Practice it on friends. Tell the advantages of your invention first, how it works, how it will be profitable for their business, why it will sell, etc. During the verbal part of your presentation, it is wise to use diagrams and charts, but keep your model hidden from view; otherwise they will be looking at your model and trying to figure it out and won't listen to you. Then at a dramatic moment bring out your model and demonstrate how it works. Do not apologize if your model is crude or an unattractive prototype, but radiate enough confidence in yourself and your invention that they will overlook any lack of "cosmetics."

Most of all, be sure your model works! Nothing can be more embarrassing and harmful than to take the time of the president, and possibly one or two top executives, to demonstrate something that does not work or falls apart during the demonstration.

Bring out your pictures and written description later, after you have made your verbal presentation. Otherwise the executives will be reading your description and looking at your pictures during your presentation.

During your presentation do not mention any faults or drawbacks of your invention, but if you are questioned about them, be prepared to defend each one or stress a countervailing advantage which offsets each disadvantage. For example, if they say, "Tooling costs will be high," say "Possibly, but I anticipate sales of $xxx in the first year and we can get a profit margin of x percent because of its uniqueness."

If you've done your best and still get a rejection, don't accept it blindly and walk away with your tail between your legs, but turn it into an asset for next time. Talk to the executives about it and learn exactly why they decided not to accept your idea so that in the future you'll be better prepared to answer and overcome the disadvantage which blocked your initial acceptance.

Lastly, you should evaluate the company to which you are demonstrating your invention just as they are evaluating you and your invention. If the company seems to be dying or run by a bunch of "fogies" who lack enthusiasm, and appear to be niggardly with capital outlays, and really do not appreciate the true value of your invention, I would not recommend accepting them even if they want your invention since you are risking a lot too when you sign up with a company. If the company doesn't promote your invention enthusiastically and correctly, it can fail in the market even if it's the greatest thing to come down the pike in 20 years.

THE OTHER WAY TO PRESENT YOUR INVENTION

The other way to present your invention is by correspondence. Because letters are easy to file and forget and because any salesman will tell you a personal presentation is a thousand times more likely to make a sale, I strongly advise against submitting an invention to a manufacturer by correspondence if you can avoid it. Try your utmost to arrange a personal demonstration as described in the previous section.

If, for geographical or other reasons, though you've done your best, you can't get a personal appointment at the manufacturer you select, you'll have to resort to correspondence to submit your invention. Your first letter should be purposely vague, short, and sweet, but enticing and designed to stimulate high interest and curiosity. For example, if you've invented a new can opener, your initial letter to your selected appliance manufacturer should look something like this:

> Mr. A.B., President
> XYZ Appliance Co.
>
> Dear Mr. B.:
>   I have developed and applied for a patent on a new and dramatically different can opener, which has only two moving parts and which can be manufactured for 80 percent of the cost of your K-1 model. If you are interested in reviewing my can opener for possible profitable manufacture by XYZ, please contact me at your earliest convenience.
>   Sincerely,

Your letter should always be individually typed and addressed to a specific individual. Find the president's name from the directories mentioned above. If you send letters to several manufacturers simultaneously, I believe it is generally advantageous to mention this in your letter (for example, "I have sent similar inquiries to two other manufacturers"), since this will show manufacturers that they have competition and that you are sincere and forthright. On the other side of the ethical fence, some inventors use a false letterhead which indicates technical competence, for example "Research Engineering Associates"; I cannot recommend this practice because it is not completely honest and may backfire when and if the truth comes out. Nevertheless there are situations where it will help.

If you receive an expression of interest from the company (amazingly enough, some companies are so stodgy that they won't be interested) they will either enclose and ask you to sign a waiver, or not mention any waiver if they have no waiver policy. If they enclose and require you to sign a waiver form, you can try to bypass it, like the persistent inventor I mentioned above did, or sign it if you find it in order and don't wish to expend the energy required to bypass the form. If no waiver is mentioned, great; you're very well situated and you might even be able to get them to sign your Proprietary Submission Agreement.

Whether or not any waiver or agreement is involved, when the time comes to submit your invention, be sure to give it all you've got. Make sure it's clear, convincing, and complete, and will keep them interested. Use the photo and description you've prepared. If you think it will be helpful, or if they ask for it, you can also submit a copy of your patent application, but omit the serial number, filing date, and claims at this stage. Follow up with phone calls and letters if you don't hear within a reasonable time; remember the squeaking wheel. If the company shows further interest, they'll tell you how to proceed. If they give a negative response, make sure they've understood your invention, its advantages, and operation before you give up on them and try another company.

If you have several companies in mind to which you wish to submit your invention by correspondence, there is nothing unethical or improper about sending inquiries to several manufacturers simultaneously. Otherwise you may waste a lot of valuable time waiting for what may be negative answers if you make sequential submissions. If you get several "nibbles" from your simultaneous inquiries, answer them all; you may wind up in the enviable position of being able to choose your manufacturer.

MAKING AN AGREEMENT

If you do sell your invention to a manufacturer, congratulations and praise are in order; you have done your job well. The next step is to sign an agreement of some sort with the manufacturer. Thus the question arises, what will be the terms of the agreement; exactly what will you sell them and for how much? There are many possibilities. Here are just a few major considerations and terms which can be written into agreements:

1. They can buy your invention, your know-how, your trademark, your patent application, and your model, as well as all your papers, outright for a single fixed sum.

2. They can just take a license under your patent application; in this case they would pay you a royalty for each unit they manufacture and sell; or they can pay you a single fixed sum in advance for a fully paid-up royalty. In this case you still own the patent rights, but receive money from them for the right to manufacture your invention under your patent. If a third party infringer is discovered, the agreement can require either you or the manufacturer to sue the infringer.

3. They can "buy" an option under which you give them the right to obtain a license under your patent application or patent within a fixed time, say 2 years. The payment for this option can be merely the company's agreement to research and develop your invention, which is a typical arrangement, or it can be a cash payment.

4. If you grant the company a license, the license can be exclusive, under which you agree to license only the company and no one else; or it can be nonexclusive, under which you license them, but also have the right to license others.

5. The license, if granted, can be for the life of the patent, or just for a limited term, say 5 years, with an option to renew for succeeding 5-year terms.

6. The license can require the payment of a minimum annual sum during each year of its existence.

7. The license rights can be sold ("assigned") by your manufacturer to another manufacturer, or any such assignment can be prohibited.

There are hundreds of other, less important considerations in licensing, which I will not treat here. Licensing, as you may have gathered by now, is a difficult, complex subject, and one that requires negotiatory as well as legal skills. Unfortunately there are no "standard" invention licensing agreements; each one must be tailor-made. Even though you can make a great invention, prepare a patent application on it, and sell it to a manufacturer, you may not be able to represent yourself adequately in negotiating a license agreement, so it is often wise to hire a patent lawyer to review any contract which is proffered to you. You will find it will probably cost several hundred dollars, but it will be money well spent. Moreover, you're on the brink of success with your invention at this stage, so why shouldn't you employ professional help now to make sure you enjoy to the fullest any success you achieve?

In fact, most reputable companies would prefer that you be represented by an attorney when you negotiate a license agreement and often will pay for your attorney. The reason is that an agreement between a sole inventor and a much larger company will not be treated as fairly for the corporation by a court as it would if the inventor were represented in negotiations by an experienced lawyer.

If you do feel confident enough to represent yourself, and you are the type of person that can go through a long license agreement in detail, and engage in nit-picking with the skill and persistence of a Philadelphia lawyer, you should read a book on the subject of licensing before proceeding to represent yourself. The books on this subject are quite expensive, so determine if your local law library has one. *Patent License Agreements* by Nordhaus is good but expensive; an economical aid that you can obtain is *Checklist for Negotiating Agreements on Patents*, etc. by Wade (see Bibliography).

HOW MUCH SHOULD YOU GET?

One of the main problems in any negotiation, which no book can ever solve, is how much to get for your invention. One rule of thumb or median license payment is a 5-percent royalty, which means that you would get 5 percent of the money received by the factory for its sales of the item embodying your invention. This is sometimes termed 5 percent of the ex-factory price.

Naturally the figure can vary up or down, depending on the uniqueness of the invention, the relation of your invention to the whole product, the volume of sales expected, the profitability, etc. For example, if you invented a new circuit for a color-TV receiver, naturally 5 percent of the ex-factory price of the TV would be far too high. But if you've invented a new type of glue or transistor, 5 percent of the ex-factory price would be far too low and 10 percent or even 15 percent would be more reasonable.

If you are offered a single lump-sum payment for all your rights (this is rare), should you take it, and if so, how much should you get? On the one side, a bird in the hand is worth two in the bush, but on the other side, your invention may turn out to be a fabulously popular one and your lump-sum payment would be only a fraction of what you would get from a fair royalty. One possibility is to estimate the sales of your invention for the life of your patent application (1 to 3 years), plus the term of the patent (17 years), apply your royalty to this figure, and take half of this as a single payment lump sum for a fully paid-up license. For example suppose you expect your widget to be sold for the next 19 years (2 years during pendency and 17 years during life of patent) for an average ex-factory price of 50 cents and an average yearly quantity of 150,000 units, and that a 5 percent royalty is fair. Applying the formula, the substitute lump-sum payment for your royalty would be $0.5 \times 19 \times 150,000 \times \$0.50 \times 5\%$, or $35,625.

The disadvantage with the alternative lump-sum calculation is that it is very hard to estimate anything about what will happen in the next 19 years. Will sales go up or down, will the product become obsolete or even more popular, will competition affect its price, etc.—these are just some of the imponderables and unknowables, so you should be extremely careful in accepting a single lump-sum payment for your rights.

While it is usually the company that writes any license agreement entered into, you should be prepared, when you present your demonstration, to name a price (slightly inflated for bargaining) or royalty and the terms you will accept. Do not ask for their offer since they may give too low a figure; you have thought about it longer, and you know more about the worth of your invention. You usually get more by dropping down a bit than trying to fight them up.

One precaution is to be sure there is an antishelving clause in any agreement. This simply means that the company cannot buy up your rights or take a license for a small sum or even nothing and then not manufacture your invention for many years. An adequate minimum royalty payment or right given you to terminate if a given minimum number of units is not sold each year or if the company doesn't actively exploit the invention are safeguards against your invention being shelved and your being deprived of your rights.

Of course, it has been rumored that sometimes a company will buy an inventor's rights for a handsome sum and then shelve the invention in order to stay with their own profitable product. I have never heard of an actual case of this being done, but if a company does want to buy your invention and shelve it or hush it up, be sure you get about what you could if it were commercially exploited.

MANUFACTURING YOURSELF

For reasons stated in Chapter 5, manufacturing a product embodying your invention—unless you already have manufacturing experience, a plant, and distribution facilities—is very difficult. Besides, you can spend your time more effectively selling your invention or patent application, rather than dealing with manufacturing and product-marketing problems. However, one authority has stated that if your idea is a great, earthshaking one, such as POLAROID film or the XEROX photocopy machine, it is best to manufacture it yourself since it would be difficult to sell it for sufficient money to get you an adequate reward.

If you do plan to manufacture yourself, I strongly suggest that you learn about the subject thoroughly beforehand so you will know what is involved and which pitfalls to avoid. The best place to obtain literature and reading material is your local SBA (Small Business Administration) office, which has scads of literature and aids available to apprise you of the problems and pitfalls. They even have a service which allows you to obtain the advice of an experienced executive free; ask for a "Counseling Request from Small Business Firm" form.

Financing any manufacturing venture of your own is a separate and formidable problem. If you have an untried and unsold product, most banks will not loan you the money to go ahead. However, if you can get orders from various local firms, the bank may loan you the money. Thus a local test marketing effort on a limited scale may be desirable. For obtaining money to finance untried products, a money lender who is willing to take more risk is needed. Such a person is usually termed a venture capitalist, who will loan you money in exchange for shares or a portion of your enterprise. The *Venture Capital Monthly* and the *Guide to Venture Capital Sources* (see Bibliography) should aid you here.

Mail-order selling is another possibility, although magazine and direct-mail advertising is expensive. Mail-order distribution houses put in their own ads, manufacture and distribute their own catalogs, and thus are valuable intermediaries for many garage-shop manufacturers. Walter Drake & Sons, Colorado Springs, CO 80940, is one of the largest, but you can obtain the names of many others by looking for ads in *Redbook, House Beautiful, Better Homes and Gardens, Apartment Life, Sunset, Holiday,* etc. These mail-order firms are always looking for new gadgets, and most of their products come from small firms. Many of them will purchase quantities of your product outright and some will take them on consignment, which means they do not pay you until and unless they sell it themselves.

Finally, don't overlook the possibility of an economical foreign manufacturer who will manufacture your invention for you to sell in the United States.

PUBLICITY AND OTHER IDEAS

Publicity is always a great aid to the inventor, whether you are going to try to sell your invention to a manufacturer, or are going to manufacture and distribute it yourself. The more publicity you obtain, the better will be your chances of obtaining financial rewards and success from your invention.

One way to obtain publicity is to hire a public-relations or marketing-research firm to promote your invention for you. There are many reputable firms who can come up with many creative and valuable ideas for a fee. However, the cost of public-relations services is very high, and therefore I do not recommend it unless you can bear the cost without difficulty.

Another alternative, definitely not recommended, but included for the sake of completeness, is to hire one of the invention-marketing or invention-developing firms that will, for a fee (usually exorbitant) send a brief printed or mimeographed blurb of your idea to newspapers, radio and TV stations, and prospective manufacturers. Having worked for several manufacturing companies and having received dozens of these blurbs from invention-developing companies, I can state from experience that they were usually put in the file-and-forget category. By following the instructions in this chapter you can do exactly what these firms can do, only better, cheaper, and with much more effectiveness. If you ever do decide to investigate one of these companies, before hiring them, ask for their past rate of success in publicizing, licensing, and selling inventions.

Another service, again not recommended, is to have your invention published in an "invention newsletter" or other invention organ or magazine for a "membership" or other fee. I doubt if any of these publications are read seriously or have ever engendered any significant license revenues for their advertisers.

If you have an invention in the drug, personal-care, or toiletry fields, it will be considered free by Product Resources International, Box 1931, Grand Central Station, New York NY 10017, which apparently serves as intermediary between inventors and manufacturers. Write to them, asking for an invention submission form and then follow the instructions.

Many magazines will feature new ideas free if you send them a clear, understandable, professional-quality photo or drawing of your invention, plus a brief, clear, and understandable description of it. They may even write a full-length feature about your invention if they think it is interesting enough. Suitable magazines are *Popular Science, Mechanics Illustrated, Popular Electronics, Better Homes and Gardens, Pageant, Parade, Playboy, This Week, True Story, Jet, Outdoor Life, House and Garden, House Beautiful, Outdoor Living, Changing Times, McCall's, Apartment Life, Argosy,* and *Sunset.* You can obtain the addresses of those you think are relevant from *Ulrich's International Periodicals Directory* in your local library.

Other sources of publicity are exhibits, trade fairs, and business shows. You pay a relatively small fee to the sponsor of the show, in return for which you are given a table or booth, or equivalent space to demonstrate your invention at the fair or show. Naturally your exhibit should be attractive, interesting, and it is preferable to have a working model or very good literature available in connection with your invention. There are exhibition-service companies that will prepare a display exhibit for you for a fee.

Do not overlook radio and TV as an excellent source of publicity. Many local radio and TV stations feature programs in which new inventors can demonstrate or discuss their inventions; or, if your invention is interesting they may feature your invention in an early morning talk show. Contact your local stations by phone, telling them that you have an interesting and very valuable invention you think they might be interested in featuring.

If your invention is or can be used in a product which the federal government might purchase, write to the General Services Administration, Federal Supply Service, 1734 New York Avenue, N.W., Washington DC 20406, telling them that you are offering a product which you feel the government can use. They will send you appropriate forms and instructions. Also, do not neglect your corresponding state and local purchasing agencies.

It may be possible to obtain a government grant from an appropriate government agency, such as the Energy Research and Development Administration or the Department of Defense, for you to research and develop your product. An excellent book on this subject is *Everything You Can Get From the Government For Free,* by C. and P. Norback.

The magazine, *Advertising Age,* has a feature called "Idea Marketplace" in each issue in which they publicize new inventions gratis. Write to them at Crown Communications, Inc., 740 Rush Street, Chicago IL 60611, sending a picture and brief description of your invention. Thomas Publications, 1 Pennsylvania Plaza, New York NY 10001 has a bimonthly called *Technology Mart* which offers a similar service.

The Invention Trade Center, 121 North Fir Street, Ventura, CA 93001, will exhibit your invention to prospective manufacturers for 6 months for $60. The ITC even has a separate security area for unpatented inventions; visitors must sign a keep-confidential agreement before they can enter.

Certain research organizations will sometimes consider and purchase rights in inventions which require additional research; two of the best known are Batelle Memorial Institute, 505 King Ave., Columbus, OH 43201, and Arthur D. Little, Inc., Acorn Park, Cambridge, MA 02104.

Lastly, do not overlook direct mail as a possible source of customers for your invention or of venture capital. Order the *Dunhill Marketing Guide to Mailing Lists* from Dunhill International List Company, Inc., 444 Park Avenue South, New York NY 10016 for information about how to begin a direct-mail order solicitation or offering of a product.

Getting the Patent Office to Deliver

CHAPTER TEN

WHAT HAPPENS AFTER YOUR PATENT APPLICATION IS FILED?

After sending your patent application to the Patent and Trademark Office, you will receive your receipt postcard back in about two to three weeks, with a stamped date and a six-digit number. The date is the filing date, and the number is the serial number of your application.

About a month later you will receive an official filing receipt, which is a small blue slip with the name(s) of the inventor(s), the title of your patent application, the examining group to which your application has been assigned, the filing date and serial number of your application, the number of claims (total as well as independent), the filing fee you paid, and your name and address. Check the information on the filing receipt very carefully; it is the information regarding your application that has been entered into the PTO's data-processing system.

If for any reason anything about your patent application is irregular, and it is not entitled to be officially filed—for example, because of an insufficient fee—the PTO will send you a letter (instead of a filing receipt) explaining the deficiency, which you should take prompt steps to correct. Once you receive the blue filing-receipt slip, your patent application is officially pending and you may label your invention and any descriptive literature, "Patent Pending."

If you haven't done so already, now is the time to send in your Statement of Prior Art (Form 5), together with copies of the references you listed on the form. Remember that the Statement of Prior Art is due within 3 months of the application's filing date. If you send in the statement after you get the filing receipt, don't forget to include the serial number and filing date on the Statement of Prior Art.

Usually about 6 months to a year and a half after the filing date, you will receive a communication from the PTO, which is known as an "office action" or official letter. It consists of forms completed by the examiner in charge of your application, describing what is wrong with your application and why it cannot yet be allowed. (Rarely will an application be allowed in the first office action after filing.) Specifically, the office action may reject claims, list defects in the specification, cite prior art, object to the drawings, etc.

To find out approximately when you will receive the first office action from the PTO, you can look in a recent issue of the *Official Gazette*. One of the initial pages will be headed "Patent Examining Groups." Look for the actual examining group to which your application is assigned, and in the column headed, "Actual Filing Date of Oldest New Case Awaiting Action," note the date opposite your examining group. You can expect to receive the first office action in about the interval between this date and your filing date.

The office action itself will specify an interval, usually 3 months from the date the office action was mailed, by which time you must file a response. Your response must amend the specification, drawing, and/or narrow or clarify your claims, and/or take whatever other action is necessary to overcome the objections and rejections in the office action. The response you file is known as an "amendment," and the entire process of correspondence (office actions and amendments) to and from the PTO is known as the patent application prosecution, although no one is "prosecuted" in the usual sense.

About 6 months after you file your first amendment, you will receive a second office action from the PTO, which usually will be a "final" action. The effect of a final action is that prosecution is substantially over; you may not send in any further amendments, except those expressly permitted by the examiner. Again you have 3 months to reply.

When you get your application in condition for allowance, you will be sent a Notice of Allowability, indicating that all of your claims are allowed. Then a formal Notice of Allowance will be sent, indicating that a base issue fee is due within 3 months. After you pay the base issue fee you will receive a receipt from the PTO, indicating the date on which your patent will issue and the number of your patent.

Shortly after the date your patent issues, you will receive your official letters patent or deed from the PTO, together with a Balance-of-Issue-Fee-Due slip; you must pay the balance of issue fee within 3 months or the patent will lapse.

GENERAL CONSIDERATIONS DURING PROSECUTION

Patent application prosecution is generally more difficult than preparation of a patent application, but by now you've gained sufficient experience in the patent field to be able to handle prosecution adequately. If you keep the following considerations in mind during prosecution, your patent application is much more likely to be allowed with broader claims, and the whole process will be much easier.

1. *Intervals Are Approximate.* Except for official periods, such as the 3-month period for response to an office action, the dates and times I've given in this chapter are only approximate and are gleaned from recent experience. They can vary quite widely, depending on conditions in the PTO at the time you file your patent application. If you don't receive any communication from the PTO for a very long time, say over 2 years after you filed your application or over a year after you file an amendment, you should check a recent *Official Gazette,* make a call, or send a status-inquiry letter to the examiner or examining group to ascertain the status of your case.

2. *You'll Be Given an Opportunity to Correct Errors of Form.* Don't worry too much about minor errors of form and procedure in dealing with the PTO. If you make an error of form or procedure, you will be given an opportunity to correct it. The PTO has so many rules and regulations that even patent attorneys who deal with the PTO all the time can't remember them all, but the PTO is fairly liberal in giving applicants, especially those who don't have an attorney, opportunities to correct nonsubstantive errors.

3. *Situations Not Covered.* If any situation occurs that is not covered in this book, and you can't find the answer by looking in the Rules of Practice or *Manual of Patent Examining Procedure*—see (6) below—call the PTO, or use common sense and do what you would expect to be the logical thing to do in such a situation. For example, if, after you've filed your patent application, you find a reference which considerably narrows what you thought your invention to be, bring it to the attention of the PTO and submit an amendment substituting narrower claims that avoid the reference. If you discover that an embodiment of your invention doesn't work, delete it from your application. If you discover a new embodiment of your invention that supersedes the present embodiments, file a continuation-in-part application (see Chapter 11). Remember that you have a continuing duty to disclose all material information about your invention to the PTO. If the examiner cites a reference against your application that is later than the filing date of your application, obviously the examiner made an error (this happens occasionally), and you should call or write to bring it to the examiner's attention so that a new office action can be issued. If you change your address, an appropriate letter (heading similar to Form 8) should be sent to the PTO.

4. *Standards of Patentability Vary.* While I have tried to give the proper standards of patentability in this book, you will appreciate that truly objective standards of patentability cannot be written, so that the actual standard you encounter when your application is examined will be very dependent upon the whims and emotions of the examiner who is assigned to handle it. While most examiners are reasonable and have generally similar standards of patentability, you will occasionally find some examiners who are extremely tough and who are very reluctant to allow any application, no matter how significant the invention, and, on the

other hand, some examiners who will allow practically anything which is even slightly different from the prior art. The solution to the problem with a tough examiner is to appeal or to be persistent; with an easy examiner, make especially sure yourself that your invention is patentable, since you don't want to have a patent with invalidatable claims issued to you.

5. *Dealing with the PTO Can Be Frustrating.* Dealing with the PTO, as with any other government agency, can often be a very frustrating experience. Since the PTO is not a competitive enterprise, sometimes its employees are lazy, incompetent, and lacking in initiative. For example, I once filed an application for an inventor whose last name was *Loe*. The filing receipt came back with the name "Lee." After several letters and calls with no response, a "corrected" filing receipt arrived; this time the inventor's name was spelled "Leo." After a few more calls and frustrations, a correct filing receipt finally arrived. As another example, the PTO occasionally "misplaces" an entire patent application, as a result of which you have to send them a new copy of your application, together with an affidavit stating that it is a true copy of what you originally filed. While it is true that there are many dedicated and competent people in the PTO, all too often frustrations and situations of the type mentioned arise. If you've ever entertained any thoughts of socialism, these will be permanently dispelled by a few years dealing with the PTO.

6. *PTO Rule Books.* During patent prosecution, you will need occasionally to refer to the PTO's Rules of Practice. These can be obtained from any government book store in a paperbound book entitled *Code of Federal Regulations—37—Patents, Trademarks, and Copyrights* (see Bibliography). In this book the PTO's patent rules are given the prefix number 1. (distinguishing them from trademark rules [2] and copyright rules [3]. For example, Patent Rule 111, referred to later in this chapter, is officially identified as Title 37 of the Code of Federal Regulations, Section 1.111, or in legal citation form, 37 C.F.R. 1.111.

   In addition to the Rules of Practice, an aid that is very useful during prosecution is the *Manual of Patent Examining Procedure* (MPEP), which is often referred to as the "examiner's Bible," and which covers almost any situation you can encounter in patent prosecution. It is an expensive, large, loose-leaf volume; it can be found in many public libraries.

7. *Never Make Negative Statements On The Record.* When dealing with the PTO, never, never say or write anything which derogates your invention, or admits that any prior-art reference shows any feature of your invention. Admittedly this may be very difficult to do in certain situations, but if you try hard enough, it can be done, and it is very important since any negative admission in the official file of your patent can be used very detrimentally against you if your patent is ever involved in litigation. If you always anticipate that your patent may later be involved in litigation, you'll do a much better job of prosecution.

8. *Be Available to Answer Office Actions.* Once you file a patent application, you will, as stated, receive an office action or other communications from the PTO, and these usually require that you file a reply within 3 months. Thus you should not go on an extended vacation to Europe or South America while your patent application is pending, since you may receive an office action while you are away, and if you fail to reply to it, your application will be abandoned.

9. *Consider Foreign Filing.* About 8 months after you file your patent application, you should consider whether you want to get protection in other countries. There are international conventions or agreements among all countries that entitle you to the benefit of your U.S. filing date on any foreign applications you file within 1 year after you file your U.S. application. So to allow time to get your foreign application prepared, you should make your foreign-filing decisions about 8 months after your U.S. application is filed (see Chapter 11).

10. *You Can Call and Visit Your Examiner.* If you have any questions about your application, or any reference which is cited against it, you are permitted to call, and/or make an appointment with and visit the examiner in charge of your application. However, usually only one or at most two applicant-initiated interviews are permitted, so don't abuse the privilege. The examiner must summarize the substance of the interview on a special form, and you must do likewise in the next paper which you send to the PTO.

11. *No New Matter Is Permitted.* Once your application is filed, you cannot add any "new matter" to it. New matter consists of any technical information that was not present in your application as originally filed. Thus it behooves you to make your application as complete as possible when you prepare it. If you do discover any new information consider a continuation-in-part application (Chapter 11).

SAMPLE OFFICE ACTION

Figs. 7a to c are reproductions of pages 76.2, 76.3, and 78 of the MPEP, showing a sample office action in an imaginary patent application. A study of the office action will enable you to deal with your first office action far more effectively.

At the top of the office action (Fig. 7a), the examiner's name (Callaghan) and his examining group (Art Unit 353) are given. Below that, in the large brackets, are the filing date, serial number and inventor's name (John A. Novel). To the right is the date the office action was mailed, which is the official date of the office action.

Below the address of the attorney (John C. Able), the first box that is checked indicates "This application has been examined," denoting that this is first office action in application No. 999,999. If it had been a second and nonfinal office action, the second box, "Responsive to communication filed

PAPER NO. 2

U.S. DEPARTMENT OF COMMERCE
Patent and Trademark Office
Address: COMMISSIONER OF PATENTS AND TRADEMARKS
Washington, D.C. 20231

T.F. Callaghan   Art Unit 353

[04/11/75   999,999]
  John A. Novel

MAILED
MAILED:
APR 19 1976

GROUP 350

John C. Able
1234 Jefferson Davis Highway
Arlington, Virginia 22202

THIS IS A COMMUNICATION FROM THE EXAMINER
IN CHARGE OF YOUR APPLICATION.

COMMISSIONER OF
PATENTS AND TRADEMARKS

☒ This application has been examined.

☐ Responsive to communication filed on _____.

☐ This action is made final.

A SHORTENED STATUTORY PERIOD FOR RESPONSE TO THIS ACTION IS SET TO EXPIRE ____3____ MONTH(S)

_____ DAYS FROM THE DATE OF THIS LETTER.

FAILURE TO RESPOND WITHIN THE PERIOD FOR RESPONSE WILL CAUSE THE APPLICATION TO BECOME ABANDONED.
35 U.S.C. 133

PART I   THE FOLLOWING ATTACHMENT(S) ARE PART OF THIS ACTION:

1. ☒ Notice of References Cited, Form PTO-892.   2. ☐ Notice of Informal Patent Drawing, PTO-948.

3. ☐ Notice of Informal Patent Application,   4. ☐
       Form PTO-152

PART II   SUMMARY OF ACTION

1. ☒ Claims ___1-11_____ are pending in the application.

   Of the above, claims _____ are withdrawn from consideration.

2. ☐ Claims _____ have been cancelled.

3. ☐ Claims _____ are allowed.

4. ☒ Claims ___1-8_____ are rejected.

5. ☒ Claims ___9-11_____ are objected to.

6. ☐ Claims _____ are subject to restriction or election requirement.

7. ☐ The formal drawings filed on _____ are acceptable.

8. ☒ The drawing correction request filed on _March 1, 1976_ has been   ☒ approved.
                                                                        ☐ disapproved.

9. ☒ Acknowledgement is made of the claim for priority under 35 U.S.C. 119. The certified copy has
      ☐ been received.
      ☐ not been received.   ☒ been filed in parent application:
                                     serial no. _888,888_ filed on _12-5-72_.

10. ☐ Since this application appears to be in condition for allowance except for formal matters, prosecution as to the
       merits is closed in accordance with the practice under Ex parte Quayle, 1935 C.D. 11; 453 OG. 213.

11. ☐ Other

Form PTOL-326 (rev. 11-75)

figure 7a Sample office action, page 1.

on _____," would have been checked; had it been a final office action, the third box, "This action is made final," would have been checked.

The next paragraph indicates that the period for response will expire in 3 months and that failure to respond will cause the application to be abandoned. Since the office action was mailed April 19, 1976, the period for response expires July 19, 1976. If the last date of the period falls on a Saturday, Sunday, or holiday, the period for response expires on the next business day.

U.S. DEPARTMENT OF COMMERCE
Patent and Trademark Office

PART III

SERIAL NUMBER **999,999**

GROUP ART UNIT **353**

NOTIFICATION OF REJECTION(S) AND/OR OBJECTION(S) (35 USC 132)

	CLAIMS (1)	REASONS FOR REJECTION (2)	REFERENCES * (3)	INFORMATION IDENTIFICATION AND COMMENTS (4)
1	1,3,4	35 U.S.C. 102	A	
2	2,5	35 U.S.C. 102	B/C	Axle assemblies of each fixed to tubular members (Fig. 2 of B, Fig. 4 of C).
3	6,7	35 U.S.C. 103	D v E+F	Obvious to extend auxiliary wheels of D (Fig. 1) laterally as in E (p. 2, ls. 1-6). Also, obvious to provide vertically adjustable wheels in D as shown by F (Fig. 3).
4	6,7	35 U.S.C. 112, 2nd paragraph	——	"Aperture" is misdescriptive in defining a sleeve within a frame member.
5	8	35 U.S.C. 103	A v E	Obvious to extend auxiliary wheels of A (Fig. 1) laterally as in E (p. 2, ls. 1-6).
6	9-11	—	—	Objected to — depend from rejected claim; will be allowed if rewritten in independent form.
7	Claim 6 would be allowed if amended to recite the specific hydraulic wheel-moving arrangement.			
8	G cited to show an analogous hydraulic wheel-moving mechanism.			

* Capital letters representing references are identified on accompanying Form PTO-892.
The symbol "v" between letters represents - in view of -.
The symbol "+" or "&" between letters represents - and -.
A slash "/" between letters represents the alternative - or -.

NOTE: Sections 100, 101, 102, 103, and 112 of the Patent Statute (Title 35 of the United States Code) are reproduced on the back of this sheet.

EXAMINER

TEL. NO. (703) -557- **3070**

Thomas F. Callaghan
Thomas F. Callaghan
Primary Examiner
Art Unit 353

—2—

figure 7b Sample office action, page 2.

Under "Part I," the check at box 1 indicates that one attachment, a "Notice of References Cited," is part of the office action. A typical Notice of References Cited, albeit from a different application, is shown in Fig. 7c.

Under "Part II—Summary of Action," the examiner has checked various boxes to indicate what action he has taken with the application. Of the eleven claims that are pending, he has rejected claims 1 to 8, objected to claims 9 to 11, approved a drawing request, and acknowledged a claim for

FORM PTO—892 (REV. 9-75)	U.S. DEPARTMENT OF COMMERCE PATENT AND TRADEMARK OFFICE	SERIAL NO. *999,998*	GROUP ART UNIT *425*	ATTACHMENT TO PAPER NUMBER *3*
	NOTICE OF REFERENCES CITED	APPLICANT (S) *STRUCK et al.*		

U.S. PATENT DOCUMENTS

*		DOCUMENT NO.	DATE	NAME	CLASS	SUB-CLASS	FILING DATE IF APPROPRIATE
	A	2717874	9-1955	VERAIN	21	102 R X	
X	B	2572144	10-1951	HEALY	340	71 X	
	C	2137376	11-1938	ALTORFER	21	DIG. 2	
	D	T881002	12-1970	JONES	96	1.6	
	E	P.P. 2400	5-1964	BOERNER	Plant	20	
	F	B207272	1-1975	DAVIDSON	75	1	
	G	1671843	5-1928	SCOTT	15	104.01 R	
	H	D238404	1-1976	OWENS	D6	5	11-13-1972
	I	DRe24841	6-1960	ROCHÉ	D8	189	
	J	Re18406	4-1932	MARINSKY	24	205.16 C	
X	K	3035319	5-1962	WOLFF	24	274 WB X	

FOREIGN PATENT DOCUMENTS

*		DOCUMENT NO.	DATE	COUNTRY	NAME	CLASS	SUB-CLASS	PERTINENT SHTS. DWG	PP. SPEC.
	L	136113	1-1950	AUSTRALIA	PAPER PRODUCTS	24	134 QA		
	M	Add.34622	11-1934	FRANCE	LORENZ	26	15 R	1	4-7
	N	19421	of 1913	UNITED KINGDOM	CROSSE	26	51.5		
X	O	1345890	7-1963	GERMANY	MUTHER	19	6		
	P	683125	3-1964	CANADA	FISHBURNE	100	216	1-5	1-19
	Q								

OTHER REFERENCES (Including Author, Title, Date, Pertinent Pages, Etc.)

R	Chemical Abstracts, Vol. 75, No. 20, Nov. 15, 1971, p. 163, abstract no. 120718k, Shetulov, D.I., "Surface Effects During Metal Fatigue", copy in Group 120 Library.
S	(500840001) Winslow, C.E.A., Fresh Air and Ventilation, E.P. Dutton, N.Y., 1926, p. 97-112, TH 7653 W5, 315-22.
T	Ballistic Missile & Aerospace Technology, Vol. 3, Academic Press, N.Y., 1964, TL 78759, p. 199, 250-108.
U	Carbowax & Polyethylene Glycols, Carbide Chemical Corporation, 1946, p. 5, copy in Group 120 Library.

EXAMINER *Richard Stone*	DATE *4-10-76*

* A copy of this reference is not being furnished with this office action.
(See Manual of Patent Examining Procedure, section 707.05 (a).)

figure 7c Citation of references accompanying office action.

"priority" of an earlier corresponding foreign application, which was filed in a U.S. parent application of the present application.

In Part III of the office action (Fig. 7b), the examiner gives his specific reasons for rejecting or objecting to the claims.

In line 1 of Part III, he has rejected claims 1, 3, and 4 under Section 102 of the patent laws (see Chapter 4) on reference A. The examiner has not made any comment, which indicates that he feels that claims 1, 3, and 4 are completely and fully anticipated by reference *A* in a manner which is too obvious to require comment.

In line 2, he has rejected claims 2 and 5 under Section 102 on reference *B* or reference *C,* and he has added a brief comment to indicate where in each reference certain features of these claims are found. The virgule or slash (/) between *B* and *C* represents "or," as indicated by the key at the bottom of the form.

In line 3, he has rejected claims 6 and 7 under Section 103 on reference *D* in view of (symbol: *v*) references *E* and *F,* and he has stated specifically why these references can be combined to render the subject matter of claims 6 and 7 obvious.

In line 4, he has rejected claims 6 and 7 under Section 112, second paragraph, because he feels the word "aperture" in these claims does not properly describe the invention.

In line 5, he has rejected claim 8 under Section 103 with an explanatory comment.

In line 6, he has stated that claims 9 to 11 are objected to because they depend from a rejected claim but will be allowed rewritten in independent form. This means that he considers that claims 9 to 11 contain allowable subject matter, and that if they are rewritten so that they include all the limitations of their parent or independent claims and do not depend on any claims, they will be allowed.

In line 7, the examiner indicates that claim 6 would also be allowed if amended (narrowed) to recite a certain feature of the invention.

In line 8, the examiner states that an additional reference (*G*) has been cited (but not used in any rejection) to show another feature of the invention.

The examiner has signed the action at the bottom and has also listed his telephone number above his official name stamp.

Referring to Fig. 7*c,* the Notice of References Cited lists eleven United States Patents, five foreign patents, and four magazine or text references. (Most office actions will cite only a few references.) All these references will be attached to the office action, except those checked in the column marked with the asterisk (*), which were furnished in a prior office action or a prior related application. To save time, the references are referred to in the office action by the letters *A* to *U.* The "Document Number" column generally lists patent numbers, except that reference *D* is a defensive publication (see Chapter 11), reference *E* is a plant patent, references *H* and *I* are design patents, and reference *J* is a reissue patent. The date column indicates the date the patent issued, or the document was published. If this date is later than your filing date, the reference is not a good reference against your application, unless it is a U.S. patent filed before your application. In the latter instance, the examiner is supposed to indicate the filing date of the patent reference in the last column, which he has done for reference *H.*

WHAT TO DO WHEN YOU RECEIVE AN OFFICE ACTION

When you receive an Office Action, don't panic or be intimidated, especially if all claims have been rejected. It is common for examiners to reject all claims, even if the rejections are not valid, in order to force you to state the essence of your invention and its true distinguishing features. Also, some examiners tend to be lazy and it's easy to issue a "shotgun" rejection in order to avoid having to spend too much time on the first office action. You'll find that even if all claims are rejected, if you approach your office action in a calm, rational, and methodical manner, as outlined below, you should not have too much difficulty with it.

After you get your office action, write the due date of your response right on the office action and also write it on your calendar so you won't forget it. It's a good idea to write your reply (amendment) well in advance of the due date so you'll have plenty of time and so you won't tend to forget it.

Also, check all your references carefully to make sure the references you've received correspond to the references in the Notice of References Cited. If there is any discrepancy, call or write the examiner at once. Mark each reference directly with its reference letter (A to U).

Next read the office action carefully and make a detailed summary of it in your own handwriting, so that you'll have it impressed in your mind.

After that, reread your application, noting all errors in the specification, claims, and drawing you would like to correct or improve.

Next, read every cited reference (except the claims-of-patent references) completely and carefully. Make sure that you take enough time completely to understand the reference and how it works. Think of each reference as a magazine or technical article, and consider everything it discloses relevant. (You should *not* normally read the claims of any cited patent since the patent has not been cited for what it claims, but for what it teaches. The claims generally only repeat parts of the specification and are not directly relevant because the owner of the patent is not charging you with infringement of his patent.) Write a brief summary of each reference, preferably on the reference itself, even if it has an adequate abstract, in order to familiarize yourself with it in your own words. If a cited reference is any publication with a date less than one year before your filing date or is a U.S. patent which has (1) a filing date preceding your filing date and (2) an issue date on or after your filing date, or up to one year before your filing date, you can, as stated in Chapter 2, "swear behind" the reference under Rule 131, and thereby eliminate it from consideration, by submitting a declaration containing facts and attached copies of documents showing that you built and tested the invention, or conceived the invention (and were thereafter diligent in building and testing it) before the effective date of the reference. See MPEP 715 for full details.

Next, make a comparison chart showing every feature of your invention across the top of the chart and listing the references down the lefthand side of the chart, as in Fig. 8.

Be sure to break up your invention so that all possible features of it, even those not already claimed, are covered and listed across the top of the chart. Then indicate by checking the appropriate boxes in the chart those features of your invention shown by each reference. This chart, if done correctly and completely, will be of tremendous aid in drafting your amendment.

Next, reread your broadest claim to see which features it recites (remember, only positively recited structure or acts count) and whether these

References	Features of my invention		
	Pivot arm	Bracket at end of arm	Bracket has screw tightener
A	X	X	
B	X		X

figure 8 Comparison chart.

features distinguish over each reference cited against this claim. When doing this, it is important to consider only the positively recited structure or acts, and not the advantages, functional statements, or whereby clauses in the claims. However, if a claim recites a means followed by a function, under Section 112, this is considered to be a positive recitation of structure.

If only one reference has been cited against your broadest claim, consider whether your claim distinguishes over this reference under Section 102, that is, are there any features recited in the claim which are not shown in the reference? If not, the claim is "fully met" or anticipated by this reference and will have to be narrowed.

If the claim recites (or has been amended to recite) novel features, consider whether these are unobvious over the reference under Section 103. Refer to the test of Chapter 4 to determine obviousness. If you consider the features obvious, you'll have to narrow the claim, either by adding more features, or reciting the existing features more narrowly.

If two or more references have been cited in combination against your broadest claim, first ask yourself whether it is proper to combine these references in the manner that the examiner has done. In order for two references to be combined for a rejection, there must be some reason or purpose for combining them, and it must be physically possible to do so. For example, if one reference shows a bicycle and another reference shows a new lightweight alloy, there would be ample reason to combine these references since it is known that bicycles should be made as light as possible and thus that one would seek to use any new lightweight alloy in a bicycle. However, if the new lightweight alloy is radioactive, it obviously couldn't be used in a bicycle since it would be too dangerous, and thus it wouldn't be physically possible in the practical sense to combine the references. Or if the alloy can't be formed in the shape of tubes, it obviously would be physically impossible to combine the references. Next, assuming that the references are combined (whether or not they can be), ask yourself if they disclose the subject matter of your claim under Section 102, and if not, are the distinctions in your claim patentable under Section 103? Also ask yourself whether there are any other errors in the examiner's logic or reasoning.

If your claim has been rejected under Section 112, the examiner feels that the language of your claim is not clear or proper, and you should try to work out alternative language which will satisfy this objection.

If you believe your broadest claim is already patentable over the prior art and that there is a serious flaw in the examiner's logic, theoretically it is permissible to leave the claim as it is and argue the patentability of your claim in order to try to get the examiner to reverse a negative judgment. But this is generally not advisable because it is difficult psychologically for an examiner to allow a claim identical to one previously rejected. Thus to save the examiner's ego, it is best to try to make some amendment to the claim, even if it is insignificant, in order to allow the examiner to save face and to state, in the next office action, that "Claim 1, *as amended,* is now considered allowable." It is usually possible to make amendments to a claim which do not narrow its scope. For example, you can recite that a member, which of necessity must be elongated, *is* elongated; you can state that a circuit is energized by a direct-current source; you can add a whereby clause to the claim stating the function of the mechanism of the claim; and you can add a longer preamble stating in more detail (but not in narrower language) the environment of your invention.

If you believe your broadest claim is not patentable and you agree with all or part of the examiner's rejection, you will have to narrow the claim by adding limitations, or by narrowing the limitations already present, in the manner outlined in Chapter 7. Look for the essence of how your invention distinguishes over the prior art and try to put this essence in your claim, but do not make your claim narrower than necessary. Often the limitation you are looking for can be found in one or more dependent claims. Show your invention and the cited references to friends or associates; often they can spot the distinguishing essence of your invention quite readily.

After you have narrowed your main or independent claim, do the same for all your other claims. Also, if you've changed your main claim, change your dependent claims so that they completely and correctly correspond in language and numbering with your main claim. If you incorporate a limitation from a dependent claim into your main claim, cancel the dependent claim. You may also think of other, narrower dependent claims to replace those which you've cancelled; refer to the comparison chart to be sure you've claimed every feature.

After the first office action, you should write the narrowest possible claims you would be willing to accept since you generally will not get any further chance to amend your claims, even if the examiner cites new art against you in a subsequent office action. So try to make your dependent claims as narrow as possible and, again, be sure all of the specific features of your invention are covered in your dependent claims.

Next, plan an outline of your response. Indicate, on a copy of your application or on separate sheets, the amendments you intend to make to your specification, your claims, your drawing, and your remarks. The "Remarks" section of your amendment should consist of a brief summary of all your amendments; a review of the rejections made by the examiner; a review of the references cited by the examiner; a summary of how you changed the claims, quoting your changes; a statement of your claimed distinctions under Sections 102 and 103 if one reference was cited; a statement of why the references can't be combined, followed by comments regarding Sections 102 and 103 if more than one reference was cited; a request for reconsideration of the examiner's position; a discussion of dependent and other main claims you have; a discussion of any technical (Section 112) rejections; any request for aid you may wish to make under MPEP 707.07(j) requesting the examiner to write claims; and a conclusion.

Think over and plan your response very carefully. Sometimes it takes even more time and effort than writing the patent application. Your remarks should simply be a long, detailed formal letter about your application, the office action, and the changes you've made.

WRITING THE AMENDMENT

Form 8 provides the initial part of your amendment. Fill in the serial number, filing date, your name, title of your application, and the examiner's name and examining unit or group art unit. The date on which you actually mail the amendment goes after "date" and the date of the office letter goes at the space indicated in the first paragraph. Put an appropriate letter (A, B, etc.), after "Amendment" to indicate which amendment it is (your first, second, etc.).

If you are going to make any changes to the specification provide the heading, *SPECIFICATION:* below the sentence printed on Form 8. Then indicate the specific places in your application where you want to make amendments and the actual amendments you wish to make. Use quotes to indicate existing words and dashes to indicate words you wish to add. For example:

Page 1, line 3, change "member" to—lever—.

Page 5, lines 12 to 14, change "member 14 . . . pivot 23" to—lever 14 is connected by way of arm 22 to bearing 23—.

Page 12, line 21, after "screw 18" insert—in contact with arm 22—.

Page 14, lines 12 to 13, delete "member 14 . . . pivot 23."

When your amendment is received, the clerk of the examining group will make each change in red ink in handwriting on the official copy of your application in the manner you direct. Thus you should insure that there is no ambiguity in your amendments. For example, if you are going to insert a phrase after the word "the" on a line and it occurs twice on the line, be sure to specify which "the" you mean.

If you want to amend your claims, provide the heading *CLAIMS:* and then indicate specifically the claim changes you desire. There are three ways to amend the claims of a patent application: (1) By word cancellation and/or insert; (2) by claim cancellation and substitution; and (3) by rewriting the claim with brackets and underscoring.

1. *The word-cancellation—and/or—insert method* should be used and is permitted only if you are cancelling words and/or are adding no more

than five words to your claim. Claim amendments made by this method are done in exactly the same manner as specification amendments, for example:

> Claim 1, line 5, change "said elongated member" to—a lever having—.

2. *The cancellation-and-substitution method* should be used if you are rewriting the claim entirely or if you have many amendments to make to the claim. To use this method, you direct the office to cancel the claim in question and substitute an entirely different claim. The new claim should be given the next-highest unused claim number. Thus, if you originally submitted 12 claims and you want to cancel claim 1 and substitute a new claim, the new claim should be number 13. For example:

> Claim 1, cancel and substitute new Claim 13 as follows:

> —13. An improved bicycle mechanism comprising [etc.]—

3. *The bracket-and-underscore method* is used when you don't have too many amendments to make to your claim and you want to point out to the examiner exactly where you are making the amendments. Under this method you retype your entire claim with the notation "(amended)" after the number of the claim (use the same number), put brackets around words to be deleted, and underscroe material to be added. If your typewriter doesn't have brackets, you're not permitted to use parentheses; you must make your brackets by hand or with virgules (slashes) and underscore lines, thus ⌐ ⌐. Some examiners don't like the bracket and underscore method of amending claims because it makes things look too confusing; I agree and therefore rarely use it. Note how the following claim reads originally (with bracketed words and without underscored words) and as amended (without bracketed words and underscored words):

> Claim 1, rewrite as Claim 1 (amended) as follows:

> 1. (amended) A method [for] of stimulating the growth rate of swine by feeding them [aspirin in an amount effective to increase their rate of growth] a daily dose of aspirin of 0.25 gram per kg of body weight.

Next add the "Remarks" portion of your amendment. Some of the rules which I'll state may seem silly, but they are the customary practice and to deviate substantially may make the examiner feel uncomfortable and take a negative attitude toward your invention.

As stated before, when writing your remarks, never admit that any prior art anticipates or renders any part of your invention obvious because this can be used against you later. Similarly never derogate your invention or any part of it.

Never get personal with the examiner, and if you must refer to the examiner always put the reference in the third person. For example, never state "You rejected . . ."; instead state "The Examiner has rejected . . ."; but better yet state "The office action rejects . . ." or "Claim 1 was rejected. . . ." If there is an error in the office action refer to the error in the *office action* and do not state that the examiner made the error. Even if you find the examiner made a completely stupid boo-boo, just deal with it in a very formal way and keep emotions and personalities out of your response. Remember, you've probably made some stupid boo-boos in your life also, and you wouldn't want your nose rubbed in them.

When referring to yourself in an office action, always refer to yourself in the third person as "Applicant" and never as "I."

Stick to the issues in you remarks. Be relevant and to the point and don't discuss personalities or irrelevant issues. Never antagonize the examiner, no matter how much you'd like to. It's not only improper; if you turn the examiner against you, it can considerably narrow the scope of claims which are ultimately allowed.

Whenever you write any new claims or make any new additions to your present claim, you must tell how they distinguish over the prior art the examiner has cited under Sections 102 and 103. Note Patent Rule 111 (*b*) and (*c*):

(*b*) In order to be entitled to reexamination or reconsideration, the applicant must make request therefor in writing, and he must distinctly and specifically point out the supposed errors in the examiner's action; the applicant must respond to every ground of objection and rejection in the prior office action (except that request may be made that objections or requirements as to form not necessary to further consideration of the claims be held in abeyance until allowable subject matter is indicated), and the applicant's action must appear throughout to be a bona fide attempt to advance the case to final action. A general allegation that the claims define a patentable invention without specifically pointing out how the language of the claims patentably distinguishes them from the references does not comply with the requirements of this section.

(*c*) In amending an application in response to a rejection, the applicant must clearly point out the patentable novelty which he thinks the claims present in view of the state of the art disclosed by the references cited or the objection made. He must also show how the amendments avoid such references or objections.

Thus you must answer every objection and rejection of the office action, even if you disagree. If you do disagree and think the office action was wrong, you must tell exactly why you disagree and why you believe it to be wrong. If you agree that a claim is obvious over the prior art, don't admit this in your response; simply cancel the claim and don't give any reason for it, or if you must comment, state merely that it has been canceled in view of the coverage afforded by the remaining claims.

Try to make a careful, complete, and convincing presentation, but don't agonize about words or minutiae, because the reality is that many examiners don't read your remarks or else skim through them very rapidly. This is because they're generally working under a quota system, which means they have to dispose of (finally reject or allow) a certain number of cases in each fiscal quarter. Thus the examiners are under time pressure and it takes a lot of time to read remarks. It is important to cover all the substantive points in the office action and to deal with every objection and rejection. If you do make an error, as stated, the PTO will almost always give you an opportunity to correct it, rather than forcing you to abandon your application.

WRITING THE REMARKS

When you write your remarks, assuming you've first made a proper outline, it's best to write a rough draft of your remarks, then wait a day or so and then put them in final form.

Your remarks should first provide a brief summary of what you've done to the specification and claims. For example, you can state: "The specification has been amended editorially and to correct those errors noted by the examiner. Claims 1 to 5 have been rewritten as new claims 13 to 18 to more particularly define the invention." If you are sending in a Request for Drawing-Correction Estimate, state here that such a request is attached to your amendment in order to correct the objection to the drawing.

Next restate the first rejection of the office action. For example, state "Claims 1 to 5 were rejected as unpatentable over references *A* and *B*." The examiner, thus oriented, saves the time it would take to reread the office action.

Next, review each of the references relied on in the rejection. One or two sentences for each is sufficient. For example: "Reference *A* (Clark patent 3,925,777) shows a clock having a sequential single-digit readout . . . [etc.]"

Next, discuss specifically how the claim in question has been amended and how it distinguishes over the references under Sections 102 and 103. For example, "Claim 1, now rewritten as new Claim 5, recites ' . . .' This language distinguishes over reference *A* under Section 102 because reference *A* does not show [etc.]. These distinctions are ones of patentable merit under Section 103 because [discuss new results]."

If a combination of several references has been cited against your claim, first state why the combination cannot properly be made and then discuss your distinctions as required under Sections 102 and 103. For example: "The combination of Smith's lever with Jones's pedal mechanism is submitted to be improper because neither Smith nor Jones suggests such a combination and one skilled in the art would have no reason to make such a combination. Moreover, the combination could not be made physically because the lever of the Smith type would not fit in or work with Jones's pedal mechanism because . . . However, even if the combination could be made, Claim 1 distinguishes under Section 102 because the combination does not show [here quote claim language], and these distinctions are patentable under Section 103 because [discuss new results]."

If your invention has achieved any commercial success or has won any praise, this is relevant, and you can mention it here and can even submit copies of advertisements for your invention.

Then request reconsideration and allowance of the claim: "Therefore Claim 1 is submitted to be allowable over the cited references and reconsideration and allowance are respectfully solicited."

If you have dependent claims which were rejected, treat these in the same manner. Since a dependent claim incorporates all the limitations of the parent claim, you can state that the dependent claim is patentable for the same reasons given with respect to the parent claim, and then state that it is even more patentable because it adds additional limitations, which you should discuss briefly.

Discuss each of the other rejections in a similar manner, that is, review the rejection, review the references, review your new claims, discuss why they distinguish, and request reconsideration and allowance.

If a technical rejection has been made (under Section 112) discuss how you've amended your claim and why your new claim is clear and understandable.

If you feel you have patentable subject matter in your application but have difficulty in writing new claims, you can request that the examiner write new claims for you pursuant to MPEP Section 707.07(j) (Chapter 7).

Last provide a conclusion, which can simply read: "For all the reasons given above, it is respectfully submitted that this application is now in condition for allowance, which action is respectfully solicited." Then add the closing "Very respectfully," followed by your signature, typewritten name, your address, and telephone number on the left-hand side. If there are two inventors, both must sign the amendment.

TYPING AND FINALING THE AMENDMENT

The amendment should be typed double spaced on legal- or letter-size paper with 1½-inch top and left-hand margins. Don't forget to keep an identical copy of your amendment in your files. I recommend typing the amendment on easily erasable paper on which you can readily make corrections, and then sending in a photocopy of the original since easily erasable paper is not acceptable by the PTO. Remember that your original signature must be on the copy you send to the PTO.

After your signature, add a "Certificate of Mailing" as follows:

CERTIFICATE OF MAILING

I hereby certify that this correspondence is being deposited with the United States Postal Service by First Class Mail in an envelope addressed to Commissioner of Patents and Trademarks, Washington, DC 20231 on [date].

_____
Inventor's Signature

Date _____

If you use this certificate, you can mail your amendment even on the last day of your response period. If you don't use the certificate, you must be absolutely sure the amendment arrives in the PTO before the last day of your response; otherwise it will go abandoned.

Don't forget to attach a postcard to your amendment reading as in Fig. 9.

If your amendment will cause the total number of claims of your application, or the number of independent claims to exceed the respective numbers in your application as originally filed, you will have to pay an additional

```
Amendment A in Application of John A. Novel,

Serial No. 999,999, filed 11 April 1975,

received today.
```

figure 9.

claims fee; use Additional Claims Fee Transmittal (Form 8*a*) and enclose a check for the appropriate amount.

IF YOUR APPLICATION IS ALLOWABLE

Hopefully you'll be sent a Notice of Allowability from the examiner after your first amendment, telling you that all your claims are allowed. This will be followed by a formal Notice of Allowance, accompanied by Base Issue Fee Due forms. You have 3 months to pay the base issue fee; the forms are self-explanatory. The base issue fee is $100, plus $10 for the first page of printed specification and $2 for each sheet of drawing.

When you receive your Notice of Allowance, review the application and drawings once again very carefully to make sure everything is correct, logical, grammatical, etc. If you want to make any amendments at this time, you can still do so, provided they do not affect the substance of the application; generally only grammatical changes are permitted after a notice of allowance. The format of the amendment should be similar to that dictated in Form 8 except that the first sentence should read, "Pursuant to Rule 312, it is respectfully requested that the above application be amended as follows:" Then make any amendments to your specification and claims in the previously used format. Under "Remarks," discuss the amendments, stating why they are not matters of substance and noting that they will require very little consideration by the examiner.

If you have amended your claims in any substantial way during prosecution, after the Notice of Allowance is received you should also file a Supplemental Declaration (Form 9) to indicate that you have invented the subject matter of the claims as amended and that you know of no prior art which would anticipate these claims.

After you're satisfied with your application and have filed any necessary Supplemental Declaration, you can pay the base issue fee on the forms provided. The application then goes to the Government Printing Office and no further changes are permitted. Be sure to send in a receipt postcard with your base issue fee transmittal. You can also place an advance order for printed copies of your patent (on a form provided) at this time.

Several months after the base-issue fee is paid, you'll receive a small pink Base Issue Fee Receipt slip, which will indicate the amount of the base-issue fee you paid and will also indicate the number of your patent and the date it will issue. A few days after your patent issues, you'll receive the deed, or letters patent. If it has more than one printed page, you'll also receive a Balance of Issue Fee Due notice; you must pay $10 more for each printed page of your specification, excluding the first page, which you've already paid for. You have 3 months to pay the balance of issue fee, but don't wait; do it right away or else you may forget and your patent will lapse. Be sure to send in a postcard with your balance of issue fee payment.

IF YOUR FIRST AMENDMENT DOES NOT PLACE THE APPLICATION IN CONDITION FOR ALLOWANCE

If your first amendment does not place the application in condition for allowance, the next Office Action will be final unless the examiner cites any new references which were not necessitated because of new limitations which you made to your claims. If you are given a second office action that is not final, you should respond to it in generally the same manner as you did the first office action. However if the second office action is made final—and it usually will be—note the provisions of Rules 113 and 116 (a) and (b), which govern what happens after a final action is sent:

RULE 113—FINAL REJECTION OR ACTION.

(a) On the second or any subsequent examination or consideration, the rejection or other action may be made final, whereupon applicant's response is limited to appeal in the case of rejection of any claim (Rule 191), or to amendment as specified in Rule 116. Petition may be taken to the Commissioner in the case of objections or requirements not involved in the rejection of any claim (Rule 181). Response to a final rejection or action must include cancellation of or appeal from the rejection of, each claim so rejected, and, if any claim stands allowed, compliance with any requirement or objection as to form.

(b) In making such final rejection, the examiner shall repeat or state all grounds of rejection then considered applicable to the claims in the case, clearly stating the reasons therefor.

RULE 116—AMENDMENTS AFTER FINAL ACTION.

(a) After final rejection or action (Rule 113) amendments may be made cancelling claims or complying with any requirement of form which has been made, and amendments presenting rejected claims in better form for consideration on appeal may be admitted; but the admission of any such amendment or its refusal, and any proceedings relative thereto shall not operate to relieve the application from its condition as subject to appeal or to save it from abandonment under Rule 135.

(b) If amendments touching the merits of the application be presented after final rejection, or after appeal has been taken, or when such amendment might not otherwise be proper, they may be admitted upon a showing of good and sufficient reasons why they are necessary and were not earlier presented.

These rules mean, in effect, that after a final action you must either appeal, cancel the rejected claims, or narrow the claims as specified by the examiner. Generally no other amendments are permitted unless you can show very good reasons why they were not earlier presented (for example, the examiner misstated a reference or cited a reference which was not necessitated by the manner in which you previously amended the claims). You may not in your response to a final rejection include any matter that raises any new issues, amends the claims in a manner other than that suggested by the examiner, requires any further search, or requires any substantial consideration.

If the examiner indicates that the case will be allowed if you amend the claims in a certain way, for example, if you cancel certain claims or add certain limitations to the claims, and you agree with the examiner's position, you should submit an amendment similar to the previously discussed amendment. However, instead of stating "Please amend the above application as follows:" (Form 8), state "It is requested that the above application be amended as follows:" This is because no amendments are made after a final action except with the permission of the examiner.

If you disagree with the examiner's position you have several choices:

1. *Interview the Examiner.* You can interview the examiner, by phone or in person, to try to come to some agreement to get the case allowed. This is often an excellent, effective choice.

2. *Amendment After Final.* You can try a further amendment or a request for reconsideration, narrowing your claims or submitting other claims. If this amendment fails, the examiner will send you a further advisory action reiterating his position, and you still will have the opportunity to exercise choices (3) or (4). Even if the examiner does not believe your amendment places the case in condition for allowance, you can still have the amendment entered for purposes of appeal if it neither raises any new issues nor requires further search or consideration.

3. *Appeal.* If you don't see any further way to improve the claims and if you believe the examiner's position is wrong, you can appeal. To appeal, you must file a notice stating that you appeal to the Board of Appeals from the examiner's final action and submit a $50 appeal fee. You must file an appeal brief within 60 days, together with a $50 brief fee. The Board of Appeals is a tribunal within the PTO consisting of senior examiners who will independently review your application and the examiner's rejections. See Rules of Practice 191 to 198 for details if you want to appeal.

4. *Continuation Application.* If you want to revise the claims further to get another round with the examiner, you can file a continuation application. Filing a continuation application is a relatively simple procedure involving writing new claims, paying a new filing fee, and sending in a special form requesting that a continuation application be prepared (See Chapter 11). You will receive a new serial number and filing date, but will be entitled to the benefit of the filing date of your original applica-

tion, and your application will be examined all over again with the new claims.

Any action you wish to take in response to a final action must be made within the 3-month period for response; otherwise the application will go abandoned. That is, you must either appeal, file a continuation application, or get the examiner to allow your application within the period for response.

If you do file an amendment in response to the final action within the 3-month period, your period for response will automatically be extended an additional month, that is, to 4 months after the final rejection, in order to give the examiner a chance to send you an advisory action to indicate whether your amendment puts the case in condition for allowance or not. However, you should be aware of this 4-month period and call to ask what action the examiner proposes to take if you haven't received a letter in sufficient time.

If all claims of your application are rejected in the final action, and you agree with the examiner and can't find anything else patentable in your application, you'll have to allow the application to become abandoned, but don't give up without a fight or without thorough consideration of all factors involved.

DRAWING AMENDMENTS

If your office action includes any objections to the drawing, these must be corrected before the case can be finally allowed. All corrections must be made by the PTO's draftsman at your expense. In addition, all drawing corrections must be requested in a separate letter and must be approved by the examiner before the office draftsman can take action. Lastly, the fee for the drawing correction must be paid in advance or charged to a PTO Deposit Account.

Since you won't be doing enough business with the PTO to open a special deposit account, you must first find out how much it will cost to have your drawing corrected in the manner you wish. To do this, if you haven't already been advised of the estimated cost, you must first file a Request for Drawing Correction Estimate (similar format to Form 8), which can read as follows:

> Please supply an estimate of the cost of correcting the drawing
> (Fig[s].＿＿) of the above application in the manner indicated in
> red on the attached photocopy.

You should attach a photocopy of your drawing indicating in red how you wish it to be corrected. If the objection to your drawing involves merely a need for cross-hatching, shading, etc., you do not have to attach a photocopy indicating the changes, but can merely request an estimate for correcting the drawing to overcome the objections raised. Often the PTO will give you an advance estimate of the cost of correcting the drawing if you are not represented by an attorney.

Once you get the estimate, you should send in the actual Drawing Amendment by itself or with your next amendment. The Drawing Amendment can also be on a form similar to Form 8 and can simply read "Kindly correct the drawing as previously indicated on the Request for Drawing Correction Estimate, dated ____. Attached is a check for $____." The minimum cost of any drawing correction is $3.

IF YOUR APPLICATION CLAIMS MORE THAN ONE INVENTION

Often patent applications claim several embodiments of an invention that the PTO regards as separate inventions. The PTO will thus require you to "restrict" the application to just one of the inventions. Even if two of your claims are directed to the same invention, but the examiner feels that the two claims are directed to subject matter which is classified in two separate subclasses, you can be required to restrict the application, that is, eliminate one set of claims. Another situation in which restriction may be required occurs when your application contains method and apparatus claims. Even when both sets of claims are directed to the same invention, the examiner will usually consider them two separate inventions and require you to eliminate either the method or the apparatus claims.

It is usually very difficult to overcome a requirement for restriction, and the rules regarding restriction practice are very complicated; they take up an entire chapter, Chapter 8, in the *Manual of Patent Examining Procedure.* Thus if you do receive a requirement for restriction, and if you want to claim both inventions, you will almost always have to file a separate application on one of the sets of claims. This separate application is called a "divisional application" because it is directed to subject matter that is divided out of your present application. A divisional application is relatively easy to file (see Chapter 11), so that if you think it is worth the cost (new filing fee plus new drawings), and if present indications are that your divisional application will comprise allowable subject matter, the easiest solution is to file the divisional application.

PROTESTS AGAINST ALLOWANCE OF YOUR PATENT APPLICATION

Most foreign countries have a practice under which they permit the public to see pending applications before they are issued in order to give the public a chance to cite prior art or otherwise object to the allowance of the application. This procedure, whereby a pending application is published, allows members of the public to object to the application or cite prior art, making what is called an opposition or, in the United States, a protest. However, there is presently no way in which the PTO can require you to allow your application to be published for protest since statutory authorization has not yet been enacted. Thus the PTO has recently been instituting voluntary protest programs under which you may be given the right to elect to have your application published for protest.

If your application is allowable at the time a voluntary protest program is running, you will be given the right to waive the secrecy of your application and have an abstract of your application published in the *Official Gazette.* Then copies of your application can be obtained by any member of the public who wants to order them; anyone can then protest against the allowance of your application by citing reasons to show why your invention is not patentable. If you do have an opportunity to have your application published for protest, I advise you to elect the procedure—the PTO will give you full instructions—since a patent application which survives the protest procedure (most do) will become a stronger patent. The disadvantages are delay, that more examination may be required, that members of the public may cite fatally damaging prior art against your application, etc., but I believe the advantages outweigh these disadvantages.

DESIGN PATENT APPLICATION PROSECUTION

Design patent application prosecution is much simpler than regular patent application prosecution, and, armed with the instructions of this chapter, you'll find it to be duck soup. Design patent applications will never require anything but the most elementary changes to the specification and claims; the examiner will tell you exactly what to do. To be patentable, the *appearance* of your design, as a whole, must be unobvious to a designer of ordinary skill over the references (usually earlier design patents) which the examiner cites. If your design has significant differences over the cited prior art designs, it should be patentable; if not, you will have to abandon your design patent application as there is no way to narrow or change the substance of the claims or drawings of a design patent application. If the examiner rejects your design as obvious in view of a reference, there is little you can do except to point out the differences in your design and argue their importance and significance.

If your design-patent application is allowed, you can select the term of protection as either $3\frac{1}{2}$, 7, or 14 years by paying a final fee of $10, $20, or $30, respectively. Most people pay the $30 fee to secure the maximum 14-year term. There is no balance of issue fee for a design patent, and once a term is selected it cannot be changed; design patents cannot be renewed.

CHAPTER ELEVEN

Your Application Can Sprout Branches — Going Abroad

WHY THE NEED FOR EXTENSIONS OF YOUR PATENT APPLICATION?

Once you have a patent application on file, isn't it either (1) approved by the PTO, so that you get a patent, or (2) rejected, in which case you have to let your application go abandoned? Unfortunately, no; there are several other possibilities of which you should be aware. (Life just isn't as simple anymore as we'd like it to be.)

A patent application is like a tree: The basic application which you file is a trunk which can sprout many branches, or new applications, which I'll cover in this chapter. Depending on the situation, the basic application can go by many names, such as "parent," "prior," "basic," or "original" application, while the extensions can be called "daughter," "continuation," "divisional," "reissue," "substitute," or "corresponding foreign" applications; if there are several successive extensions the basic application is called the "grandparent" or "great-grandparent" application.

The following are the different situations in which you may want to file extension applications:

1. If you want *another round with the examiner* or a chance to try a new and different set of claims after a final action, you should file a *continuation application.*

2. If your basic application was held to have two inventions and you've had to restrict it to one of these inventions and you want to *file a separate application on the "nonelected" invention,* you should file a *divisional application.*

3. If you have made *an improvement of your basic invention* you should file a *continuation-in-part (CIP) application.*

4. If you have received a patent, but you want to *revise the claims of the patent* or correct significant errors in the specification of your patent for some valid reason, you should file a *reissue application.*

5. If you want to obtain *patent protection in other countries,* you should consider *foreign-filing* corresponding applications from your basic U.S. application.

6. If you can't get or for some reason don't want a patent once you have filed your application, but want to be sure no one else will ever get a patent on the invention, you can *publish your patent application* by converting it to a *defensive publication.*

7. If you abandon your application and *later refile a new application* on the same invention, the new application is termed a *substitute application.*

CONTINUATION APPLICATIONS

In the *Manual of Patent Examining Procedure* (MPEP), Section 201.07, a "continuation" is defined as "a second application for the same invention claimed in a prior application and filed before the [prior application] becomes abandoned." A continuation application is almost always filed after a final rejection when you want to have another round with the examiner, that is, when you want to try a new set of claims or have claims reviewed which the examiner has refused to examine because you submitted them after a final action.

In the "old days," patent prosecution proceeded at a leisurely pace, with the examiner often sending four or five office actions before final rejection. However, in recent years (since the late 1960s), the PTO instituted its "compact prosecution" practice in which the examiner almost always makes the second office action final. The purpose of this change in procedure was to obtain more income for the PTO (or to reduce the amount of work the PTO performed) and to shorten the backlog of pending applications. However, most patent lawyers find that two office actions often are not enough to define the invention adequately, reach an issue with the examiner, and complete the prosecution in a proper manner. Therefore continuation applications are often filed nowadays, especially since the process has been made very simple by Rule 60 and a special continuation/divisional application request form (Form 10).

Remember that a continuation application must cover the same invention as the parent or basic application, and that the parent or basic application should be abandoned when the continuation is filed. The continuation application is entitled to the filing date of the parent application for purposes of overcoming prior art, although the continuation receives its own filing date and serial number. You can file a continuation of a continuation; in fact it is theoretically possible to file an unlimited sequence of continuation applications, but note that if an issue has been reached in the parent application, the examiner can and usually will make the first office action in a continuation application final.

When a patent issues on a continuation application, the heading of the patent will indicate that it is a continuation application. Also the filing date and serial number of the parent, original, or basic application will be given in order to apprise the public of the patent's *effective* filing date.

If you want to file a continuation application, it is simply necessary to complete and file Form 10, together with a new filing fee and a preliminary amendment containing the new claims you desire to prosecute. To complete Form 10, check "continuation" in paragraph 1 and fill out all the other blanks in the form. Also check the space before paragraph 6a. Attach a check for $65, a receipt postcard (see Chapter 8), a Preliminary Amendment (Form 11), and, if the preliminary amendment will cause the application to have more than one independent claim or more than ten total claims, an Amendment Transmittal (Form 8a) and a second check for extra claims. For the preliminary amendment on Form 11 you should leave the serial number and filing date blank, but insert the serial number and filing date of the parent application in the parenthetical portion of the heading.

The PTO will prepare the continuation application in response to Form 10; this will consist of an exact copy of the prior application as filed except that all claims will be cancelled except Claim 1. Therefore the preliminary amendment should include all the amendments to the specification you made in the parent case. And it should also direct cancellation of Claim 1. Then insert the new claims you desire, numbered in sequence after the highest numbered claim of the prior application. Under "Remarks" in the preliminary amendment you need merely state, "The above amendments were made in the parent case and the above new claims are being submitted as part of the continuation application; these claims are submitted to be patentable over the art of record in the parent case." Be sure to include all the claims you desire in the preliminary amendment since the first office action may be a final action if the examiner does not cite any new prior art. Note (Item 6A) that the PTO will transfer the drawings from your parent application and abandon it as of the date of transfer.

As with a regular application, you will receive your postcard back with the stamped serial number and filing date of your continuation application; thereafter you will receive the blue filing receipt and first office action in due course.

If the claims finally allowed in a continuation application, or divisional application (see section below) differ significantly from the claims originally presented in the parent application, a Supplemental Oath (Form 9) should be filed before the base issue fee is paid.

DIVISIONAL APPLICATIONS

As stated in MPEP 201.06, "a later application for a distinct or independent invention, carved out of a pending application and disclosing and claiming only subject matter disclosed in the earlier or parent application, is known as a divisional application or 'division.' " Divisional applications are filed when the PTO holds that two separate or distinct inventions were claimed in the parent case and you wish to file a separate application on the claims that were not prosecuted in the parent case. Divisional applications are so called because they cover subject matter which is "divided out" of the parent case.

A divisional application is entitled to the filing date of the parent case for purposes of overcoming prior art, although, like the continuation, it receives its own serial number and filing date. A patent issuing on a divisional application will show the serial number and filing date of the parent application. The parent application of a divisional application can either issue as a patent or become abandoned if you feel it is not patentable over the prior art, but remember that the divisional application must be filed while the parent is pending. There can be a division of a continuation application and a continuation of a divisional application.

One pitfall in patent law, which fortunately is encountered very infrequently, is the "double patenting" trap: One should never obtain two patents on the same invention since both can be held invalid under the doctrine of double patenting. However, due to a special statute, a patent issuing on a divisional application filed after the examiner has required the parent application to be restricted to one of two inventions can never be held invalid for double patenting.

As in the case of a continuation application, the drawing(s) can be transferred from the parent application if the parent is to be allowed to become abandoned. However, since the parent of a divisional application usually is not to be abandoned—that is, usually will issue as a patent—new drawings for the divisional application must be supplied. Fortunately there are several firms in the Arlington area that can make a photolithographic copy in India ink of the drawing of the parent application, which you can use for the divisional application. If any figures of the drawing are not relevant for the divisional application, the firms can even remove them. Two of the firms are Quality Patent Printing, Box 2404, Arlington, VA 22202, and Kirby Lithographic Co., 409 Twelfth Street, S.W., Washington, DC 20024. These firms will send you appropriate authorization forms to enable them to borrow your drawing from the PTO; the charge is only about $10 to make a duplicate of a patent drawing.

To file a divisional application, fill out Form 10 as indicated for a continuation application, but in paragraphs 1 and 5 check the word "divisional." If your parent application is to be abandoned, check box 6a; if you are filing new formal drawings, check box 6b.

You should accompany Form 10 with a check for the $65 filing fee, a receipt postcard, and a preliminary amendment (Form 11). In the preliminary-amendment form leave the serial number and filing date blank, but include the serial number and filing date of the parent case in the parenthetical portion of the heading.

Insofar as possible, you should amend the specification of the divisional case to include any amendments made in the parent case, but you should cancel any subject matter not pertinent to the invention of the divisional case; frequently there will be no subject matter that can be cancelled without affecting the disclosure of the divisional case. In the claims portion of the preliminary amendment you should cancel Claim 1 and then insert any claims you wish to direct to the divisional invention. These claims may simply be "nonelected" claims of the parent case. Remember that if the claims exceed one independent or ten total, an Amendment Fee Transmittal (Form 8a) and a second check for the extra claims fee should also be sent.

CONTINUATION-IN-PART APPLICATIONS

As defined in MPEP 201.08, "a continuation-in-part is an application filed during the lifetime of an earlier application by the same applicant, repeating some substantial portion or all of the earlier application *and adding matter not disclosed* in the earlier application." Continuation-in-part applications are not common. They are used whenever you wish to cover an improvement of your basic invention, for example, if you have discovered a new material, better design, etc.

Generally the parent application should be allowed to go abandoned when a CIP is filed, but if you do want the parent application to issue, you must be sure that the claims of the CIP application are patentably different—that is, they define subject matter which is unobvious over that of the parent application—or else the CIP and parent application patent can both be held invalid for double patenting.

The advantage of a continuation-in-part application over a separate application is that the CIP is entitled to the filing date of the parent application for all subject matter common to both applications; if any claims of the CIP cover the new subject matter of the CIP, such claims are entitled to the filing date of the CIP only. If your "improvement" of your basic application is different enough to be unobvious over the basic invention, an entirely separate application, rather than a CIP, can be filed, but it's better to use a CIP application since the common subject matter gets the filing date of the parent application.

You can file a CIP of a continuation or divisional application or vice versa in either case. It is also theoretically possible to file an unlimited number of successive CIP applications to cover successive improvements; some inventors have filed chains of CIPs with as many as eight or more applications, each of which issued into a patent.

CIPs are sufficiently rare that I have not provided any form, but if you do wish to file a CIP, you must retype your specification and supply new drawings if the parent application is to issue. The CIP should be filed in a similar manner to any other application, except that the first sentence of the application should state that it is a continuation-in-part of the prior application, a special declaration (Form 3.18[a] of the Patent Rules [Title 37, Code of Federal Regulations]) should be used.

REISSUE APPLICATIONS

As stated in MPEP 201.05, "a reissue application is an application for a patent to take the place of an unexpired patent that is defective in some one or more particulars." Parts 1400 to 1401.12 of the MPEP discuss reissue applications extensively.

If you have received a patent and believe that the claims are not broad enough, that they are too broad (you have discovered a new reference), or that there are some significant errors in the specification, you can file an application to get your patent reissued at any time during the 17 year duration of your patent. The reissued patent will take the place of your original patent and expire the same time as the original patent would have. However, if you wish to broaden the claims of your patent through a reissue application, you must do so within 2 years from the date the original patent issued. Moreover, anyone who manufactures anything after the original patent issues and before the reissue issues that would infringe the broadened claims is entitled to "intervening rights," which will preclude a valid suit against this person for infringement of the reissue patent's broadened claims.

To file a reissue application you must reproduce the entire specification of the original application (a copy of the printed patent is acceptable), putting brackets around matter to be cancelled and underlining matter to be added. When the reissue patent issues, it will include the brackets and underlining. You must also supply a request for a title report on the original patent ($3 charge) and offer to surrender the original patent deed. You must provide a detailed showing in your oath as to why you believe the original patent to be wholly or partially inoperative or invalid; use Form 3.31(a) of the Rules of Practice. Reissue patents are relatively rare and are identified by the letters RE followed by a five-digit number, for example, "Patent RE 26,420."

FOREIGN FILING

All of the nations of the world that have a patent system have signed treaties stating, in effect, that if you file a patent application in any one country, you may file a corresponding application in any other country within 1 year of your original filing date and be entitled to your original filing date in the other country. Thus you have 1 year after you file your U.S. application to file foreign patent applications and be entitled to your U.S. filing date. However, you should not wait the whole year, but should take action in about the eighth to tenth month after your U.S. filing date so that you will have time to prepare correspondence and have appropriate translations made by your foreign correspondents. On the other hand, you shouldn't act too soon; a special statute prohibits foreign filing without a special license until 6 months after your U.S. filing date (in order to give the government time to see if you've filed on anything which should be made a military secret).

Foreign patent prosecution and practice is complicated and expensive, and therefore should be undertaken only for inventions that have attained or show extremely good promise of attaining commercial success. Also, foreign applications should only be filed in countries where a significant market for products embodying the inventions is likely to exist.

Except for Canada, whose patent laws and practice are practically identical to U.S. practice, almost all foreign countries have patent laws and practice greatly different from ours. Some of the main differences are as follows: In foreign countries patents expire 15 years (Italy) to 20 years (Israel) from the filing date, rather than 17 years from the issue date. Some foreign countries examine patent applications for novelty and some do not; the latter (nonexamining countries) simply issue a patent on every application filed and leave it up to the courts to determine whether the invention was novel and unobvious. Once a patent issues, annual maintenance fees, which increase each year, must be paid or else the patent will lapse. Moreover, in some foreign countries (France, West Germany, Italy, Australia, the Netherlands), annual maintenance fees must be paid while the application is pending! Also, some foreign countries require that patented inventions be "worked" (put into commercial use) on pain of compulsory licensing at government-set fees.

SEPARATE CONVENTION APPLICATIONS

There are now two ways to obtain corresponding patents in foreign countries. The first and older way is to file a separate corresponding application in each foreign country in which you wish to obtain a patent. Such applications must be filed within 1 year of and claim "priority" of your U.S. filing date. These applications are termed "Convention" applications since they are made under the International Convention for the Protection of Industrial Property, a treaty done in Paris in 1883 and revised several times since then. A foreign patent agent in each country you select can prepare an appropriate convention application; you must send the agent a copy of your U.S. application, special drawings (which can be made by the same companies which make drawings for U.S. divisional applications—see *Divisional Applications*, above), a power of attorney, details of the U.S. application, and sometimes an assignment and/or a certified copy of your U.S. application; the last can be obtained from the PTO. The cost for filing a foreign application in each country is high, namely about $500 to $1000, depending on the country, on the length of your application, and on whether a translation is required.

If you wish to correspond directly with the foreign patent agents yourself, you will first have to get the name of a patent agent in each country. Most U.S. patent attorneys are associated with one or more patent agents in each country, but if you do not know any and cannot find the names of any though a U.S. patent attorney or someone who is familiar with foreign patent agents, there are several other ways to obtain the names of foreign patent agents. One way is to look in the telephone directory of the city where the patent office of the foreign country is located. In Canada it is Ottawa; in the United Kingdom, London; in France, Paris; in Germany, Munich; in Sweden, Stockholm; in Japan, Tokyo; in Italy, Rome; in Australia, Canberra and Sydney. Most large libraries have foreign telephone directories. Another way is to inquire at the consulate of the country; most foreign countries have consulates in major U.S. cities. A third possibility is to hire a local patent attorney to do the work for you, although this involves an intermediary's costs. Because of the complicated nature of foreign filing, many patent attorneys even use their own intermediaries, namely specialized patent-law firms in New York, Chicago, or Los Angeles, which handle foreign filing exclusively. A fourth possibility is to hire a British firm of patent agents to do all your foreign filing. A last possibility is to look in the *Martindale-Hubbell Law Directory* (in any law library) which lists some foreign patent agents in each country. Whichever way you get your foreign patent agent, be careful, however, because some foreign patent agents, like some U.S. patent attorneys and agents, are not competent.

The easiest way to file a Convention application, once you have the name of an agent in the country in which you wish to file, is to send the agent a copy of your U.S. application, asking for all the necessary forms and requirements. Almost all foreign patent agents will correspond with you in English, but be sure to allow plenty of time before the 1-year deadline in order to give yourself time to obtain all the necessary documents and to give the agent time to translate the application and reformat it for filing in the agent's country.

PATENT COOPERATION TREATY (PCT) APPLICATIONS

In Washington in 1970, a new and separately operable Patent Cooperation Treaty was done; under this treaty, which was not implemented until 1978, patent applications may be made in foreign countries by filing "international" applications with the "International Bureau," which was formed under the treaty and is represented in the United States by the Patent and Trademark Office. By filing international applications under the PCT, you will (to a great extent, at least) save the expense of having your application prepared in multiple formats and prosecuting separate applications in the respective countries, but most countries will still require you to pay their own filing and other fees, provide a translation of your application if their language is different from English, and file an appropriate national oath or declaration.

As this book goes to press, not all of the PCT procedures have been finalized but most major countries have ratified the PCT and enough information is now available to provide you with general guidance on filing PCT applications. The most important preparations can be made when you first prepare your U.S. application; as noted in Chapters 6 and 8, the original application should be prepared in the new international format if there is any chance you may want to file it abroad later. If you don't prepare your original U.S. application in international format, you'll have to retype it and redo the drawings in international format in order to file a PCT application. The main differences between the PCT and U.S. national formats (both of which are now acceptable for U.S. applications) are the drawing size and margins, location of page numbers, and spacing between typed lines; all of these differences were detailed in Chapter 8.

Assuming your application is in the proper format, the first step to take to file corresponding foreign applications under the PCT is to obtain a "Request" (Form PCT/RO/101) and transmittal letter (Form PTO 1382) from Box PCT, Patent and Trademark Office, Washington, DC 20231. Complete the forms (full instructions will be attached), requesting the PTO to prepare a certified copy of your U.S. application for use with your PCT application, and attach a check payable to the Commissioner of Patents and Trademarks for the international application filing fees as computed on the Request (about $416 for filing in three foreign countries; about $270 of this will be refunded later because the U.S. and international searches usually will be duplicative), plus the fee for the certified copy (30 cents per page of your application, plus $1 for certification). Then mail the letter, Request, and check to Box PCT, c/o the PTO, which is a designated receiving office for the International Bureau in Geneva. Like Convention applications, the international (PCT) application should be filed within 1 year of your U.S. filing date.

You'll receive a filing receipt and separate serial number for your international application, and the application will eventually be transmitted for filing to the countries you have designated on your Request form. Although the subsequent procedures are not yet clear, obviously you'll have to have separate correspondence with the designated countries, including filing translations, separate oath or declaration forms, and separate national filing fees, where appropriate. You'll probably have to engage the services of independent patent agents in the respective countries to assist you in completing the filing in their countries and with any subsequent prosecution which is required. The separate foreign countries will rely to a great extent on the international search they'll receive from the International Bureau (in most cases this will be an adoption of the U.S. search), so you'll save what used to be the agonizing, extremely expensive job of separately prosecuting an application in each foreign country in which you elected to file.

DEFENSIVE PUBLICATIONS

If you have filed a U.S. application and for some reason do not wish it to issue as a patent or cannot obtain a patent on it, but want to be absolutely sure that no one else will ever be able to obtain a patent on it (for instance, you are manufacturing a product embodying the invention), you can elect to have an abstract of your application published in the *Official Gazette* and have your entire application opened to public inspection. This will cause it to become a prior-art reference, which will preclude anyone else from obtaining a patent on the invention, provided no application on the invention has been filed earlier.

To convert a pending application to a defensive publication, it is simply necessary to file a paper requesting that an abstract of the disclosure be published, authorizing the application to be laid open to public inspection, expressly abandoning the application as of 5 years from your filing date, and waiving all rights to an enforceable patent. (The 5-year term before abandonment is to allow you to revive the application in case you discover that anyone gets a patent on the invention and you want to get into interference with that person.) Full details of the defensive-publication program are provided in MPEP 711.06. There is no fee to convert your application to a defensive publication.

Defensive publications are cited by "*T-*" number, which indicates the volume number of the *Official Gazette* in which the abstract was published and the number of the abstract; for example, Defensive Publication T-869-031 refers to the defensive publication number 31 in volume 869 of the *Official Gazette*.

SUBSTITUTE APPLICATIONS

The term "substitute" is defined in MPEP 201.09 as "an application which is in essence a duplicate of an application by the same applicant which was abandoned before the filing date of the later case."

I hope you never have to file a substitute application since it does not get the benefit of the filing date of the earlier case. This is because it was not filed while the earlier case was pending. Thus any prior art which issues after the filing date of the earlier case and before the filing date of the substitute case is good against the substitute case. Substitute applications are rarely filed since most people who wish to file a continuation application do so while the parent application is pending. If, however, you somehow allow your application to become abandoned and you cannot successfully petition the Commissioner of Patents to revive the application (see Chapter 13), you still may be able to get protection on the invention by filing a substitute application, assuming significant prior art hasn't been published in the meantime.

CHAPTER TWELVE

Now That You've Gotten the Patent

WHAT TO DO JUST BEFORE YOUR PATENT ISSUES

Several months after you pay the base-issue fee (Chapter 10), you'll receive a small, orange base issue fee receipt, which will indicate the number and issue date of your patent; this date will be about 1 or 2 months after the date you receive the base issue fee receipt. If your invention hasn't yet been licensed or sold, or even if it has, but you want additional publicity, you should now prepare a press release to accompany copies of your patent for transmittal to the various media. The press release should be done on a letter-size sheet and should be captioned with your name, address, and telephone number, and should carry the head "For Release On [date of your patent issuance]." Below that, put an attractive, eye-catching and stimulating headline, such as "Midgeville Inventor Gets Patent on Jam-Free Bicycle Mechanism."

Then write several brief, concise, but clearly worded and interesting paragraphs about you and your patent, telling what problems it solves, how it is used, when it was invented, any commercial success it has had to date, and any other information you think the public and prospective manufacturers might be interested in, including some biographical facts about yourself. Remember that newspaper articles are cut from the bottom up, so be sure the first paragraph includes all the essentials, the second paragraph gives information that is somewhat less essential, etc.

Several days after the Tuesday on which the patent issues, you will receive your patent deed, which will include a fancy jacket, red seal, and blue ribbon; you'll also receive the printed copies of your patent if you ordered them when you paid your base issue fee. If you don't receive printed copies, make sufficient photocopies from the deed for distribution with your press release. Send copies of the press release and patent to local radio and TV stations, newspapers, and magazines. Also send copies to any trade or subject-matter magazines; for example, if your patent relates to a bicycle, send copies to bicycle magazines; if it relates to an electronic circuit, send it to electronic magazines, etc. Also send copies of your PR and patent to organizations, clubs, churches, and other groups to which you belong since the issuance of a patent to you would be a matter of personal interest to organization members.

About two weeks before the patent issues, you should also send a copy of your PR alone (you won't have the patent yet) to Stacey V. Jones, Patent Columnist, New York Times, 229 West 43d Street, New York, NY 10036. Mr. Jones writes a column for each Saturday's *The New York Times* that features or describes several of the more interesting patents which issued the preceding Tuesday. If your invention is interesting enough (in his opinion), he may feature your invention in his column.

If you have sales blurbs promoting your invention, you should, at this time, change them to indicate that your invention is "patented" rather than "patent pending."

If you or a licensee of yours is manufacturing a product embodying the invention, you should consider marking your product with the patent number; see *Patent Number Marking* below.

BE WARY OF OFFERS

Soon after being awarded a patent, a client of mine received an offer by mail, advising that an article about her patent was published and offering to send her a copy of the article for $3.95. After anxiously sending in her money, she received the "article," a photocopy of a page from the PTO's *Official Gazette* showing the usual main drawing figure and claim of her patent! Fortunately she was able to obtain a refund by threatening to call in the FTC and postal inspectors, but you may not be so lucky; new rackets are originated all the time.

Another offer frequently received by patentees, usually about a year or more after their patent issues, states something to the effect that, "Your patent was cited in a recently issued patent; if you send us $10 we'll send you a copy of the recently issued patent, which you should review for a possible infringement, interference, improvement of your invention, etc." This type of offer does provide a somewhat useful service, albeit at a high cost. Personally I wouldn't accept the offer since most all patents which have earlier patents cited as references are very different and extremely unlikely to be of any value to the owner of the earlier patent.

WHAT RIGHTS DOES YOUR PATENT GIVE YOU?

The grant of a patent gives you, or the person or corporation to whom you "assigned" (legally transferred) your patent or patent application, a 17-year monopoly on the invention *defined by the claims of the patent*, beginning with the date of issuance of the patent. This monopoly gives you the right to sue anyone who makes, uses, or sells your invention. (This monopoly is not renewable.) If your suit is successful, you'll recover damages for the period covered by the patent and also get an injunction, precluding the infringer from using your invention in the future, during the remaining term of the patent. Damages will generally be equivalent to a reasonable royalty you could have gotten had you licensed the patent. The injunction is an order signed by a federal court, which, if violated, can subject the violator to contempt-of-court sanctions, including imprisonment and fines. In exceptional cases—if the infringer's conduct was flagrant or in bad faith—you may also be able to recover attorney fees and/or triple damages.

The right to exclude others from using the patented invention (that is, the right to get an injunction against anyone who uses your invention) is generally used to license others (that is, to force them to pay you royalties under a formal agreement for their use of your invention).

Occasionally, companies or individuals who manufacture a patented invention use their patent to enforce a monopoly; that is, they feel they can make more money by charging whatever the traffic will bear, rather than a competitive price, even though they would receive royalties by licensing others. It is sometimes regarded by antitrust attorneys as dangerous to use a patent to create a monopoly (even though a patent gives one the right to do this) since the courts have a bias against monopolies, and if the patent monopolist is charged with any violation of the antitrust laws, having used a patent to create a monopoly will militate against the defendant in the eyes of most judges.

Some inventors think that a patent gives them the right to manufacture the invention covered by the patent. This is not true. Patent rights aside, you can manufacture anything you choose, so long as you don't duplicate anyone's trademark. Thus you have a right to manufacture the invention even without the patent. What a patent does do is give you the right to exclude others from making, using, or selling your invention. Moreover, if you make an invention covered by a patent, you still must comply with all other government regulations, statutes, and court decisions, such as clean-air provisions, drug regulations, Product Safety Commission regulations, product-liability considerations, antitrust laws, etc. The patent does not give your product any privileged status or position.

A patent is personal property and can be sold, given away, willed, or even executed upon by your creditors, just like any other item of personal property. Even though it is personal property, the actual patent deed you receive from the Patent and Trademark Office has no inherent value; thus you need *not* put it in your safe-deposit box or take any steps to preserve it against loss. Your ownership of the patent is recorded in the PTO (just like the deed to your house is recorded by your county's Recorder of Deeds), so that if you lose the original deed, you can still get copies of the printed patent or specially certified copies showing that you are the owner. Most inventors, however, like to keep their patent deed in a safe and conspicuous place since it is a handsome and impressive document.

During the 17-year term from its date of issuance, your patent is termed an in-force patent; after this term it is an expired patent, and the subject matter of the claims is considered to be in the public domain. Whether your patent is in-force or expired, it still is a valid publication that the PTO may cite against others applying for a patent on the same or a related invention.

As a patent's term comprises a strange number of years (17), you may be interested in knowing how this term originated. At the time in post-Colonial America when the patent statutes were being enacted, some legislators favored a 14-year term, in conformance with the medieval British Statute of Monopolies, while some favored 20 years as a longer and rounder number. The two groups met each other half way and compromised on the present 17-year term, although the United Kingdom has subsequently changed its term to 16 years from filing.

WHAT TO DO WHEN YOU GET THE PATENT

Patents almost always issue on a Tuesday, every week of the year. Thus your patent will be mailed to you on the Tuesday of its issuance, and you will receive it a day or so later. When you receive the deed (and printed copies if you've ordered them) you will, as stated in Chapter 10, receive a notice indicating a balance-of-issue fee, which is due within 3 months. Pay this right away on the forms provided so you won't forget about it, remembering to include a receipt postcard.

Then proofread your patent carefully with a friend. Look at the information in the heading of the patent—serial number, filing date, title, your name, etc.—to make sure all is correct. Then read the patent word for word against your file of the specification, including your amendments. Mark down all of the errors you find in the printed patent. All too often you'll find several errors.

If you find errors, but none of them is significant, that is, if the meaning you intended is obvious and clear, the PTO will not issue a certificate of correction, but you should make the error of record in the PTO's file of your patent. To do this, simply write a "make of record" letter to be put in the file of your patent, listing the errors you found. This letter should be captioned similarly to Form 12, but should be headed, "Notation of Errors in Printed Patent" and should list all the errors in the patent.

If any of the errors you discover are significant, that is, if the meaning is unclear because of a wrong reference numeral, missing or transposed words, failure to include an amendatory change of significance, etc., you are entitled to a certificate of correction. If the errors are the fault of the printer, the certificate of correction will be issued free; but if you've spotted any errors that are your fault, that is, if they are in your file of the patent as well as the printed patent, you still can get a certificate of correction provided the error is of a clerical or minor nature and occurred in good faith. Examples are a wrong reference numeral, an omitted line or word, etc. A certificate of correction to correct your error will cost $15.

If you wish to obtain a Certificate of Correction in either case, fill out Forms 12 and 13. In Form 12 (the request letter), insert the patent number, issue date, and the date you mailed the form. Check paragraph 2 if the error is the fault of the PTO; check paragraph 3 if the error is your fault. If you check paragraph 3, tell why the error occurred, for example, "[Specifically], applicant erroneously typed "43" instead of —34— at page 1, line 15."

In either case (whether you checked paragraph 2 or 3), below paragraph 3 list the places in the application file where the errors occurred, for instance:

Page 1, line 15

Page 2, line 3

Then add "Very respectfully," followed by your name and address in the usual manner. Add a $15 check if you've checked paragraph 3 on Form 12.

Form 13 (the actual certificate form) should accompany Form 12 in duplicate and should be completed with the patent number, date, and inventor(s). In the body of the form, as close to the top as possible, type neatly and clearly the locations in the patent where errors occurred (corresponding to your list on Form 12) and how the copy should be read. Do this in the same manner as you would write the changes in an amendment, for example: "Column 1, line 13, change "12" to —21—; Column 4, line 38, change "said transistor" to —diode 18—; etc." Then write the patent number again and your name and address at the bottom of the page. Leave a 2-inch blank space at the bottom of the form.

When the PTO issues the certificate of correction, they will sign and seal the form, and return it to you for attachment to your deed and printed copies of your patent. They will also make photographic copies for attachment to all copies of the patent in the PTO's stores.

PATENT NUMBER MARKING

A special section of the patent laws (Section 287) states that products embodying a patented invention may be marked with the legend, "Pat." or "Patent" followed by the patent number. If you so mark your product, you can recover damages from any infringers you sue from the date you began marking. If you do not mark the product with your patent number, you can recover damages only from the date you notified an infringer of infringement, or from the date you filed suit against the infringer, whichever is earlier. However, you must mark your product with the actual number of the patent; the legend "Patented" alone is not enough.

The actual marking should be done on the product itself, on its package, or by means of a label affixed to the product. If you do not manufacture any product embodying the invention, or if the invention relates to a process that is not associated with a product and hence cannot be marked, you can recover damages from an infringer for the entire period of infringement without marking.

The disadvantage of patent marking is that anyone who wants to copy your product can easily see the number of your patent, order the patent, read its claims, and design around your claims or some other flaw in your patent. If you don't mark, the potential infringer can still probably get this same information, but only through a lot more expense and effort, so that human inertia may help you. Many companies, therefore, favor *not* marking their patented products, or simply marking them "Patented," relying on their familiarity with the field to enable them to discover any infringer and notify the infringer promptly so that significant damages will not be lost.

ADVERTISEMENT IN OFFICIAL GAZETTE

If you still haven't licensed or sold your invention by the time your patent issues, you can advertise the availability of your patent for license or sale in the *Official Gazette.* You simply send a letter to the Commissioner of Patents and Trademarks, Washington, DC 20231, asking to have the availability of your patent for license or sale listed, together with a check for $3. While this possibility is mentioned for the sake of completeness, I do not recommend it since it probably will have little effect; I've never heard of anyone licensing or selling a patent through an Official Gazette advertisement.

IF YOU DISCOVER AN INFRINGER

If you discover anyone making, using, or selling the invention defined by the claims of your patent, you have, as stated, a right to sue, and if successful, you can recover damages for past infringement and an injunction against making, using, or selling anything embodying your invention in the future. In addition, if an infringer's conduct is flagrant, i.e., infringement is willfully continued after an attorney confirmed infringement, or without any reasonable defense—you can also recover triple damages and attorney fees.

The statute of limitations on patent infringements is 6 years, which means that you cannot recover damages more than 6 years back from the date you filed suit. However, if you are aware of an infringement, you should act rapidly; otherwise the infringer can claim having been lulled into believing you would not sue under your patent, and thereby "estop" your suit. Also, if you're selling a product embodying the invention and you didn't mark it with the patent number, the 6-year term of damages can be considerably shortened by application of Section 287 (see *Patent Number Marking* above). You can bring suit even after your patent has expired and still go back 6 years during the time the patent was in force, provided you had some valid reason for waiting the full 6 years.

If the infringer of your patent is a company or individual who is making products embodying your invention under a government contract, you can sue only the government in the Court of Claims in Washington. Moreover, you can't get an injunction prohibiting the company from manufacturing your invention; you can recover only damages since the infringing device may be useful for national defense.

If you discover what you believe to be an infringement, you should obtain as many details and particulars about the infringing device or process as possible. You should procure evidence, such as service manuals, photographs, actual samples of the infringing device, advertisements, product-catalog sheets, etc., and study these carefully against the claims of your patent. Remember that all of the elements of the main or broadest claims of your patent must be met by the infringing device (Chapter 7). Even if the infringing device has additional elements, it still will infringe. For example, if your claim recites three elements, A, B, and C, and the infringing device has four elements, A, B, C, and D, it will infringe. But if the infringing device has two elements, A and B, it will not infringe. Similarly, if the supposed infringing device has three elements A, B, and C', it will not infringe, provided element C of your claim does not read on element C' of the infringing device.

Even if your claims do not literally read on the infringing device, but the infringing device is the equivalent of your invention in structure, function, and result, it still may be held to infringe under the "doctrine of equivalents." Moreover, if your claims don't read on the infringing device, but the infringing device is a specially made component that is only useful in a machine covered by your patent, the infringer may be liable under the doctrine of "contributory infringement." However, even if your claims literally read on the infringing device, but the infringing device has a different structure, function, or result than your invention, the device may be held not to infringe your invention under the "negative doctrine of equivalents."

As you've gathered by now, the subject of infringement is complicated, and it may be necessary to consult a patent attorney (not a patent agent) to determine whether an infringement actually exists.

Two further facts about infringements are worth noting here: (1) The PTO doesn't care about and has no responsibility in regard to infringements, so if you discover an infringement, it is totally your responsibility to bring the infringer to heel; the PTO won't aid you in any way. (2) If your patent is owned by joint inventors or owners, any joint inventor or owner can make, use, and sell the patented invention without accounting to the other joint owner, so you can't maintain a valid suit against your joint owner for "infringing" your patent.

If you do confirm an infringement, you can write a letter in which you ask the infringer to stop infringing your patent and to pay you royalties for the past, or you can offer the infringer a license under your patent for future activity and again ask for a settlement for the past. However, your letter may go unanswered, and your demands may not be acceded to. The infringer can simply continue infringing, or stop infringing and pay you nothing. In this case you will have to sue for patent infringement if you want to recover damages or an injunction.

Suits for patent infringement must be brought in federal court where the infringer (who may be a corporation) resides, or is headquartered, or where the infringer has any place of business and has made, used, or sold the patented invention. Thus you should, if possible, select an attorney whose office is in one of these locations. You can sue the retailer or purchaser of the invention as well as the manufacturer; suits against the retailer or customer are sometimes brought in order to get a jurisdiction that is favorable, or close to the patent owner. If a suit is brought against the retailer or customer of a patented invention, the manufacturer of the patented invention will usually step in and defend or reimburse the customer's suit, and indeed has a duty to do so under the Uniform Commercial Code.

Patent infringement suits are very expensive and can cost each side $50,000 or more in attorney fees, travel and deposition expenses, witness fees, and telephone and secretarial expenses. Thus the law works very much in favor of the wealthy or large corporations since they are far better equipped to defend and maintain patent infringement suits than a single individual would be. Therefore, if you discover an infringement, it may be to your advantage not to sue and to accept a settlement that is less than you think you are owed. If you do sue, be well aware of the costs through trial and be sure you can afford them. The courts give sympathy to the individual inventor in patent litigation, but the plaintiff still must be able to afford to bring and maintain the suit.

Some inventors have brought suit by themselves for patent infringement, but this is extremely difficult without legal training. If you are considering such a possibility, read a book on the subject, such as *Patent Litigation: Procedure and Tactics* by R. S. White, before you act.

Lastly, you should know that if you are manufacturing or using an invention covered by your patent, it does not give you immunity from infringing someone else's broader patent. For example, you may have a specific improvement patent or a special metal or gear used in a machine that you manufacture. Nevertheless you could be charged with infringement of the entire machine by one who owns a more basic patent covering the whole machine. Your patent is no defense against that patent owner's charge of infringement.

DEFENSES AGAINST A PATENT

Most people are surprised to learn that patents, even though duly and legally issued, can be declared invalid, nonenforceable, or noninfringed. In other words, a patent doesn't give you an invincible weapon, which can ride herd over and crush all infringers; rather a patent is a weapon, which, like any other, can be defeated if it has weaknesses or if it isn't used in the proper manner.

The sad fact is that over 50 percent of the patents that do get to court are held invalid, but this doesn't mean that 50 percent of all patents are invalid since the figure doesn't count the patents that don't get to court because the infringer saw the impossibility of invalidating them or didn't want to spend the $50,000 or more necessary to fight the patent.

An accused infringer of a patent can avoid liability in three different ways:

1. By showing that the claims of the patent aren't infringed

2. By showing that the patent is not enforceable

3. By showing that the patent is invalid.

Non-infringement (1) has already been covered above. A patent can be declared nonenforceable (2) if the owner of the patent has misused the patent in some way or has engaged in some illegal conduct that makes it inequitable for the owner to enforce the patent. There are old maxims in the law stating that "He who wants equity must do equity" and that "One must come into a court of equity with clean hands." Some examples of inequitable conduct that will preclude enforceability of a patent are false marking (marking products with patent numbers that don't cover the patent marked); illegal licensing practices, such as false threats of infringement; various antitrust violations; extended delay in bringing suit, which works to the prejudice of the accused infringer; and fraud on the PTO, such as withholding a valuable reference from your Statement Of Prior Art, or failing to disclose the full and truthful information about your invention in your patent application.

Patents can be invalidated (3) by prior-art references that the PTO didn't discover or use properly; by showing the specific machine covered by the patent to be inoperable; by showing that the disclosure of the patent is incomplete, that is, that it doesn't teach one skilled in the art to make and use the patented invention; by showing that the claims are vague and indefinite under Section 112; by showing that the patent was issued to the wrong inventor, etc.

As you can imagine, the subject of patent invalidity is also complex and difficult. In fact, it has been said that if enough money is spent, almost any patent can be "broken." However, patents are respected in many quarters and *billions* of dollars change hands in the United States each year for the licensing and sale of patent rights.

ECONOMIC ASPECTS OF A PATENT

As stated, a patent can be used to enforce a monopoly or to obtain license revenues if you wish to allow others to manufacture the invention. However, there is generally no sense in using the patent to enforce a monopoly unless you manufacture or use a product or products embodying the invention yourself.

If you license others to make the invention and don't manufacture the invention yourself, you can grant an exclusive license to one manufacturer or you can grant nonexclusive licenses to several manufacturers. In the case of an exclusive license, the royalty is higher, and an annual minimum should be required; but generally more licensing revenue can be obtained by granting many nonexclusive licenses, at a lower royalty.

If you manufacture the invention yourself and license one or more other manufacturers, you will have a competitive advantage in the marketplace; their costs will be higher because they have to pay you royalties. However, they may still be able to give you price competition since royalties are generally a small part of the cost of manufacture, and they may effect more important manufacturing economies that will overcome their royalty burden. Thus it often happens that licensees charge less for the product than the licensor, but this is sometimes because their product is inferior.

If you obtain a patent and are manufacturing the invention and wish to use your patent to enforce a monopoly, other manufacturers will wish to compete with you if your product is a profitable one, regardless of the strength of your patent. Only if your patent is a very strong one,—that is, if it is a pioneer invention in the field, it has broad claim coverage, there is no significant prior art extant, and it is not vulnerable to attack on any other grounds—will you be able to preclude competition; but be aware that a profitable, already engineered product will almost certainly spur imitators who will use whatever means they can to break your patent or design around it.

If your product is not broad and basic, and you still wish to enforce a monopoly, the competition generally will try to design around your patent's claims, which may take them a significant time to do because of the difficulties of engineering and testing. It thus behooves you to market your product as intensely as possible in the initial time period since the establishment of market leadership in a competitive field has a tremendous economic advantage, regardless of the competition that comes later. This is especially so if your product has a powerful, catchy, and easy-to-remember trademark, such as CROCK POT or HULA HOOP. There is a risk, however, because the competition, in attempting to design around your patent, may actually come up with a significant improvement of the invention that not only will avoid infringing your patent, but also will offer significant advantages over your invention, which can be an asset sufficient to override your initial market leadership.

I cannot stress strongly enough that a patent is only one tool to be used in marketing, and is not an invincible weapon that will keep out all competition to give you dominance in the field for 17 years. An example may best illustrate what I mean. Two clients of an antitrust lawyer colleague of mine invented an accessory, which none of the large manufacturers made, to go with a widely used consumer product. The inventors obtained a patent on the accessory; the patent had relatively narrow claim coverage. The inventors then manufactured the accessory for several years, establishing market leadership and enjoying handsome profits. However, they did not maintain an aggressive sales operation, and one of the large manufacturers of the basic item, viewing the success of the inventors' accessory, decided to manufacture its own accessory, which they did by designing around the inventors' patent. Because of the inventors' slackened sales effort and the large manufacturer's sizable and established sales force, and its ability to sell the accessory with the basic product, the inventors' sales soon faltered to a very small fraction of their former level. The inventors were most upset and couldn't understand how the situation could occur; they thought that once they had their patent, they would be free of competition for 17 years. The sad truth is that they were not adequately apprised by their patent attorney that a patent is only one tool in marketing, that the claims of a patent can be designed around (especially if the claims are narrow), and that success inevitably will breed competition, regardless of patents.

PRODUCT CLEARANCE

Suppose you want to manufacture a specific product or perform a specific process commercially. You have some reason to believe it may be covered by an in-force patent because someone else makes or performs the product or process, or the product or process is unusual. How do you find out whether you can manufacture or perform the product or process with impunity?

Unfortunately, there is no way to be 100-percent sure, because no search can cover pending patent applications, but I can give you some pretty specific instructions and guidelines.

If the process or product you wish to duplicate is already manufactured or used, look at the product, the literature accompanying it, and the packing material to see if any patent number is given. If you can get the patent number, order the patent from the Patent and Trademark Office. If the patent was issued over 17 years ago, it's expired, and the invention is in the public domain; you can manufacture or use the product or process with impunity.

If the patent is in force, read the claims carefully, diagramming them if necessary, to know exactly what is covered. You shouldn't look primarily at the drawings of the patent, but rather you must take the trouble to read and analyze the claims. If what you want to manufacture is not covered by the claims, and if you feel there is probably no other more basic patent on the thing you wish to manufacture, you are free to do so.

If the product or process you wish to manufacture is simply marked "Patented" and carries no number, your task is more difficult. You can write to the company, asking for the number and date of their patent, or whether their patent is in force, but they're not bound to answer, and you'll have given away your hand by communicating with them. You can have a (relatively cheap) search made in the PTO of all of the patents issued to the company in question, but there is no guarantee that this will uncover the patent since the patents may not be owned by the company in question; the manufacturer may simply be a licensee. The best way to determine whether an in-force patent is applicable is to make a search in the relevant classes and subclasses of the PTO, or have someone make the search for you. The search should seek to find any patents on the invention in question. This will involve a greater expenditure, but at least you will be fairly certain of your position. (If, however, there is a patent pending on the product or process, there is no way to obtain any details, even if the manufacturer marks the product "patent pending"; thus not all risks can be eliminated.)

If the product or process you wish to manufacture has been known or used in the marketplace for over 17 years, you can be pretty sure that no in-force patent will be applicable, or that even if one is applicable, it is just about to expire anyway.

If there is an in-force patent applicable, and you still wish to manufacture the product, you have several alternatives.

You can manufacture or use the product or process and hope that the patentee won't catch you. If you do this it is wise, as well as good accounting practice, to keep reasonable royalty reserves (see Chapter 9 for how to determine a reasonable royalty) in case you're ever caught. Also, you should analyze the patent, or have a patent attorney do so, to set up defenses to show that you were not a "willful" infringer since willful infringers may be subject to triple damages or attorney fees in a lawsuit. If you do manufacture without a license, be aware that the patent owner may discover and sue you and get an injunction against you prohibiting you from further manufacture. Although the idea of manufacturing without a license may seem deceitful, risky, and improbable, you should be aware that it is done all the time in the industry; the infringer simply takes the full-speed-ahead-and-damn-the-torpedoes attitude and hopes to be able to negotiate a favorable settlement or break the patent if caught.

You can also ask the patent owner for a license to manufacture under the in-force patent. However, here you take the risk, if you aren't familiar with the patent owner's practices, of being refused a license, and moreover you'll have shown your hand so that if you do manufacture, the patent owner will be looking out for you and will certainly sue or accuse you of infringement in short order.

You can also make an extended validity search to try to "break" the patent. You should use a professional, experienced searcher to do this and should expect to spend several hundred dollars or more in order to make the widest and most complete search possible. Also, you should order a copy of the PTO's file of the patent (at 30 cents per page) to see if there are any weaknesses or flaws in the patent that are not apparent from the printed patent itself. Again, the services of an attorney should be employed here, because breaking patents is tricky art and requires a highly skilled practitioner.

Your last alternative is to review the claims of the patent and then try to design around them. Often the claims of a patent, upon analysis, will be found to have one or more limitations in them that can be eliminated in your product or process so that you can make the patented invention even cheaper than the patentee; alternatively, you can design around one of the elements of the patent and make an improved device and get your own patent on it.

Unless there is an in-force patent covering an item, anyone is free to make and manufacture identical copies of it, provided that one doesn't copy the trademark of the product, and provided the shape of the product itself is not so unusual or fanciful, such as the shape of the FOTOMAT huts, that the shape itself is considered a trademark.

I am reminded of the story of one manufacturer's effort to copy a small hardware item by having it manufactured cheaply in the Orient. He sent the item overseas with instructions to make several thousand identical copies of the item. Since he didn't give any further instructions, the Oriental manufacturer did as instructed, manufacturing and shipping back several thousand copies of the item, including a faithful copy of the embossed trademark of the manufacturer's competitor. The manufacturer then had to spend significant money obliterating the trademark, thereby losing his entire profit in the process.

Some Odds and Ends to Consider

In this chapter I'll delve into some miscellaneous topics which, although not generally used in the exploitation and development of inventions, are useful as background knowledge and in certain special situations that may arise.

APPEALS

As explained in Chapter 10, if you've received a final office action with which you disagree, and you are unable to change the examiner's mind, and you don't think you can present any better claims in a continuation application, you can appeal to the Board of Appeals, a tribunal of examiners-in-chief in the PTO. To appeal you first must file a Notice of Appeal, a simple form which appears as Form 31 in the back of the Rules of Practice. The Notice of Appeal must be accompanied by a $50 appeal fee and must be filed within the period for response to the final action. This period is normally 3 months from the date the final action was mailed, but this period is automatically extended to 4 months if you file a response to the final action within the 3-month period.

Within 2 months of filing the Notice of Appeal, you must file an appeal brief, together with a second $50 brief fee. The brief must be filed in triplicate and should contain a description of the invention and a copy of the claims on appeal. See Rules 191 to 198 for further details. If you wish to have an oral hearing before the board, you must request it at the time you file your brief, but oral hearings are not encouraged. If you do have a hearing, you will be allowed 20 minutes for oral argument, and 15 minutes will be allowed for the examiner's presentation.

After you file a brief, the examiner occasionally will allow the case, but if not, will file a brief, too (termed an "Examiner's Answer"). You may then file a reply brief limited to any new arguments raised in the Examiner's Answer.

If the Board of Appeals disagrees with the examiner, they will issue a written decision, generally sending the case back with instructions to allow the case. If they agree with the examiner, their decision will state why they believe the case is unpatentable.

If the Board of Appeals upholds the examiner and you still believe your invention is patentable, you can take a further appeal within 60 days of the date of the board decision either to the Court of Customs and Patent Appeals (CCPA) in Washington, or by filing suit against the Commissioner of Patents and Trademarks in the U.S. District Court for the District of Columbia. The district court route is used when an applicant desires to present some new evidence regarding the patentability of an invention. If the suit is lost in the district court, you can appeal to the United States Court of Appeals for the District of Columbia Circuit, and if suit is lost in the CCPA or the court of appeals, you can even request the United States Supreme Court to hear your case, although the Supreme Court rarely hears patent appeals.

If the examiner has issued a ruling on a matter other than the patentability of your claims—for example, has refused to enter an amendment or has required the case to be restricted to one of several inventions—and you disagree with this position, and the examiner has refused to budge after you have requested reconsideration, you can't appeal, but you can petition the Commissioner of Patents and Trademarks to overrule the examiner; see *Petitions to the Commissioner* below.

ASSIGNMENTS

As I've mentioned before, both a patent application and a patent can be sold, given away, or otherwise transferred; even a partial interest in each can be transferred. However, in order to transfer a patent or patent application, a written document, termed in the law an "assignment," is required.

Documents for assignment of a patent application or patent are not provided in this book since they are generally used only in connection with the sale of a business or when an employed inventor files a patent application. As stated in Chapter 9, if you are able to sell your invention to a company, a far more complex document, namely a license agreement, will usually be used. However, there are short assignment documents in the PTO's publication, *General Information Concerning Patents*, but these assignments are only useful in transferring the U.S. rights to a patent or patent application; thus it's best to get professional legal advice in situations where a patent application or patent is to be assigned, since you may wish to transfer foreign rights, and many other factors may require the use of a more complex document.

An assignment document should be recorded in the PTO after signature, preferably as soon as possible so that the new owner's name can be associated with the patent application or patent in the PTO's records. Also, if an assignment is not recorded within 3 months and the former owner of the patent application or patent makes a subsequent (fraudulent) sale of the patent application or patent, the second new "owner" of the patent application or patent could hold a superior interest to the first owner. The fee for recording an assignment is $20; when the PTO records an assignment, it simply photographs it, stamps it with the date and location (reel and frame numbers) of the photographs, and returns the recorded assignment back to the new owner, just as your county recorder will do with the deed to your house.

If a patent application is assigned before the base issue fee is paid, the assignment information should be included on the base issue fee—transmittal form so that the name of the new owner, as well as the inventor's name, will appear on the patent. If a patent is assigned, there is no way to have the PTO print the new owner's name on the patent.

COPYRIGHTS

A copyright is a right given by law to exclude others from publishing or copying literary, dramatical, musical, or artistic works. While a patent effectively can protect ideas per se (assuming the claims are drawn broadly enough), a copyright can protect only an author's or artist's particular form of expression of ideas, and not ideas per se. Thus, for example, while a copyright can protect the particular arrangement of words which constitute a book or play, it cannot protect the plot, theory, or message of the book or play. Some specific works that are copyrightable are books, poetry, plays, songs, catalogs, photographs, advertisements, labels, movies, maps, drawings, sculpture, prints and art reproductions, game boards and rules, and recordings. Certain materials, such as titles, slogans, lettering, ideas, plans, forms, and nonoriginal material, are not registerable for copyright, although certain common-law (ancient judge-made law) rights may exist. U.S. government publications, by custom, are not copyrighted and may almost always be freely copied and sold by anyone, if desired.

It is important to distinguish between a common-law copyright and a registered copyright. As soon as a work is created, and assuming it was not published without a copyright notice, common law can be employed to protect the work against theft and unauthorized duplications. But it is wise to register the copyright (by filling out the appropriate form and sending a copy of the work and the proper fee to the Copyright Office) because registration gives the copyright owner strong, clearly defined, statutory rights in federal courts. Under the copyright laws, which have been recently revised, the old common-law right of "fair use" has been codified; this allows limited, noncommercial copying of a copyrighted work, whether registered or not.

As indicated, a work can be published before the copyright is registered without loss of rights, provided it contains a copyright notice; this consists of the word "Copyright," or the symbol ©, together with the author's or copyright owner's name and the date, for example "Copyright 1978 Mary

Jones." It is desirable also to add the words "All rights reserved" to secure full foreign rights. While it is advisable to register the copyright as soon after publication as possible, there is actually no time limit for doing so; however, a lawsuit under the copyright laws cannot be brought until registration has been effected. Under the new copyright law, all works can be registered for copyright before publication, if desired.

The Copyright Office is technically part of the Library of Congress and is not associated with the Patent and Trademark Office or the Department of Commerce. Unlike the PTO, which examines patent applications and trademark applications for novelty, the Copyright Office does not make novelty examinations or searches to determine whether a similar work has already been copyrighted; all works which are sent to the Copyright Office are registered, provided the formal requirements are met. Thus the registration of a copyright is merely the recording of a claim of originality, and does not provide a presumption of originality, as does a trademark registration or patent. In fact it has been said that the Copyright Office would even register a copyright on the Bible, if an application were filed!

Under the new law, the Copyright Office provides just four basic application forms: Form SR for sound recordings, Form VA for works in the visual arts (photos, maps, sculpture, labels, etc.), Form PA for works of the performing arts (music, plays, movies, etc.), and Form TX for all other forms of expression (books, poetry, catalogs, advertising copy, periodicals, etc.). The registration fee is $10, and full instructions are provided on the application forms. The forms and circulars of general information can be obtained free by writing to Copyright Office, Washington, DC 20559.

The term of a copyright registration was formerly 28 years, renewable for another 28 years, but the new copyright law was approved in October 1976 and took effect January 1978. For works renewed after 1977 it changed the second term to 47 years.

For works created after 1977, one of two terms is applicable. For copyrightable work created for the author's own benefit, the single term of the copyright is the author's life plus 50 years. If the copyrightable work was created by an author commissioned or hired by another, the single term of the copyright is 75 years from publication or 100 years from creation of the work, whichever term is shorter.

Most patent attorneys handle copyrights, but many authors and artists secure their own copyrights since the procedures are so simple. There are also lawyers who specialize in copyright litigation.

DEPOSIT ACCOUNTS

If you do a good deal of business with the PTO, it is advisable to open a deposit account. Such an account costs $10 to open, and a minimum $50 balance must generally be restored each month. The PTO pays no interest on its deposit accounts, but does issue monthly statements. All PTO services and fees (such as filing fees, drawing amendments, issue fees, etc.) can be charged to a deposit account, except that copies of patents must be ordered by check or with 50-cent patent-order coupons, which can be purchased through a deposit account.

To open a deposit account with the PTO, simply send a letter to the Commissioner of Patents and Trademarks, Washington, DC 20231, with a check for at least $50, requesting that a deposit account be opened in your name. The PTO will open the account and send you appropriate forms and information on how to use the account.

INTERFERENCES

An interference is a proceeding in the PTO that is instituted to determine priority of inventorship when two or more inventors have claimed the same invention. An interference can be instituted between two or more patent applications, or between one or more patent applications and one or more patents. (Interferences between patents are very rare and can only be tried in federal court.)

An interference is a very complex proceeding so that unless you're an exceptional individual, if your patent application is ever involved in an interference, you should seek professional legal help, although it will be very expensive. Rules 201 to 287 govern interferences. The best advice I can give is to be well prepared, in case your application ever becomes involved in interference; record all steps in your invention development (conception, building, etc.) carefully as outlined in Chapter 2. Interferences are handled by a PTO tribunal termed the Board of Patent Interferences.

As stated earlier, the winner in an interference will not, unfortunately, be the first to file a patent application on the invention; rather it is the first to "reduce his invention to practice" (file a patent application *or* build and test the invention), *unless* the other party conceives the invention first and has been diligent in effecting a reduction to practice.

The PTO generally institutes an interference when they discover two patent applications claiming the same invention. However, since the PTO is such a large, complex, and populous organization, and since its employees do not always do perfect work, mistakes are sometimes made, and an application that should have been involved in an interference with another application may be allowed to issue as a patent without an interference being declared. If this occurs and an examiner or a patent applicant sees the patent which claims the same invention as a pending application, an interference can be declared with the patent, provided the patent has not been out for more than 1 year. An interference with a patent is instituted by first presenting the claims of the patent in the patent application so that both the patent and the patent application will contain identical claims. Thus if you see a patent which *claims* your invention, you can get your pending application into interference with the patent by copying the claims of the patent in your application, identifying the patent from which you copied the claims to the examiner, and showing how your application supports these claims.

On the other hand, if you are granted a patent, be aware that there may be patent applicants whose applications contain the same invention as yours; all such persons have 1 year from your patent's date of issuance to copy your claims in their applications to get into interference with you.

INVENTION DEVELOPERS

Invention developers are companies or organizations that generally run ads in newspapers, magazines, etc. stating "Inventions and Ideas Wanted!" These companies will require you to pay them a relatively large fee, in return for which they will try to sell your invention or have it manufactured, sometimes also taking a part (for example, 20 percent) of your invention, and sometimes also hiring a patent attorney or agent to prepare a patent application on your invention for you.

The fees charged by invention developers are generally relatively high ($1000 to $2000 and up) because they have very high overhead and advertising expenses. I believe that the fees charged are exorbitantly high in relation to the services rendered, and moreover, many invention developers are downright incompetent and dishonest. If I were an inventor, I would avoid all invention developers like the plague.

If you do encounter invention developers, before paying any money or signing on the dotted line, I suggest you ask what percent of their clientele have had inventions licensed through them and how much royalty income they have obtained for their clients in relation to fees received. If they balk at answering these questions, you know they have something to hide. California now has a regulatory statute that requires invention developers to provide this information, but unfortunately most states have not been so diligent in policing the field.

As stated in Chapter 9, the marketing efforts of almost all invention developers leave much to be desired. Generally, they will do little more than write a brief blurb describing your invention and send it to prospective manufacturers in the appropriate fields. If you follow the advice in Chapter 9, you should be able to do a far better job, at a very small fraction of the cost of what you would pay an invention developer.

INVENTORS' ORGANIZATIONS

In recent years many inventors' organizations have developed or sprung up in order to provide inventors with information and ideas, and to provide various seminars and trade fairs where inventions can be exhibited. As far as I am aware, all these organizations are legitimate and honest, and provide reasonable value for the membership or other fees charged. Some of these organizations are: American Society of Inventors, 1317 Spruce Street, Philadelphia, PA 19107; Inventors Workshop International, 16218 Ventura Boulevard, Encino, CA 91436; California Inventors Council, P.O. Box 376, Main Office Station, San Francisco, CA 94101; Intellectual Property Owners, Inc., 1800 K Street, N.W., Washington, DC 20006, and Oregon Inventors Council, P.O. 3288, Eugene, OR 94703. The last organization, which is associated with the University of Oregon, will do a commercial evaluation of your invention for a $25 fee.

PATENT AGENTS, ATTORNEYS, AND LAWYERS

A *patent agent* is an individual with some technical training (generally an undergraduate degree in engineering) who is licensed by the PTO to prepare and prosecute patent applications. A patent agent cannot appear in court and cannot handle the licensing of inventions, patents, or patent applications; cannot handle trademarks; and cannot handle infringement suits.

A patent attorney or patent lawyer has all the powers of a patent agent, and in addition is licensed to practice law by the bar of at least one state. Thus, patent attorneys and lawyers must be licensed by two authorities, the PTO and a state bar. (In California a patent *lawyer* is licensed to practice law in the California courts, and a patent *attorney* generally is licensed by a state other than California and thus cannot practice before the California courts, but may handle licensing agreements and trademarks.)

All patent agents and attorneys (including patent lawyers) are listed in the PTO's publication *Attorneys and Agents Registered to Practice Before the U.S. Patent and Trademark Office* (A&ARTP).

All active patent agents and attorneys are either in private practice (a law firm), or employed by a corporation or the government. Most attorneys in private practice charge about $60 to $125 an hour. But many corporate-employed or retired attorneys also have private clients and charge about one-third to one-half of what their downtown counterparts charge. To find these "discount" attorneys (whose services are usually just as good or better than those of the law firms), look in the geographical section of A&ARTP for corporate-employed or retired attorneys in your area; the latter can usually be identified by having an address in a residential, rather than downtown section. Many corporate-employed and retired attorneys will be delighted to help you with the preparation and/or prosecution of your patent application, so that, as stated earlier, if preparing and prosecuting a patent application seems too formidable to you, you can do much of the work yourself and use a corporate-employed attorney for the rest. You may be able to get your patent issued for one-tenth the cost and know exactly what is going on in addition. A&ARTP also indicates those attorneys and agents who are employed by the federal government; under a special statute these attorneys and agents may not accept private clients.

The PTO gives its "agent's examination" for license to practice patent law about once every 10 months. To take the examination, one must have a technical undergraduate degree or equivalent technical training and experience, or be a licensed attorney.

THE PATENT AND TRADEMARK OFFICE

The PTO is located in a complex of modern, medium-rise buildings in Arlington, Virginia, informally called "Crystal City." Although, as stated, all mail must be addressed to Commissioner of Patents and Trademarks, Washington, DC 20231, the PTO is physically located at South 26th Street and U.S. 1 (Jefferson Davis Highway) in Arlington, Virginia, about half a mile due west of the Washington National Airport. The PTO is technically part of the Department of Commerce (which is headquartered in Washington), but the PTO is generally autonomous.

The PTO employs about 1200 examiners, all of whom have technical undergraduate degrees, in such fields as electrical engineering, chemistry, or physics. Many examiners also are attorneys. The PTO also has about an equal number of clerical, supervisory, and support personnel. The Commissioner of Patents and Trademarks is appointed by the President, and most of the high officials of the PTO have to be approved by Congress. Most patent examiners are very well paid; a journeyman examiner (10 years experience) usually makes $30,000 to $35,000 a year.

PETITIONS TO THE COMMISSIONER

The Commissioner of Patents and Trademarks has power to overrule almost anyone in the PTO except the Board of Appeals and the Board of Patent Interferences. Thus, if you think you've been treated unfairly or illegally, you can petition the Commissioner to overrule a subordinate. For example, if the examiner has made a ruling regarding your patent application (other than a rejection of claims), you can petition the Commissioner to overrule this ruling. If you forgot to pay your base issue fee or balance of issue fee in time, you can petition the Commissioner within 3 months of the due date to accept a delayed payment of the fee. Also, if you've failed to respond to an office action in time, you can petition the Commissioner to revive your abandoned application ($15 fee). If you would like your patent application examined ahead of its turn because you're sick or old, an infringement is occurring, you need a patent in order to get capital, or your invention relates to the use of energy or ecology or safety (such as recombinant DNA), you can petition to have your application made special; see MPEP 708.02 for the requirements.

If you do petition the Commissioner for any reason, you must make your grounds as strong and as complete as possible. Generally, most petitions must be accompanied by a verified showing, which means a statement signed by you and either notarized or containing a declaration such as that in the last paragraph of Form 4 of this book.

PLANT PATENTS

Many people are surprised to learn that patents can be obtained on plants. If you've developed a new, asexually reproduced plant, you can get a patent on it, generally in the same manner as you get a regular 17-year apparatus patent. In a plant patent application only one claim is permitted and color drawings or photos can be used. See Rules 161 to 167 if you wish to file a plant patent. Copies of plant patents in color cost $1.

TRADEMARKS

A trademark is any word, name, symbol, or design used by a merchant to identify his goods and distinguish them from others, that is, a trademark is a brand name. While the media often refer to trademarks as "trade names," a trade name more properly means the name of a business, such as "Procter & Gamble," although certain trademarks (such as FORD) are also trade names. In addition to trademarks, there are service marks, certification marks and collective marks, which are used to identify services, give certifications, and identify organizations, in the same way as trademarks are used for branding goods.

If you wish to adopt a trademark and use it on goods, you may do so with almost any word or design, provided it isn't already in use for similar goods. To determine whether a trademark is already in use, a search should first be made in the PTO's trademark files or in commercial directories to be sure there is no existing similar mark. There are also specialized trademark-search organizations that do trademark searches cheaply and efficiently.

If you adopt a unique trademark and apply it to your goods, it's entitled to common-law protection, which means that you can sue anyone who uses a similar mark for similar goods for unfair competition to halt use of the mark. You do not have to register your mark in order to bring and win such a suit. However, if you do adopt and use a trademark on your goods, you should register it in your state trademark office, and the Patent and Trademark Office. Once your mark is registered, it will be much easier to sue infringers since the registration gives a presumption of exclusivity and ownership.

If you do wish to register a trademark in your state, it must have first been used in intrastate commerce. Write to your state's secretary of state for forms and instructions. If you wish to register a trademark federally, it must have first been used in interstate commerce; write to the Commissioner of Patents and Trademarks for an appropriate form. Trademark application forms for the PTO are provided for corporations, individuals, and partnerships.

It is very important to use a trademark properly once you've adopted it as a brand name for your goods. Before it's registered, you should indicate it's a trademark by providing the superscript "TM" after the mark. Once the mark is registered, provide the superscript ® or indicate that the mark is registered in the U.S. Patent and Trademark Office ("Reg. U.S. Pat. & T.M. Off."). Word trademarks should always be used as brand names, that is, they should be used as adjective modifiers in association with the general name of the goods to which they apply, and should not be used as a substitute for the name of the goods. For example, if you're making and selling can openers and have adopted the trademark AJAX, always use the words "can opener" after AJAX and never refer to an AJAX alone. Otherwise the name can become generic and be lost, as happened to "cellophane" and "aspirin."

Trademarks can also be "weak" or "strong," depending upon how unusual the mark is. Weak marks are more difficult to police or register than strong marks. Examples of weak marks are SUPREME, ROYAL, and MAJESTIC; these terms are descriptive or are very common and in wide use. An example of a strong mark is KODAK, a very unusual, artificial term. While strong marks are easier to police and register, they are harder to promote and advertise.

THE MAIN POINTS TO REMEMBER

Now that you've reached the end, I feel it would be useful to review what I consider to be the main points to remember and keep in mind when working with inventions and patent applications. If you follow these main points, the rest will fall into place easily or can readily be accomplished, but if you don't follow these main points, even perfect compliance with the rest will avail you little.

1. Keep good, clear, complete, and witnessed records of your conception, development, building, and testing of your inventions.

2. Make your patent application as complete as possible; tell the truth, the whole truth, and nothing but the truth about your invention, and tell the PTO about all prior art, knowledge, and use of which you are aware.

3. Make your claims as broad as possible; eliminate as many elements as you can from the broadest claims and write the remaining elements in as broad a manner as possible.

4. Never say anything negative or detrimental about your claims or invention and never admit that the prior art shows any feature of your invention.

5. Persevere with your invention and the development of it. The more and the harder you work on your invention the greater will be your chances of success.

6. If you need additional information, turn to a source in the Bibliography, ask an examiner or clerk at the PTO what to do, or as a last resort, ask a patent agent or attorney.

7. Remember the "one-year rule" (Chapter 4): you *must* file your patent application within one year after any publication or offer of sale of anything which embodied your invention.

8. Do your commercial evaluation carefully and do reevaluations from time to time.

9. Try to file a patent application before trying to sell your invention to any prospective manufacturer, and when you do try to sell it, stress its profit potential above all else.

10. Include the narrowest possible claim in your application after the first office action and be sure to do your amendment meticulously and completely.

11. Make your foreign filing decisions about 8 to 10 months after your U.S. filing date.

Good luck and successful inventing!

Bibliography

It has been said that knowing where to look is half the battle of knowing the law. With this in mind, this chapter is provided to help avoid having to hire a patent lawyer in case you encounter any situations or problems which this book does not cover. I've also provided a number of resources and publications I feel will be of interest to inventors and other creative people. I provide comment generally where the title of the book or source isn't self-explanatory. Most books which can't be found in a general or business library may be found in a law library.

Government Publications

Annual Index of Patents. Issued yearly in two volumes: *Patentees* and *Titles of Inventions.* U.S. Government Printing Office (GPO), Washington, DC 20402. Comes out long after the end of year to which it pertains, for instance, in September. Available in search libraries.

Answers to Questions Frequently Asked about Patents. U.S. Patent and Trademark Office (PTO), Washington, DC 20231. Free.

Attorneys and Agents Registered to Practice before the U.S. Patent and Trademark Office. Annual. GPO. Contains alphabetical and geographical listings of all attorneys and agents. $5.00*

Classification Definitions. Many loose-leaf volumes. Contains definitions for each of 66,000 subclasses. Available in search libraries.

Code of Federal Regulations (Title 37—Patents, Trademarks, and Copyrights). Revised annually. GPO. Contains U.S. Patent and Trademark Office's patent and trademark rules, forms, and drawing symbols; also contains Copyright Office's rules. A must for all who prosecute their own patent applications. $3.00.

Federal Government, rev. ed., 1974, Library of Congress, GPO. Lists government information resources and government-sponsored information analysis centers. $4.25.

* Prices where given were current at press time, but, check before ordering since increases have been occurring frequently.

General Information Concerning Patents. Revised periodically. GPO. 75 cents.

General Information Concerning Trademarks. Revised periodically. GPO. $1.50.

Guide for Patent Draftsmen. GPO. Not needed if *Code of Federal Regulations* (Title 37—Patents, Trademarks, and Copyrights) is purchased. 65 cents.

Index to Classification. Loose-leaf. Contains 66,000 subclasses and cross-references arranged alphabetically. Available in search libraries.

Manual of Classification. Loose-leaf. Contains 300 search classes for patents arranged numerically, together with subclasses in each class. Available in search libraries.

Manual of Patent Examining Procedure. Revisions issued several times per year. GPO. Called "the patent examiner's bible," the *MPEP* provides answers to almost every conceivable question about patent prosecution. $19.65 (including revisions for indefinite period).

Monthly Checklist of State Publications. Library of Congress; GPO. Lists publications prepared by state governments.

Patents and Inventions: An Information Aid to Inventors. GPO. $1.75.

Patent Laws. GPO. $2.10.

Patent Official Gazette. Issued each Tuesday. GPO. Contains drawing and main claim of every patent issued each week, miscellaneous notices; lists inventors, assignees, etc. $300, first class, per year.

Questions and Answers about Plant Patents. PTO. Free.

Questions and Answers about Trademarks. PTO. Free.

Small Business Administration. The SBA's list of free publications has three sections: "Management Aids," "Small Marketer's Aids," and "Small Business Bibliographies." Listed are dozens of excellent, concise business pamphlets, such as no. 82, *Reducing the Risks in Product Development.* Order from your local SBA office or SBA, Washington DC 20416.

Trademark Official Gazette. GPO. Lists trademarks published for opposition and registered each week. $88.40 per year.

U.S. Government Organization Manual. GPO.

Law Books Relating to Patents

Corpus Juris Secundum, vol. 69, *Patents.* A legal encyclopedia which will answer almost any question on patent law. West Pub. Co., St. Paul, 1958 (supplemented annually). Any law library.

"International Patent Planning," *Harvard Business Review,* March-April 1967, pp. 56–72.

Journal of the Patent Office Society. Monthly. Box 2600, Arlington, VA 22202. Contains articles on patent law and advertisements by patent services, for instance, drafts persons, drawing reproducers, searchers. Subscription $7.00 per year.

Kayton, I. *Patent Preparation and Prosecution Practice.* Six volumes. Patent Resources Institute, Washington, DC 20006, 1976. $350.

Landis, J. L. *The Mechanics of Patent Claim Drafting,* 2d ed., 1974, Practicing Law Institute, 810 Seventh Avenue, NY 10019. $35.

Martindale-Hubbell Law Directory, Martindale-Hubbell, New York. Annual. Lists patent attorneys by geographical area (including some foreign) and gives ages, colleges, and sometimes other information about attorneys. Any law library.

Milgrim, R. M. *Trade Secrets.* Matthew Bender, New York, 1967, $50.

Nordhaus, R. C. *Patent License Agreements.* Jural, Chicago 60626, 1976. $30.

Wade, W. *Check List for Negotiating Agreements on Patents, Know-How, Trademarks and Joint Ventures.* Advance House, Box 334, Ardmore, PA 19003, 1965. $5.

White, R. S. *Patent Litigation, Procedure & Tactics.* Matthew Bender, New York, 1974. $50.

General Interest Books Relating to Patents and Inventions

Clark, R. W. *Edison—The Man Who Made the Future.* Putnam, New York, 1977. $12.95.

Dorl, R. T. *Strategy for Patent Profits.* Noyes Dev. Corp., Park Ridge, N.J., 1967.

Gilmore, F. E. *How to Invent.* Gulf Pub., Houston, 1959. $5.50.

Inventing: How the Masters Did It. Moore Pub., Durham, N.C., 1974. $8.95.

Lessing, L. *Man of High Fidelity: Edwin Howard Armstrong.* Lippincott, Philadelphia, 1956. Biography of the inventor of frequency modulation; he committed suicide because of the delays and difficulties of patent litigation against the large radio companies, but his widow eventually collected millions in settlements.

McNair, E. P. *How to Become a Successful Inventor: Design a Gadget in Your Spare Time and Strike It Rich.* Hastings House, New York, 1973. $7.95.

Paige, R. E. *Complete Guide to Making Money with Your Ideas and Inventions.* Barnes & Noble, New York, 1976. Excellent guide to invention marketing. $2.95 paperback.

Poole, W., and G. Poole. *Men Who Pioneered Inventions.* Dodd, Mead, New York, 1969. Studies of seventeen great inventions.

Pratt, F. *All about Famous Inventors and Their Inventions.* Random House, New York, 1955. $4.39.

Walsh, J. E. *One Day at Kitty Hawk.* Crowell, New York, 1975. The story of the development and sale of rights to the airplane. $10.00.

Publications Relating to Business

Adams, A. B. *Apollo Handbook of Practical Public Relations.* Apollo Editions, New York, 1970. How to get publicity. $2.65 paper.

Aljain, G. W. *Purchasing Handbook.* McGraw-Hill, New York, 1973. How to run a purchasing department. $29.50.

Applied Sciences and Technology Index. H. W. Wilson Co., Bronx, NY 10452. Lists engineering, scientific, and industrial periodicals by subject.

Ayer Directory of Newspapers and Periodicals. Annual. Ayer Press, Philadelphia, PA 19106. Lists United States newspapers and magazines geographically.

Bacon's Publicity Checker—Magazines, Bacon's Publicity Checker—Newspapers. Annual. Bacon Pub. Co., Chicago. Classifies all sources of publicity.

Bootstrap Newsletter. Box 506, Cupertino, CA 95014.

California Manufacturers Register. Annual. 1115 S. Boyle Ave., Los Angeles, CA 90023. 72–50.

Carson, G. B. (ed.) *Production Handbook.* Ronald Press, New York, 1972. $27.50.

Coman, E. T. *Sources of Business Information.* University of California Press, Berkeley, CA 94729, 1964. $11.

Conover Mast Purchasing Directory. Conover Mast, Denver, CO 80206. Annual. Three volumes. Manufacturers listed alphabetically and by products. Also lists trademarks.

Cossman, E. J. *How I Made a Million in Mail Order.* Prentice-Hall, Englewood Cliffs, NJ, 1963. $8.95.

Dible, D. M. *Up Your Own Organization.* Entrepreneur Press, c/o Hawthorn Books, New York. How to start and finance a business. $14.95.

Dun & Bradstreet Reference Book. Six issues per year. Lists three million businesses in United States and Canada. D&B also publishes specialized reference books and directories, e.g., *Apparel Trades Book* and *Metalworking Marketing Directory.*

Entrepreneurs Magazine. International Entrepreneurs' Assn., 631 Wilshire Blvd., Santa Monica, CA 90401. Predicts new business opportunities and needs. $3 sample copy.

Frey, A. W. (ed.) *Marketing Handbook.* Ronald Press, New York, 1965. Guide to selling goods and services. $19.95.

Grant, M. M., and N. Cote. *Directory of Business and Financial Services.* Special Libraries Assn., NY 10003.

Guide to American Directories. 9th ed. B. Klein Pubs., New York, 1975. Lists directories by industry, profession, and function.

Guide to Venture Capital Sources. Capital Publishing Co., Chicago, IL 60603. $42.50.

Hofheimer, F. S. *Mailing Lists Catalog.* 29 E. 22d St., NY 10010.

Idea Source Guide Newsletter. Box 66, Fairless Hills, PA 19030.

International Yellow Pages. R. H. Donnelley Corp., NY 10017. Similar to local Yellow Pages, but provides foreign business listings.

MacRae's Blue Book. MacRae's Blue Book Co., Hinsdale, IL 60521. Sources of industrial equipment, products, and materials. Also lists trademarks.

Moneymaking Opportunities Magazine. 13263 Ventura Blvd., Studio City, CA 91604.

Nicholas, T. *How to Form Your Own Corporation without a Lawyer for Under $50.* Enterprise Pub., Wilmington, DE 19810. $14.95.

Nicholas, T. *Where The Money Is and How to Get It.* Enterprise Pub., Wilmington, DE 19810, 1976. $14.95.

Potentials In Marketing Magazine. 731 Hennepin Avenue, Minneapolis, MN 55403.

Standard & Poor's Register of Corporations, Directors & Executives. Annual. Three volumes.

Synthesis Magazine. Box 157, Manhattan Beach, CA. Business ideas.

Thomas Register of American Manufacturers. Thomas Pub., NY 10001. Eleven volumes. Similar to *Conover Mast Directory* above.

Trademark Register of the United States, Annual. Trademark Register, Washington Bldg., Washington, DC 20005. Lists all registered trademarks by subject matter classes. $49.

Ulrich's International Periodicals Directory. R. R. Bowker Co., NY 10036. Lists periodicals by subject.

Venture Capital Monthly. S. M. Rubel Co., Chicago, IL.

Books Relating to Self-Improvement

I believe that the real key to success and happiness (in inventing as well as life), lies principally within each individual's own mind. A positive, optimistic attitude, hard work and perseverance, the willingness to take full responsibility for one's own destiny, and living and thinking mainly in the present time—rather than luck, inherited abilities, and circumstances—are principally responsible for success and happiness. I have therefore provided a list of books whose main purpose is to prime you with the attitudes to secure such success and happiness, so that you'll be able to use *Patent It Yourself!* as effectively as possible.

Berkowitz, B., and M. Newman. *How to Be Your Own Best Friend.* Ballantine, New York. 1971, $1.50 paperback.

Branden, Nathaniel. *The Psychology of Self-Esteem.* Nash, Los Angeles, 1971. $1.95 paperback.

Dyer, W. W. *Pulling Your Own Strings,* Funk and Wagnalls, New York, 1978. $8.75.

Dyer, W. W. *Your Erroneous Zones.* Funk & Wagnalls, New York, 1976. $2.25 paperback.

Ellis, A., and R. A. Harper. *A New Guide to Rational Living.* Wilshire Book Co., Los Angeles, 1975. $3 paperback.

Hill, N. *Think and Grow Rich.* Wilshire Book Co., 1976. $3 paperback.

James, M., and D. Jongeward. *Born to Win.* Addison-Wesley, Menlo Park, CA, 1971. $5.95 paperback.

Karbo, J. *Lazy Man's Way to Riches,* 17105 S. Pacific, Sunset Beach, CA 90742. 1976. $10 (refundable if dissatisfied) paperback.

Maltz, M. *Psycho-Cybernetics,* Wilshire Book Co., N. Hollywood, CA. 1960. $2 paperback.

Forms

* The forms on pages 166 through 199 (with the exception of Form. No. 7 which is entirely mine) are adapted from United States government material and are included here for the use of the reader. They may be copied manually on a typewriter or mechanically reproduced on a copying machine.

form 1   Request letter for Disclosure Document Program.

```
                                    _____
                                    Date


Commissioner of Patents and Trademarks
Washington, District of Columbia 20231

                    Request for Participation In
                    Disclosure Document Program:
                    Disclosure of_____
                                        Your Name
                    Entitled_____
                                    Title of Disclosure


Sir:

        Attached is a disclosure of my above-entitled inven-
tion (consisting of_____sheets of written description and
_____separate drawings or photos), a $10 check, a stamped,
addressed return envelope, and a duplicate copy of this letter.

        It is respectfully requested that this disclosure be
accepted and retained for two years (or longer if I later refer
to it in a paper filed in a patent application) under the Dis-
closure Document Program.


                        Very respectfully,



                        _____
                        Your signature



                        _____
                        Print name



                        _____
                        Address


                        _____


Enclosures:
  As stated above
```

form 2   Reference letter for Disclosure Document Program.

IN THE UNITED STATES PATENT AND TRADEMARK OFFICE

Ser. No.:_____

Filed:_____

Inventor(s):_____

Title:_____

Group Art Unit:_____

Examiner:_____

_____

Disclosure Document Reference Letter

Commissioner of Patents and Trademarks
Washington, District of Columbia 20231

Sir:

A disclosure document as identified below was previously filed in the Patent and Trademark Office. As this disclosure relates to the above patent application, it is requested that this Disclosure Document be retained and referenced to the above application.

Disclosure Document Title:_____

Disclosure Document Number:_____

Disclosure Document Filing Date:_____

Very respectfully,

_____
Signed name

_____   _____
Date   Typed name, Inventor

_____
Address

_____

form 3   Transmittal letter for patent application.

                                                    Date _____

Commissioner of Patents and Trademarks
Washington, District of Columbia 20231

Sir:

        Attached for filing are the following patent

application papers:

        Inventor(s):_____

                     _____

        Title:_____

              _____

        Pages of Specification and Claims:_____

        Sheets of Drawing_____

        Date Application was signed:_____

                              Base Fee = $65

        Total Claims_____-10=_____x 2= $_____

    Independent Claims____-1 =_____x10= $_____

        Check Enclosed for Total: $_____

                        Very respectfully,

_____   _____
Signature of Inventor #2   Signature of Inventor #1

_____   _____
Typed Name of Inventor #2   Typed Name of Inventor #1

_____   _____
Address   Address

_____   _____

form 4 Declaration for patent application.

DECLARATION

Original Application

As a below named inventor, I declare that the information given herein is true, that I believe that I am the original, first and sole inventor if only one name is listed at 201 below, or a joint inventor if plural inventors are named below at 201–203, of the invention entitled:

....

....

which is described and claimed in the attached specification, that I do not know and do not believe that the same was ever known or used in the United States of America before my or our invention thereof or patented or described in any printed publication in any country before my or our invention thereof, or more than one year prior to this application, or in public use or on sale in the United States of America more than one year prior to this application, that the invention has not been patented or made the subject of an inventor's certificate issued before the date of this application in any country foreign to the United States of America on an application filed by me or my legal representatives or assigns more than twelve months prior to this application and that no application for patent or inventor's certificate on this invention has been filed by me or my legal representatives or assigns in any country foreign to the United States of America. I acknowledge a duty to disclose information of which I am aware and which is material to the examination of this application.

SEND CORRESPONDENCE TO:	DIRECT TELEPHONE CALLS TO: (name and telephone number)

		LAST NAME	FIRST NAME	MIDDLE NAME	
201	**FULL NAME OF INVENTOR**	LAST NAME	FIRST NAME	MIDDLE NAME	
	RESIDENCE & CITIZENSHIP	CITY	STATE OR FOREIGN COUNTRY	COUNTRY OF CITIZENSHIP	
	POST OFFICE ADDRESS	POST OFFICE ADDRESS	CITY	STATE OR COUNTRY	ZIP CODE
202	**FULL NAME OF INVENTOR**	LAST NAME	FIRST NAME	MIDDLE NAME	
	RESIDENCE & CITIZENSHIP	CITY	STATE OR FOREIGN COUNTRY	COUNTRY OF CITIZENSHIP	
	POST OFFICE ADDRESS	POST OFFICE ADDRESS	CITY	STATE OR COUNTRY	ZIP CODE
203	**FULL NAME OF INVENTOR**	LAST NAME	FIRST NAME	MIDDLE NAME	
	RESIDENCE & CITIZENSHIP	CITY	STATE OR FOREIGN COUNTRY	COUNTRY OF CITIZENSHIP	
	POST OFFICE ADDRESS	POST OFFICE ADDRESS	CITY	STATE OR COUNTRY	ZIP CODE

I further declare that all statements made herein of my own knowledge are true and that all statements made on information and belief are believed to be true; and further that these statements were made with the knowledge that willful false statements and the like so made are punishable by fine or imprisonment, or both, under section 1001 of Title 18 of the United States Code, and that such willful false statements may jeopardize the validity of the application or any patent issuing thereon.

SIGNATURE OF INVENTOR 201	SIGNATURE OF INVENTOR 202	SIGNATURE OF INVENTOR 203
DATE	DATE	DATE

form 5   Statement of prior art.

Inventor(s):

Serial No.   Group Art Unit:

Filed: Examiner:

Title:

STATEMENT OF PRIOR ART

Commissioner of Patents and Trademarks
Washington, DC 20231

Sir:

The following listed prior art has come to the attention of applicant(s). This prior art is believed relevant to, but patentably distinguishable from, the present invention and is being cited pursuant to Rule 97. A copy of each prior-art publication is enclosed and its relevance is discussed below.

form 6 Design patent application, first of three pages.

DESIGN PATENT APPLICATION

PETITION

Commissioner of Patents
Washington, District of Columbia 20231

Sir:

The undersigned petitioner(s) pray(s) that letters patent may be granted to the undersigned for the new and original design set forth in the following specification. The Filing Fee of $20 is attached.

SPECIFICATION

Be it known that the undersigned inventor(s) has (have) invented a new, original, and ornamental design entitled

"_____
                          Title
_____"

of which the following is a specification, reference being made to the accompanying drawing(s), forming a part hereof.

       Fig. 1 is a _____
               Type of view
       Fig. 2 is a _____
               Type of view

    I(we) claim the ornamental design for a_____

_____as shown.
    Title of design

                        _____
                             Signature

                        _____
                             Signature

form 6   Design patent application, second of three pages.

DECLARATION

The undersigned petitioner(s), declare(s) that she, he, or they is or are citizen(s) of the United States and residents of _____ and _____

          City and State

_____, respectively, that she,

    City and State

he, or they verily believe(s) herself, himself, or themselves to be the original, first, and sole/joint inventor(s) of the design entitled "_____

                             Title

_____" described and claimed in the foregoing specification; that she, he, or they do(es) not know and do(es) not believe that the same was ever known or used in the United States before her, his, or their invention thereof, or patented or described in any printed publication in any country before her, his, or their invention thereof, or more than one year prior to this application, or in public use or on sale in the United States more than one year prior to this application; that said design has not been patented in any country foreign to the United States on an application foreign to the United States on an application filed by her, his, or their legal representatives or assigns more than six months prior to this application; and that no application for patent on said design has been filed by her, his, or their representatives or assigns in any country foreign to the United States.

form 6   Design patent application, last page.

The undersigned petitioner(s) declare(s) further that all statements made herein of her, his, or their own knowledge are true and that all statements made on information and belief are believed to be true; and further that these statements were made with the knowledge that willful false statements and the like so made are punishable by fine or imprisonment, or both, under Title 18, U.S. Code, Sec. 1001, and that such willful false statements may jeopardize the validity of this application or any patent issuing thereon.

_____
Date

Send correspondence to -

_____
Signature

_____
Typed name

_____
Address

_____

_____
Date

_____
Signature

_____
Typed name

_____
Address

_____

form 7   Proprietary Information Agreement.

PROPRIETARY INFORMATION AGREEMENT

_____ (Recipient) acknowledges that
the attached document(s)-- _____ --
contain valuable proprietary information of_____
and understands that these documents and the information contained thereon are therefore furnished to Recipient under the
following conditions:

1. The documents and the information contained thereon
   shall be used solely for evaluating a proposal from or
   supplying a quotation or component to _____.

2. Recipient agrees not to disclose these documents or the
   information thereon to any person outside recipient's
   organization or to any person within recipient's organization not having a bona fide "need to know" same.

3. Recipient shall exercise due care to safeguard these
   documents and the information contained thereon or derived therefrom from access by unauthorized persons.

These terms shall not apply to any information which Recipient
can document was in or enters the public domain without fault
of Recipient or was in or comes into recipient's possession
without restriction.

_____   _____
        Date   Recipient

form 8 Amendment.

Ser. No.:

Filed:

Inventor(s):

Title:

Examiner and G.A.U.:

AMENDMENT

Date:_____

Commissioner of Patents and Trademarks
Washington, District of Columbia 20231

Sir:

    In response to the Office Letter mailed_____,

19___, please amend the above application as follows:

form 8a   Additional claims fee transmittal.

IN THE U.S. PATENT AND TRADEMARK OFFICE

Serial No.:

Filed:

Inventor(s):

Title:

Examiner and G.A.U.:

ADDITIONAL CLAIMS FEE TRANSMITTAL

Date:_____

Commissioner of Patents and Trademarks
Washington, District of Columbia 20231

Sir:

    Attached is an amendment for the above application.

A check for $_____for additional claims fee is enclosed,

calculated as follows:

CLAIMS AS AMENDED

			HIGHEST NO. PREVIOUSLY PAID FOR	PRESENT EXTRA	RATE	ADDITIONAL FEE
	CLAIMS REMAINING AFTER AMENDMENT					
TOTAL CLAIMS		MINUS		=	X $2	=
INDEP. CLAIMS		MINUS		=	X $10	=
			TOTAL ADDITIONAL FEE FOR THIS AMENDMENT →			

_____

_____
                          Inventor(s)

form 9 Supplemental declaration.

IN THE UNITED STATES PATENT AND TRADEMARK OFFICE

Serial No.:

Filed: Group Art Unit:

Applicant(s):   Examiner:

Title:

SUPPLEMENTAL DECLARATION

As an applicant in the above-identified application
for Letters Patent I declare as follows: (1) The subject
matter of said application in its present form was part of my
or our invention; (2) such subject matter was invented before
I or we filed said application and before the filing date of
any original or parent application from which said application
is derived; (3) I do not know and do not believe that such
subject matter was ever known or used in the United States before my or our invention thereof or patented or described in
any printed publication in any country before my or our invention thereof, or more than one year before said application
or any original or parent application thereof or in public use
or on sale in the United States for more than one year before
said application or any original or parent application thereof;
(4) said invention has not been patented or made the subject of
an inventor's certificate issued before the date of said application, or any original or parent application thereof, in any
foreign country on an application filed by me or us or by my
or our legal representatives or assigns more than twelve months
prior to said application, or any original or parent application thereof; (5) all statements made herein of my own knowledge are true and all statements made on information and belief are believed to be true and these statements are made with
the knowledge that willful false statements and the like so
made are punishable by fine or imprisonment, or both, under 18
U.S.C. Sec. 1001, and that such willful false statements may
jeopardize the validity of said application or any patent issuing thereon.

Date_____   _____

Date_____   _____

Date_____   _____

form 10 Continuation/division application form, one of two pages.

IN THE UNITED STATES PATENT AND TRADEMARK OFFICE

_____
Date

Commissioner of Patents and Trademarks
Washington, District of Columbia 20231

Sir:

1.   Please prepare a ( ) Continuation/( ) Divisional

application under Rule 60 of pending prior application of

_____, Ser. No. _____, filed
         Inventor(s)
_____19___, Title "_____."

Said prior application was in charge of Examiner _____

_____in G.A.U. _____.

2.   Please prepare a copy of the prior application.

3.   Please cancel all claims of the prior application,

except Claim 1.

4.   A check for the filing fee of $65 for one inde-

pendent claim is enclosed.

5.   Please amend the specification by inserting before

the first line the sentence:-- This is a ( ) Continuation/

( ) Division of application Ser. No._____, filed_____

_____,19___.--

( ) 6a.   Transfer the drawing(s) from the prior

application (base-issue fee has not been paid) to this appli-

cation and abandon said prior application as of the filing date

of this application.   A duplicate of this sheet is enclosed for

insertion in the file of the prior application.

form 10   Continuation/division application form, second of two pages.

( )6**b**. New Formal drawing(s) (____sheets) are (is) enclosed.

7. A preliminary amendment is enclosed. (Claim numbering begins with next number after highest numbered claim of prior application.)

The undersigned declare(s) further that all statements made herein of his/her/their own knowledge are true and that all statements made on information and belief are believed to be true; and further that these statements were made with the knowledge that willful false statements and the like so made are punishable by fine or imprisonment, or both, under Section 1001 of Title 18 of the United States Code and that such willful false statements may jeopardize the validity of the application or any patent issuing thereon.

Correspondence Name
and Address:

_____

_____

_____   _____

_____   Inventor(s)

IN THE UNITED STATES PATENT AND TRADEMARK OFFICE

Ser. No.:

Filed:

Inventor(s):

Title:

Examiner and G.A.U.:

[A ( ) Continuation/ ( ) Division of

  Ser. No.   , Filed   ]

PRELIMINARY AMENDMENT

                                    Date:_____

Commissioner of Patents and Trademarks
Washington, District of Columbia 20231

Sir:

    Prior to examination, kindly amend the above application

as follows:

form 12 Request for certificate of correction.

IN THE UNITED STATES PATENT AND TRADEMARK OFFICE

Patent No.:

Issued:

REQUEST FOR CERTIFICATE OF CORRECTION

Date_____

Commissioner of Patents and Trademarks
Washington, District of Columbia 20231

Sir:

1. The above patent contains significant error, as indicated on the attached Certificate of Correction form (submitted in duplicate). These errors arose at the respective places in the application file indicated below.

( )2. Since such error arose through the fault of the Patent and Trademark Office, it is requested that the Certificate be issued at no cost to applicant.

( )3. Such error arose through the fault of applicant(s). A check for the $15 fee is enclosed. Such error is of a clerical or minor nature and occurred in good faith and therefore issuance of the Certificate of Correction is respectfully requested. Specifically,

form 13 Certificate of correction.

UNITED STATES PATENT AND TRADEMARK OFFICE
CERTIFICATE OF CORRECTION

PATENT NO. :

DATED   :

INVENTOR(S) :

It is certified that error appears in the above—identified patent and that said Letters Patent are hereby corrected as shown below:

MAILING ADDRESS OF SENDER: PATENT NO. _____

Index

Litigation, anticipating, during prosecution, 108
Local manufacturers, 91
Location of infringement suit, 145
Log book for consultants, 25
Lump-sum payment for invention rights, 100–101

Machine, 28–29
  claim to, 67, 70
Magazines:
  as prior art, 33
  publicity in, 103
Mail-order classification of invention, 39n.
Mail-order firms, selling and, 102
Mailing:
  amendment, 121
  invention disclosure to yourself, 14
  patent application, 87
Main points to remember, 159–160
Maintenance fees for foreign patent, 135
Manual of Classification, 39, 162
Manual of Patent Examining Procedure, 77, 107, 108, 126, 162
  Sec. 201, 130, 131, 133, 138
  Sec. 707.07(j), 117, 121
    quoted, 77
  Sec. 708.02, 158
  Sec. 715, 114
  Sec. 1400, 133
Manufacture, articles of, 28–29
  claim to, 67, 70–71
Manufacturer(s):
  duty to indemnify customer, 145
  prospective, 48, 91–93
  smaller, advantages of, 91, 92
  waiver form, 48, 93–96
Manufacturing:
  doing it yourself, 28, 50, 51, 53, 101–102
  of a patented product without a license, 149–150
Market, foreign, for products, 134
Market leadership, 90
Market novelty, 48
Market research firms, 102
Marketing:
  before filing, 54
  of invention, 4, 47, 89–104
  by invention developer, 156
  of patented product, 148
  test, 54–55, 102
  of unfiled invention, 48–51
Marking of product:
  with patent number, 140, 143–144
  patent pending, 149
Martindale-Hubbell Law Directory, 136, 162
Massaging shower heads, 3
Material information, duty of disclosure, 85
Means clauses in claims, 69, 72, 75, 114

Mechanics of Patent Claim Drafting, The (Landis), 77, 162
Methods, 28–39
  [*See also* Process(es)]
Military secrets, 134
Misuse of patent, 146
Model of invention, 90
Molecular diagrams, 62
Monopoly from patent grant, 28, 60, 140–141, 147–148
Morality as requirement for patentability, 30
Multiple inventions in patent applications, 126
Multiplicity of claims, 75

Narrowing claim, 116, 134
National Catalog of Patents, 43
Naturally occurring articles, 29
Negative aspects of invention, 22, 23
Negative doctrine of equivalents, 145
Negative limitation in claim, 74
Negative opinions on commerciality, 18
Negative statements in application, 108, 160
New claims in continuation application, 129
New embodiment of invention, 107
New issues in amendment after final action, 124
New matter in patent application, 109
New uses, 28–29
  claim to, 67, 71
New York Times, patent column, 140
Nonelected claims, 133
Nonelected invention, 129
Nonenforceability defense to suit, 146, 147
Noninfringement defense to suit, 145
Nonobviousness, 31–33, 115
Nonpatentable subject matter, 28–30
Non sequitur in claim, 74
Norback, C., 104
Norback, P., 104
Nordhaus, R. C., 100, 162
Not invented here (NIH) syndrome, 92–93, 96
Notarization of invention disclosure, 12–13
Notice of Allowability, 106, 122
Notice of Allowance, 106, 122
Notice of Appeal, 151
Notice of References Cited, 111–114
Novelty examination of copyright material, 154
Novelty requirement, 20, 30–31, 73
Numbering of patent publications, 134, 137, 143–144

Objection in office action, 113, 119
Objects of invention, 57, 63
Obviousness, 31–33, 49, 115
Offers:
  of license to infringer, 145
  to patentee, 140
  of sale of invention, 33, 54, 160